D1809325

MILITARY OPERATIONS AND THE MIND

9780773547186

C JSCSC Library R

Date: 27.2.17

Class Mark: 72.6(71)BEL

Hobson Library

303667

Military Operations and the Mind

War Ethics and Soldiers' Well-Being

Edited by
Stéphanie A.H. Bélanger and Daniel Lagacé-Roy

McGill-Queen's University Press
Montreal & Kingston • London • Chicago

© McGill-Queen's University Press 2016

ISBN 978-0-7735-4717-9 (cloth)
ISBN 978-0-7735-4718-6 (paper)
ISBN 978-0-7735-9906-2 (ePDF)
ISBN 978-0-7735-9907-9 (ePUB)

Legal deposit second quarter 2016
Bibliothèque nationale du Québec

Printed in Canada on acid-free paper that is 100% ancient forest free
(100% post-consumer recycled), processed chlorine free

This book has been published with the help of a grant from the
Canadian Federation for the Humanities and Social Sciences,
through the Awards to Scholarly Publications Program, using funds
provided by the Social Sciences and Humanities Research Council
of Canada. Funding has also been provided by the Canadian
Institute for Military and Veteran Health Research.

McGill-Queen's University Press acknowledges the support of the
Canada Council for the Arts for our publishing program. We also
acknowledge the financial support of the Government of Canada
through the Canada Book Fund for our publishing activities.

Library and Archives Canada Cataloguing in Publication

Military operations and the mind: war ethics and soldiers' well-being/
edited by Stéphanie A.H. Bélanger and Daniel Lagacé-Roy.

Includes bibliographical references and index.
Issued in print and electronic formats.
ISBN 978-0-7735-4717-9 (hardback). –
ISBN 978-0-7735-4718-6 (paperback). –
ISBN 978-0-7735-9906-2 (ePDF). –
ISBN 978-0-7735-9907-9 (ePUB)

1. Military ethics – Canada – Case studies. 2. Military ethics – Canada –
Decision making – Case studies. 3. Command of troops – Moral
and ethical aspects – Canada – Case studies. 4. Soldiers – Canada –
Psychology – Case studies. 5. Soldiers – Health and hygiene – Canada –
Case studies. 6. Well-being – Canada – Case studies. I. Bélanger,
Stéphanie A. H., editor II. Lagacé-Roy, Daniel, 1960–, editor

U22.M565 2016   174'.9355   C2016-900334-5
                                          C2016-900335-3

This book was typeset by Interscript in 10.5/13 Sabon.

Contents

Tables and Figures

Abbreviations

AEP	Army Ethics Programme
BOI	Board of Inquiry
CAEP	Canadian Army Ethics Programme
CAF	Canadian Armed Forces
CALWC	Canadian Army Land Warfare Centre
CDS	Chief of Defence Staff
CFD	Chief of Force Development
CFOPP	Canadian Forces Operational Planning Process
CIDA	Canadian International Development Agency
CIMVHR	Canadian Institute for Military and Veteran Health Research
CA	Comprehensive Approach
CO	Commanding Officer
COA	Course of Action Development
CONOPS	Concept of Operations
DEP	Defence Ethics Programme
DFAIT	Department of Foreign Affairs and International Trade
DND	Department of National Defence
DRC	Democratic Republic of the Congo
DRDC	Defence Research and Development Canada
ELM	Elaboration Likelihood Model
ECS	Environmental Chief of Staff
ESMM	Ethical Sensitivity Mindfulness Model
FAST	Foreign-Deployed Advisory and Support Teams
FCM	Four Component Model
LOAC	Law of Armed Conflict
MND	Minister of National Defence

MSF	Médecins Sans Frontières
NATO	North Atlantic Treaty Organization
NCO	Non-Commissioned Officer
NDHQ	National Defence Headquarters
NGO	Non-Governmental Organization
NORAD	North American Aerospace Command
OMB	Organizational Misbehaviour
OPME	Officer Professional Military Education
ORB	Organizational Retaliation Behaviour
OT	Organizational Transformation
PME	Professional Military Education
PVO	Private Volunteer Organizations
RCAF	Royal Canadian Air Forces
RCN	Royal Canadian Navy
RDIT	Rest's Defining Issues Test
RLE	Religious Leader Engagement
RMCC	Royal Military College of Canada
ROE	Rules of Engagement
RWA	Right-Wing Authoritarianism
SDO	Social Dominance Orientation
START	Stabilization and Reconstruction Task Force
STI	Sexually Transmitted Infection
TED	Technology, Education, and Design
TL	Transformational Leadership
UMP	Unit Morale Profile

Acknowledgments

We would like to thank McGill-Queen's University Press, and especially Ms Jacqueline Mason for her thorough guidance and dynamic encouragements. We would like to thank the Canadian Institute for Military and Veteran Health Research, who made this publication possible, as well as its team, for their cheering support: specifically, Lauren Hanlon, the communications director, who magically coordinated all the meetings, roundtables, and conferences surrounding the production of this book. We would also like to thank the Royal Military College of Canada for encouraging us in our efforts to advance research in military ethics and moral injuries. More specifically, we want to thank Officer Cadet Bruno Gravel, whose constant and diligent work helped us bring the written project from its first draft to its final state, as well as Officer Cadets Jérémie Fraser, Benjamin Fortier-Dion, and Luc Bilodeau, for their unconditional support and hard work.

We would like to thank all our colleagues from the Canadian Armed Forces, especially the Canadian Forces Health Services Group, as well as the Defence Ethics Programme. The multiple actors involved in these important institutions have been encouraging us through their continued presence and wise guidance since the start of this project. We would like to thank all the Defence Scientist experts in military ethics, as well as our colleagues from many universities across Canada for their rigorous, scientific, yet sensitive and collaborative approach to military ethics and moral injuries.

On the international scene, we would like to thank our colleagues at both the European and the North American chapters of the International Society for Military Ethics for their support and encouragement. Their enriching conferences and extremely well-informed publications, and also their deep friendship, have been a true inspiration for us.

Our final and most profound acknowledgment goes to all those who serve, to all those who have served, and to their families. Please accept this book as a token of our profound appreciation.

MILITARY OPERATIONS AND THE MIND

Introduction

STÉPHANIE A.H. BÉLANGER

This book is the first of its kind, as it offers a Canadian perspective on the impact of war ethics on the well-being of service men and women. As a joint initiative between the Royal Military College of Canada and the Canadian Institute for Military and Veteran Health Research, it brings together researchers and practitioners from across the country to address the impact of ethical issues on the well-being of those who serve.

RMCC is renowned for its rigorous and continuous contributions to fundamental and applied research in military ethics, on both the national and international scenes. The novelty of this current initiative stems from its scope: enhancing the well-being of serving members by providing them with the best education and training in military ethics before and after deployments, while abroad and at home. This book aims to better inform politics and public policies and to enhance the well-being of its main stakeholders: the soldiers, sailors, and airmen and women as they are called to serve in the most singular, often harsh, and sometimes dangerous conditions.

This book considers ethics based on a performative definition, reflecting the way it is being approached in the latest *DND and CAF Code of Values and Ethics*: to "set a standard of expected behaviours for all personnel of DND and the CAF."[1] More specifically, we define and approach ethics in this collection as an aim to clarify the nature of right and wrong, as a reflection on morality, and as an application of the rules of conduct by which soldiers and the military culture live. Our assumption is that when a course of action involves uncertainty or conflicting values, or may cause harm, regardless of the action chosen, it can have a significant impact on the well-being of those involved. This impact comes from a disconnect either in the values shared between the leaders and the troops, or between the values shared more broadly by the Canadian troops and the ones shared by other players involved. The relationship of causality between ethical behaviour and well-being will be explored through-out the collection by different authors, each with an original and yet integrated approach.

Well-being, like ethics, is an emerging field of research that has also been studied from different angles depending on the discipline. We opt for a broad definition that is in line with the work being done at the Canadian Institute for Military and Veteran Health Research in this specific field, and that is well captured in this quote: "stable wellbeing is when individuals have the psychological, social and physical resources they need to meet a particular psychological, social and/or physical challenge."[2] Hence, in the context of this book, the ethical challenge could weaken the individual's capacity to find the resources that would help them overcome it. More specific-ally, we would like to borrow from Farnsworth's definition, which has the advantage of distinguishing moral emotions from moral injuries: "Moral emotions are experienced and regulated within a context of social connection. However, moral emotions can be func-tionally distinguished from nonmoral emotions in that they are con-cerned primarily with the preservation of social relationships. Moral injury, which is characterized by the violation of deeply held per-sonal and societal moral standards, is thus likely to be accompanied by strong moral emotions related to the perceived characteristics and contingencies of the morally injurious event."[3]

This emerging field is distinct from other typical fields in military, historical, philosophical, and behavioural studies that address the ethics of soldiers while in operations as well as at home, by integrat-ing into the analysis of ethical issues the well-being component. Furthermore, it offers a specific focus on the lives of the soldiers not only during operations overseas, but also while at the regiment. Such an approach has never been used before from this specific perspec-tive, nor in all three elements.

We hope that this book will lay the groundwork for many publi-cations on military ethics and well-being, not only using the Canadian perspective but also on the international scene. This book aims to address this field of study from a Canadian perspective. Moreover, a recent study showed that Canada is, actually, taking the lead on integrating military ethics and well-being.[4] This emerging field of study will soon be growing through the coordinated efforts of researchers from across Canada, as well as through their relationships with their counterparts on the international scene.

PART ONE: THE ETHICS OF DECISION-MAKING AND ITS REPERCUSSIONS ON THE SERVICE MEN AND WOMEN IN THE THREE ELEMENTS: LAND, SEA, AND AIR

The first part of this book discusses various ethical considerations and challenges that are specific to each one of the three elements where the men and women of the Canadian Forces may serve: aboard ship, in an aircraft, or while supporting land operations. The Comprehensive Approach model offered by the Canadian Army Land Warfare Centre opens more discussions on broader organizational considerations.

In "Exploring Ethical Choices at Sea Based on Two Case Studies," Stéphanie A.H. Bélanger and Ethan Whitehead emphasize the new challenges faced by the military since the publication of the new *Department of National Defence and Canadian Armed Forces Code of Values and Ethics* (2013). Military members anticipate – and are trained – to work in extremely stressful environments where, as opposed to the vast majority of other professions, the use of force is an expected part of their work. This chapter explores two case studies from a naval environment and discusses the theoretical background to the foundation of decision-making in the Royal Canadian Navy, as well as the impact of ethical decision-making and ethical leadership on the well-being of sailors.

In his chapter titled "Ethics of Command – Theory and Practice: An RCAF Perspective," Joe Sharpe continues the discussion on the importance of bringing together theories and experience. This discussion contributes directly to our understanding of the ethics of command from the more specific perspective of the Royal Canadian Air Force. The challenge can be arduous when mission necessity and individual ethics end up on a collision course, a situation that can arise in unexpected and unanticipated ways. Furthermore, this chapter deals with the friction between legal obligations and ethics experienced by senior RCAF officers, and will provide future commanders with a starting point from which to think about challenging areas of command responsibility. This area of conflict has been seen in recent wars (such as Iraq, Kosovo, Afghanistan, and Libya) when air power is delivered by physically removed actors via air or space with the intent of influencing the behaviour of people or the course of events on the ground.

Peter J. Gizewski and Heather Hrychuk, who are both Defence Scientists from Defence Research and Development Canada, as well as Colonel Richard Dickson from the Canadian Army Land Warfare Centre, recognize in their chapter titled "Military Ethics and the Comprehensive Approach: Ensuring Effective Responses to Security Challenges" the need to practice a more coherent, holistic, and collaborative approach to operations as the challenges of governance and security operations are becoming ever more evident – both in Canada and elsewhere. In fact, officials in Canada and a number of other countries (e.g. the United States, the United Kingdom, and other NATO allies) are increasingly calling for the adoption of a more "Comprehensive Approach" to operations. Such an approach would see diplomatic, developmental, commercial, and, of course, defence resources aligned with those of numerous other agencies, coordinated through an integrated campaign plan and applied in areas of operations as needed. When combined with a solid programme of training and education in ethics, the result would be more effective responses to the security challenges confronted.

PART TWO: ETHICS AND LEADERSHIP: TENSIONS AND RESOLUTIONS BETWEEN FORCE PROTECTION AND MISSION SUCCESS

The second part of this book brings these reflections to the managerial level and offers models on how to better train the leaders responsible for the lives or deaths of their troops in highly complex and often violent situations. The management of ethical risk in decision-making is of crucial importance in the success of operations.

The aim of the chapter titled "Managing Ethical Risk in the Canadian Armed Forces" is to describe the problem ethical risk poses for military effectiveness, and to suggest measures for managing that risk. Peter Bradley and Shaun Tymchuk address the concept of "ethical risk" and more specifically how to manage it. The authors outline a three-stage model for assessing ethical threats at the societal, organizational, and individual levels. Furthermore, they show how surveys and organizational reporting measures can be used by military leaders in this assessment process to help identify where their organizations are ethically vulnerable.

This vulnerability has its impact on the leaders; given the (in)famous instances of unethical behaviour by leaders, significant research attention has been devoted to understanding the ethical dimension of leadership in terms of the ethical behaviour of leaders (i.e., the moral person) and the expectations of ethical behaviour from followers by leaders (i.e., the moral manager). Thus, in their study titled "Antecedents of Ethical Leadership: Can We Predict Who Might Be an Ethical Leader?" Damian O'Keefe, Victor Catano, E. Kevin Kelloway, Danielle Charbonneau, and Allister MacIntyre explore how ethics training might influence participants' ethical sensitivity, which, in turn, might have an impact on how they view the ethicality of their leaders.

PART THREE: INTEGRATING ETHICAL SENSITIVITY AND ETHICAL RISK-TAKING IN OPERATIONS

The third part brings these reflections to the operational level, proposing some methods of measurement of ethical sensibility. This section also suggests an integration of ethical considerations directly into the Operational Planning Process to better inform the soldiers of their commander's intent with regards to ethical issues as they are called to make important ethical decisions in their extremely dangerous work environments.

To better improve their ethical decision-making process, leaders need to recognize the ethical dimensions of an issue before they begin reasoning and making ethical decisions. Allister MacIntyre, Joe Doty, and Daphne Xu provide, in their chapter titled "Ethical Sensitivity during Military Operations: Without Mindfulness There Is No Reasoning," a review of existing literature on ethical sensitivity followed by a discussion of their proposed model of ethical sensitivity – the Ethical Sensitivity Mindfulness Model. An example of ethical sensitivity could be how one's actions affect others in terms of moral implications, reactions, feelings, and one's ability to differentiate a moral or ethical dilemma as a breach of social norms. It is important to note that individuals can be exposed to ethical issues and not be sensitive to or aware of them – a form of mindlessness. This chapter aims to review current measures of ethical sensitivity, and concludes with the authors' proposed approach to measuring it.

These measures of ethical sensitivity are of great importance given the challenges present in the conflict environment in which the Canadian Armed Forces have operated and continue to routinely operate, including the complex settings that create many ethical predicaments. As analyzed by Howard G. Coombs in "The Continuing Evolution of Post–Cold War Operational Ethics in the Canadian Armed Forces," these challenges, in combination with a professional ethos that puts successful accomplishment of assignments as one's *raison d'être*, create ethical risk. Furthermore, orders and instructions are created and issued through military planning processes, which in and of themselves do not create the space for ethical discourse. However, Coombs suggests that with minor changes to such systems as the Canadian Forces Operational Planning Process, this oversight can be rectified in a fashion that will continue to allow for military accomplishment and, at the same time, ensure that the ethical risk is examined.

PART FOUR: CULTURAL CLASHES AND DECISION-MAKING

This book ends by offering some historical grounds to further the reflections on the ethical sensitivities that service men and women face on a regular basis, and proposes a model of how to better evaluate their ethical sensitivity and ultimately provide them with better-informed ethical training.

Allan English offers an historical perspective to controversial sexual behaviour involving Canadian service personnel. "Sex and the Soldier: The Effect of Competing Ethical Value Systems on the Health and Well-Being of Canadian Military Personnel and Veterans" examines key factors using three case studies in an effort to help us understand this type of conflict more fully so that we may mitigate its negative effects. The selected case studies include aspects of controversial sexual behaviour involving Canadian service personnel that have generated highly visible emotional responses and official reactions – thereby enabling the reader to discern more easily differences in ethical codes and gaps between value systems. This chapter demonstrates how competing ethical value systems in the CAF can have adverse effects on the mental health and well-being of Canadian military personnel and veterans. It concludes with suggestions on how to mitigate these adverse effects, in order to reduce the number of situations that may potentially cause harm to Canadian military personnel and veterans.

The last chapter, "Understanding How Soldiers Make Ethical Choices," provides a summary of the relevant literature and proposes a model of ethical decision-making that integrates individual dual-process approaches to decision-making with socio-cultural influences at the group and organizational levels. Deanna L. Messervey and Karen D. Davis, both Defence Scientists, propose a model to better understand how soldiers make ethical decisions so that militaries can promote ethical decision-making that is congruent with military values. In doing so, this chapter introduces a case study using CAF harassment policy to underscore the role of the military environment, including values, climate, and culture, in contributing to how soldiers think and behave.

ABOUT THE CONTRIBUTORS

To conclude, this collection illustrates how theory in military ethics is only as good as its practice shows it to be successful. This is why, at the end of the book, a particular focus is being brought to bear on the background of the authors, who all met numerous times in order to brainstorm and bring together their theories and practices. After these meetings, researchers had a better sense of what specific topics needed the practitioners' expertise and could be tailored into well-informed documents, allowing them to enhance the resources they offer to serving members. Some of the authors are academics, some are Defence Scientists, some are reservists, some are veterans; and all have soldiers' well-being at heart. They share a common goal: to address issues in military ethics and moral injuries in order to better serve military personnel through cutting-edge and yet clear and accessible evidence-based research.

NOTES

1 *The DND and CF Code of Values and Ethics*, http://www.forces.gc.ca/en/about/code-of-values-and-ethics.page (accessed 19 August 2015).
2 Rachel Doge, Annette P. Daly, Jan Huyton, and Lalage D. Sanders, "The Challenge of Defining Wellbeing," *International Journal of Wellbeing* 2, no. 3 (2012): 222–35.
3 Jacob K. Farnsworth, "The Role of Moral Emotions in Military Trauma: Implications for the Study and Treatment of Moral Injury," *Review of General Psychology* 18, no. 4: 249–62.

4 M.M. Thompson, *Moral Injury in Military Operations: A Review of the Literature and Key Considerations for the Canadian Armed Forces* (Toronto: Defence Research and Development Canada, 2015).

Preliminary Considerations

DANIEL LAGACÉ-ROY

The study of ethics and war in the military has a long tradition. One of the first discourses on ethics and war in the Western tradition is that of Thucydides (ca. 460–ca. 400 BC), a general, political philosopher, and historian, known for relating the Peloponnesian War (431–404 BC).[1] His writing tends to reflect more on the account of historical facts, at the expense of presenting an argument on the moral implications of certain decisions made by the parties involved. However, his interpretation of the Peloponnesian War indicates that some "version[s] of events" describe the ethical conduct of war in his time. The debates around the decision "to put to death all males of military age in the city [of Mytilene]"[2] and the "use of bodies as a strategic bargaining tool"[3] speak to decisions with ethical implications and relate to realities that could resonate today. In today's language, they could be called "treatment of prisoners" or "treatment of civilians." To a certain extent, moral implications – then and now – in the context of war reveal similarities that transcend historical periods and timeframes. In fact, a quick scan over the history of war seems to show patterns that illustrate decisions to go to war and conduct at war that are similar across a spectrum of events.[4] It seems that, since Thucydides' time, every written account on war – whether written by historians, philosophers, dramaturges, or by the participants themselves – questions or justifies a given way of conducting war. It is in this tradition that we, today, offer a collection that aims at reviving the debate over the conduct of war in the context of Canadian war culture, while exploring means to better prepare the service men and women for whom the war theatre is not a rhetorical exercise, but a lived experience. Our soldiers are not only the ambassadors of our concepts of a just war; they embody them. This book addresses the impact of our indoctrinated war culture on their well-being, in the hope of enhancing their level of moral preparedness.

In Canada, there is an expectation that Canadian Armed Forces members shall conduct themselves ethically. It was always implicitly understood that ethical conduct would be embraced by military members both in garrison and in theatre. While there was no "official" statement of defence ethics prior to the 1990s, this unwritten expectation was part of the military fibre. We may argue that the military Code of Discipline and the military Code of Conduct were guidelines that served to model the conduct of military members and to help achieve ethical standards. In fact, these two Codes still serve as guidelines for behaving ethically and lawfully. However, the need for a specific ethical *code* began to surface in the late 1970s. Retired Lieutenant-Colonel Charles Cotton claims, in his 1979 report "Military Attitudes and Values of the Army in Canada," that military members need a "short ethical code about how members of the military ought to behave and about what their basic beliefs should be."[5] Cotton's assessment of the need for a "military ethos" has influenced the shaping of the current *Statement of Defence Ethics*.

It is well known that the 1990s were a period of turmoil for the CAF. It would be difficult to deny the importance of that period, or to refute that it became a point of reference for justifying and rationalizing the changes that followed. Most authors in this book would make reference to this period as an unavoidable cataclysm. The CAF *raison d'être* was challenged all the way to its core. The CAF were confronted with reductions in force strength and resources, and an increase in operational tempo.[6] Challenges also came from advanced technologies, the more diverse population from which new recruits are enrolled, and inevitable mission requirements.[7] Nevertheless, some particular events were key players in strengthening the criticism of the military establishment: the lack of accountability, trust, confidence, and responsibility, and of openness and transparency at the senior leaders' level. In addition to the lack of professionalism from the upper echelons, the mission in Somalia ended with a painful tragedy. Some authors in the book discuss this tragedy at length. The Somalia incident embodies in itself the "dysfunctional atmosphere" that existed in the CAF at that time.[8] The explanation of such a "dysfunctional atmosphere" centres on the leadership's failure to address the visible gap between professionalism and ethical conduct.

This brief account of the troubled period of the 1990s reveals that the lack of ethical guidance by senior leaders damaged the image of the CAF. It was visible in the way they tangibly expressed their leadership, or lack thereof, and the way subordinates understood military values and beliefs. As a result, defining the military ethos became imperative. In addition, leader development was recognized as an important condition for ensuring constant adaptation to a changing world. It is clear that these two aspects (military ethos and leader development) are part of the same equation that defines the nature of ethics in the CAF.

The military ethos as it is usually understood by military members stems directly from the *Statement of Defence Ethics*. We have to look back at the proposed ethos statement from retired General Ramsey Withers (then Chief of Defence Staff) in 1981 to recognize that the need to define the CAF ethos was already envisaged prior to the 1990s. However, the severe scrutiny in 1994 following the Somalia incident reinforced the need to revisit the ethos statement.

The creation of a Defence Ethics Programme (DEP) in the late 1990s seemed to answer the needs of military members for ethical training. It was provided to all military members (and civilian employees) and focused on ethical obligations and principles for guiding ethical decisions and conduct. While this programme responded to the lack of concrete training and, to a certain extent, education, it still lacked the necessary advanced research and a discerning assessment of the ethical situation in the CAF. In my opinion, this gap became more noticeable when situations such as sexual misconduct required a more in-depth analysis, including an understanding of different situational factors inherent to military life.

The various chapters in this book are good examples of the advanced research and in-depth analysis needed in addition to the DEP. To some extent, each chapter contributes to the body of knowledge by providing different perspectives on how soldiers make ethical choices. More specifically, they speak to the underpinning foundation of ethical decision-making. The importance of the presentations derives from their desire to highlight critical facts to help understand the requirements enforced on military members. These requirements specify the type of framework in which military members operate, and become, in many cases, their only point of reference. The impact of such a framework reveals the approach by which ethical and unethical decisions are made.

The concept of ethics is complex. In *The Ethical Imagination*,[9] Margaret Somerville said: "Complexity requires being comfortable with ambiguities, ironies and contradictions – in short, being comfortable with uncertainty." Military conduct is especially prone to uncertainty in conditions where action is inescapable and its consequences profound. Hence, the challenge for us does not rely solely on recognizing situations' complexity, but on the ability to deal adequately with it.

Military members are invited to embrace an "ethical identity." Such an identity is paramount if the purpose of ethics in the military is to instil in members the profound goal of aspiring to be "ethical persons." To achieve this, it needs to be recognized that people are active agents who have to take responsibility for their own actions when facing ethical dilemmas. The thinking required for this cannot be replaced by frameworks or ready-made methods of ethical resolution.

According to Michel Foucault, the ancient Greek philosophers understood ethics as a way of being. An ethical person was visible to others.[10] Military members are recognized as ethical agents by the way they are and behave. It is this way of being and behaving that authors in this book have tried to capture, by describing ethical situations faced by military members and explaining how they have responded to them.

I hope that the contents of this book enhance your understanding of military ethics and provoke discussions that continue to add to the body of knowledge. Enjoy!

NOTES

1 Thucydides, in *The Ethics of War*, ed. Gregory M. Reichberg et al. (Malden, MA: Blackwell Publishing, 2006).
2 Ibid., 12.
3 S. Nevin, "Military Ethics in the Writing of History: Thuycydides and Diodorus on Delium," in *Beyond Battlefields: New Perspectives on Warfare in the Graeco-Roman World*, ed. Edward Bragg et al. (Cambridge: Cambridge Scholars Publishing, 2008), 99.
4 Thucydides, in *The Ethics of War*, ed. Reichberg et al.
5 C.A. Cotton, "A Canadian Military Ethos," *Canadian Defence Quarterly* 12, no. 3 (Winter 1982/83): 10–13.
6 F. Pinch, "Canada: Managing Change with Shrinking Resources," in *The Postmodern Military: Armed Forces after the Cold War*, ed. C.C. Moskos et al. (New York: Oxford University Press, 2000), 161.

7 B. McKee, *Canadian Demographic and Social Trends* (Ottawa: DND, Directorate of Strategic Human Resources, 2002).

8 Two books, one in English and one in French, describe with accuracy this period: S. Taylor, *Tarnished Brass: Crime and Corruption in the Canadian Military* (Winnipeg: Lester Publications, 1996), and M. Purnelle, *Une armée en déroute* (Montreal: Liber Publications, 1996).

9 M. Somerville, *The Ethical Imagination* (Toronto: Anansi Press, 2006), 203.

10 M. Foucault, "The Ethics of the Concern for Self as a Practice of Freedom," in *Michel Foucault: Ethics, Subjectivity and Truth*, ed. Paul Rabinow (New York: The New Press, 1997), 286.

PART ONE

The Ethics of Decision-Making and Its Repercussions on the Service Men and Women in the Three Elements: Land, Sea, and Air

1

Exploring Ethical Choices at Sea Based on Two Case Studies[1]

STÉPHANIE A.H. BÉLANGER
AND ETHAN WHITEHEAD

INTRODUCTION

Are people held to the same ethical standards regardless of their profession? Does society expect the same ethical values from a police officer and a tradesman, or from a florist and a lawyer? Despite the differing societal responsibilities of these professions, in everyday life there is an expectation that citizens of all professions and trades will adopt similar ethical standards. Yet, the question remains: does society hold certain professions more accountable for their actions, expecting them to behave according to additional guidelines? Or do certain professions face additional hardships in making ethical decisions based on their unique work environments? This chapter discusses the ethical standards applied to members of the Canadian Armed Forces, specifically those of the Royal Canadian Navy (RCN). It will focus on the distinct characteristics and impact of the application – or absence – of ethical decisions and ethical leadership on the well-being of the men and women who serve in the RCN.

The CAF and the Department of National Defence have undertaken the study and application of ethical leadership by many means, and on numerous occasions, including, in 1997, the founding of the Defence Ethics Programme. Since 2012, this programme is being restructured to better reflect the modern ethical challenges faced by both military and civilian DND employees. The new *Department of National Defence and Canadian Armed Forces Code of Values and Ethics*[2]

(2013) is a manual that brings together the values described in the *Values and Ethics Code for the Public Sector*[3] (2012) manual, as well as the values described in the manual *Duty with Honour: The Profession of Arms in Canada*[4] (2003). Additionally, more changes have been added for serving members. For instance, the older manual that first came into force in 2003 promoted the values of "Duty," "Honour," "Courage," and "Loyalty." The new manual, published in 2013 (and still incomplete in 2014; the second chapter, on military operations, is still under review), replaced "Duty" with "Stewardship" and "Excellence," making the values more applicable both to service men and women, and to civilians working for DND. The underpinning philosophy behind the new *Code of Values and Ethics* is that civilian employees and service members should adopt and behave according to the same code. However, one may ask: do civilian employees face the same reality as the soldiers who risk their lives on the front line? Yet, there is a societal expectation that the soldiers, while at the front lines, should behave according to the same moral standards as the civilians left behind.[5] And it is on the very specificity of the nature of the job of service men and women that this chapter will focus.

The research done on "military ethics" suggests that military members are considered not only civilians but also members of a profession dually embracing the values of their respective societies and the values promoted by their military profession. It suggests specificity to this particular kind of ethics.[6] Nevertheless, it seems that military members are expected to use the same ethical standards as the rest of society, despite the fact that they anticipate – and are trained – to work in an extremely stressful environment where, as opposed to the vast majority of other professions, the use of force is an expected part of their work. They could be called into harm's way at any time, and be asked to protect the innocent with the same energy, the same efficacy, and the same rigour as when they are called to use force to eliminate the enemy. The unique nature of their profession creates, rather than breaks, a tension between their professional persona and an independent, and yet intimately related, societal entity.[7] In the military, unethical behaviour by even the lowest-ranking soldier can have a negative strategic effect, a greater impact on the social perception based on the nature of the profession, as witnessed, to use a very obvious example, by the impact of the images of Private Lynndie England, a "strategic private" at the Abu Ghraib prison in Iraq. But there are also so many more common behaviours that are under great scrutiny, such as the trial of Brigadier-General Ménard, the former Afghan mission commander who was court-martialled over an in-theatre sexual liaison with a subordinate.[8] Ethical leadership is approached by the Department itself, but also by public scrutiny, as a concept that means much more than a prescribed behaviour; it is a mentality, a way of being, that embraces a large spectrum of behaviours affecting each individual at all ranks and at every moment of their decision-making processes. In both cases, even though at a very different scale, when these soldiers' involvement in unethical and morally reprehensible acts came to light, it cast doubt on the actions of all military service personnel involved in the conflict.[9]

The Navy has also had its share of public embarrassments, one of the most obvious being the Tailhook scandal.[10] This 1991 incident consisted of the alleged sexual assault of approximately eighty-three women and seven men by over one hundred United States Navy and Marine Corps officers at the annual Tailhook Association Symposium in Las Vegas, Nevada. Upon investigation into this incident, the leadership was blamed for its lack of connection with the social realities: "Senior naval officials did not know themselves within a larger cultural framework or the potential fragility of their service's political status and social makeup."[11] Given not only the large impact of unethical behaviour (professional entity) on public perception (societal entity) – but more importantly, given the negative impact of the leaders' lack of social awareness of the behaviour of their troops – the study of "military ethics" becomes essential to the understanding of the nature of the profession of arms. It becomes, by the same token, essential in providing leaders with well-informed guidelines for the ethical training of service members. The intention of this chapter is to bring together theories and experience through case study analysis and evidence-based considerations. Background to the foundation of decision-making in the RCN, as well as the effects of ethical decision-making and ethical leadership on service men and women, will be discussed.

BACKGROUND

Ship structure usually means that one role of the various officers and senior non-commissioned officers on board is to formulate recommendations to the Commanding Officer (CO), and then to seek his or her approval to carry those actions out. Responses to emergencies are routine responses as well. The officers' development as junior leaders aboard ship tends to depend heavily on the character of their CO.

Ethical leadership in the RCN is greatly influenced by events that occurred in 1949.[12] In a period of a few weeks, three ships on active deployment experienced collective insubordination, commonly referred to as mutiny, consisting of coordinated "sit-ins" and non-violent protests that were quickly resolved. The Mainguy Report (1949) details the results of an investigation about the causes of these mutinies. Grievances voiced by the crews of the ships were varied; however, they can each be traced back to a lack of ethical decision-making and a lack of ethical leadership by the senior offi-cers of the respective ships. For decades after these events, every officer of the RCN that passed through officer training school stud-ied the report detailing the mutinies in order to gain an understand-ing of the leadership and ethical failures of the past and to avoid such a disaster happening again.[13] Despite best efforts, though, ethi-cal misconduct is still bound to occur. The recent scandals surround-ing the behaviour of some of the leaders of HMCS *Whitehorse* that caused her withdrawal from an international exercise in July 2014 can serve as an example. The ship was ordered home from an inter-national naval exercise following allegations of drunkenness, sexual misconduct, and shoplifting against three of the ship's sailors.[14] The incidents prompted Vice-Admiral Mark Norman to launch an inter-nal review of naval policies and procedures. All levels of the military are held responsible for ethical decisions at sea, at home, and in port.

ETHICAL LEADERSHIP WHILE AT SEA

The CAF, as with most organizations, has experienced various instances of unethical leadership, the Mainguy Incident being one.[15] The CAF Leadership Doctrine defines leadership as "directing, moti-vating, and enabling others to accomplish the mission professionally and ethically, while developing or improving capabilities that contrib-ute to mission success."[16] If there are isolated cases of unethical lead-ership, the harm to the institution can be minimal if readily addressed. However, many examples[17] show that when leaders move away from ethical principles, it can have devastating effects on the entire organi-zation. In a broad sense, there is a risk of weakening public trust in, or the "trustworthiness" of, the CAF.[18] In a more intimate sense, the psychological well-being of subordinates can be affected by the moral characteristics of their leaders. The ship as a whole under the CO's command becomes one indivisible entity, dependent on her or his leadership approach and decision-making processes. The following case study will demonstrate the influence of a CO's leadership and has been modified to protect the identities of those involved, but the principles remain the same: even a small breach of ethical leadership, not necessarily a spectacular one, can have a profound impact on the ship's company if not managed properly.

Case Study Example

Following two weeks of intensive mine countermeasure (MCM) exercises with multiple allied nations, four MCM ships were alongside in a foreign port for some rest and recovery for the crews of all ships. As is customary, the commanding officers of each ship gathered their respective crews to give them the standard "don't do anything stupid" and "remember, you represent the Navy" speech. Due to the format of the MCM ships, they were able to form what is referred to as a "nest," which means that there was only one access point for all four ships, where a single crew could maintain a duty watch, allowing a greater number of the sailors to take advantage of shore leave. As a result, the Officer in Tactical Command (OTC) of the four ships was not required on duty and went ashore. In accordance with Ship Standing Orders (SSOs), he left the instruction that the identification card of every person who came on board was to be checked without exception.

As the night wore on, the members of the ships' companies went ashore to find drinking establishments. The remaining duty watch was set up and established. As is usually the case, an Ordinary Seaman was posted as Access Point Sentry (APS), with the Quarter Master at the bow, reachable by VHF radio. Around 0100 the OTC returned, visibly inebriated. In accordance with SSOs and the OTC's orders, the APS requested identification from the OTC and his party. The APS, who was new to his ship, did not recognise the captain of the other ship. At this point the OTC became belligerent, making statements to the effect of "don't you know who I am?" and "I'm the Captain, I don't have to show my ID."

Not wanting to cause conflict, the APS radioed the Quarter Master, requesting the Officer of the Day to the bow to deal with the escalating situation. When the Officer of the Day arrived on scene, the drunken captain had started making threatening remarks and gestures toward the APS. The Officer of the Day recognised the OTC and his party. With great effort from the Officer of the Day and the OTC's Operations Officer, the OTC was calmed and brought on board his ship and taken to his cabin.

The events were to such a scale that, by the end of the port visit, every member of each ship in the group had heard of the altercation. This had the effect of lowering morale on board all the ships, but particularly on the inebriated captain's ship. Tensions on board his ship started to run high, with murmurs from the junior ranks about why the double standard existed, as such behaviour would not have been tolerated from them.

Discussion

This vital influence of the leader's personal character puts a lot of pressure on the social credibility, or ethos, of the leader. It is therefore desirable that this ethos is maintained through a high level of attributes considered positive by social standards.[19] Adding to this pressure is the isolation of the crew from the rest of the world for long periods of time, often repeatedly more than three months in a row for exercises, and more than six months in a row for missions. These extreme situations tend to increase the gap that separates the sailors from the "civilians" and to reinforce the importance of the experience aboard ship in their lives – more specifically, of the effects of ethical decision-making and ethical leadership on the well-being of service men and women. In such a confined and isolated environment, as demonstrated in the case study above, morale-shattering news travels fast – it takes only a matter of hours for news of the CO's indiscretions to reach all members of the crew, and as is common of such things, for it to become embellished with each retelling. As the news of the leader's misconduct circulates and his ethos is jeopardized, it quickly leads to a decrease in the crew's respect for him, and a weakened trust in the chain of command as a whole.

ETHICAL DECISION-MAKING UNDER OPERATIONAL PRESSURE

Ethical decision-making during operations still holds many mysteries despite extensive research into the field.[20] According to existing research, "more training cannot eliminate dilemmas that are ethically insoluble. The only real solution is acknowledging that these dilemmas will arise during war and attempting to limit the kinds of situations that give rise to these dilemmas."[21] Just like soldiers, sailors often have to make difficult decisions under pressure, and can feel almost as if they might as well "flip a coin."[22] In any operational context, leaders have an obligation to minimize the risk into which they send their serving members. Upon enrolment, CAF members resign their right to refuse to obey a lawful order that might put them in harm's way. The clause of unlimited liability is not without an "obligation" from the government down to the CAF leaders to insure that "the demand will only be forthcoming when there is a genuine national interest at stake,"[23] and that the troops will not be sacrificed unnecessarily. This responsibility of the government is to be approached more in the sense of a "social" than a "legal" covenant.

Ambiguous situations are no less frequent at sea than in the other two elements. In the Navy this is due, among many factors, to the complex international laws that allow or forbid a foreign ship to cross "the line" into foreign territories, and to frequent encounters with military, merchant, civilian, and unidentifiable ships that can originate from any country. How does a CO decide if he or she should intervene with a foreign vessel? When is the decision to send a boarding party or a medical team made? Where does the mandate start and where does it stop? All of these factors have to be taken into consideration, often in a heartbeat, and each one of them will most likely involve engaging the troops in a potentially extremely fragile, if not explosive, and thus dangerous, situation.

The following case study is based on a scenario reported to the authors by a sailor who was required to obey an order that he considered to be extremely complex due to the moral weight he felt he had to bear. Master Seaman Finamore, who was a Leading Seaman at the time of the event, gave a public speech in Halifax in April 2012 at a reception hosted by the Honorable Myra Freeman. He related his experience as a medical technician aboard HMCS *Charlottetown* during NATO Operations in Libya in the summer of 2011.[24] Master Seaman Finamore agreed to share an electronic copy of his public speech with the authors of this article. With his permission, the following case study recollects the story in the seaman's own words:

Case Study Example

My name is LS David Finamore. I joined the Canadian Forces seven years ago as a Medical Technician. I most recently spent six months aboard HMCS *Charlottetown* off the coast of Libya during the Gadahfi crisis.

Being deployed on a warship, despite the warm climate of Libya, is no five star cruise. Patrolling mine-filled areas and having missiles fired at you from shore were only some of the hazards we faced. Aside from hostile threats there was also a need to provide humanitarian assistance whenever possible. One morning I awoke to the following humanitarian situation:

Picture a forty-foot lobster style fishing vessel in the middle of the Mediterranean Sea. Now picture that same boat filled with upwards of 300 Libyan refugees. Their vessel had broken down and our ship was required to assess the situation as no surrounding ports would allow them entry. This assessment would dictate whether or not the refugees would be taken aboard our ship, which in turn would bring them onto Canadian soil and make them our complete responsibility. As part of the assessment team I was sent over to their vessel with a radio and a stethoscope. I was given roughly 1 hour to do a rapid triage and general medical assessment of all the refugees. Of the 300 plus refugees there were three pregnant women, ten infants, many elderly men and women and only one man who spoke English. You can imagine that this was no easy task as I was literally walking on people as I made my way through the vessel. Upon completion I communicated my findings back to the ship where the decision was made by the Captain that we would mechanically fix their vessel and send them back on their way.

This outcome weighed heavily on me as I know that the information from my medical triage played a large role in shaping the Captain's decision. I had completed the triage to the best of my abilities given the challenging circumstances and all the refugees were clinically well enough to continue travelling. However, my concern was how much longer their journey might be and what that might mean for the health of the young and old aboard the vessel.

That is only one of many situations a Medic may find himself in; having to make difficult, practical and professional decisions quickly and efficiently. But this is what we are trained to do.[25]

Discussion

The medic involved in this scenario, when asked about how he was able to perform under such extreme conditions, stated that he "just did his job."[26] Although soldiers and sailors alike are trained to obey orders, one can wonder if the obedience brings any additional stress when the member understands the implications of their actions on the bigger picture, rather than following blindly. Although Finamore's task – to medically assess the hundreds of civilians, including elderly, women, and children, within the hour to determine if they required medical treatment – was straightforward in nature, it bears its moral implications. Saying "yes" involves a huge responsibility for the government of Canada, which risks being put into a delicate political situation. Saying "no" involves acknowledging that it is likely that many will die. However, in this case, the medic understood his part in the CO's decision on what might be life or death for these people. He was able to provide his assessment as directed; however, due to operational restrictions, he found himself questioning how accurate an assessment could be made in such a short timeframe. He was therefore left to act as best he could within his restrictions. Given the complexity of the moral implications of the situation in which this sailor was placed, he would still have to deal with the psychological impact, called "concern" in his own testimony, after the fact. The nature of the work performed by the members of the CAF is such that this type of situation is not unrealistic for any branch. Ethical leaders understand that their sailors or soldiers live with the consequences of the decisions they make, and call it "Duty" – now transformed to "Excellence." "I just did my job" has become the hallmark of their hard work achieved with pride under extreme physical and psychological pressures.

CONCLUSION

While much progress has been made by the CAF since the first implementation of the Defence Ethics Program in 1997, there is still much work to be done. At the end of the day, despite the common ethical standards, being a serving member in the military does not equate to being a civilian. The military requires its members to follow societal expectations while accomplishing tasks and missions significantly outside of that society's scope. Military members must abide by civilian rules in addition to the military regulations (Queen's Regulations and Orders) and the applicable international laws (Geneva Conventions and the Laws of Armed Conflict). Less pressure is imposed upon them when they are trained in such a way that the work environment encourages ethical behaviour, rather than promoting a "laisser faire"

. When serving members are put under extreme pressure, their …mination to persist beyond a "normal" human's emotional capacity meets the expectations of their training, but may result in psychological challenges. Our military members remain, in fact, emotional human beings merely supressing, ignoring, and neglecting their instinctive emotional responses.[27]

The operational planning process, which will be discussed in the third part of this book, cannot ignore the importance of integrating ethical values prior to giving final orders, even in extremely stressful and pressing situations. Furthermore, in operations or during training, when the cleavages between ranks, trades, or genders are emphasized by double standards, the morale of the troops is dismantled and ethical values are left aside until they vanish completely. Many other case studies could have been used to illustrate the importance of strong leadership at all ranks. Some might expect it to be normal for a select few of our serving members to adopt a rogue attitude because it is the nature of the beast. However, this would be absolutely unconscionable. On the other hand, one would be deluded to assume that there is no problem in the CAF; that all serving men and women work together and respect one another at all times, with no possibility of rogue behaviour. Leadership simply cannot turn a blind eye to the complexity and the unique nature of the Armed Forces, where civilians are called to voluntarily revoke their freedom, requiring them to train to be able to use a machine gun and to distribute bottles of water to children at the same time, especially when leaders are potentially held to different standards than are those they lead. Acknowledgment of the unique nature of the job, combined with an acute awareness of the service's political status, will enhance the efficacy of the ethical education of all troops.

NOTES

1 The authors, both serving members of the Navy Reserve of the RCN, have the advantage of being able to enrich their "Naval" ethical experience through their civilian lives; one teaches military identity and ethos at the Royal Military College of Canada, and the other one practices the ethical values in his work environment as a registered nurse. The opinions expressed in this article reflect the research of the authors and do not necessarily represent the opinion of the Canadian Army, the Canadian Armed Forces, or the Department of National Defence. This chapter would not

have been possible without the precious help of Bruno Gravel, Research Assistant.

2 National Defence and the Canadian Armed Forces, "The DND and CF Code of Values and Ethics," http://www.forces.gc.ca/en/about/code-of-values-and-ethics.page (accessed 28 April 2015).

3 Treasury Board of Canada Secretariat, "Values and Ethics Code for the Public Sector," http://www.tbs-sct.gc.ca/pol/doc-eng.aspx?section=text&id=25049 (accessed 28 April 2015).

4 "Duty with Honour: The Profession of Arms in Canada National Defence of Canada," http://www.21armystuff.30wl.com/pd/Duty-with-Honour-The-Profession-of-Arms-in-Canada-2009-e.pdf (accessed 28 April 2015).

5 See for instance the reflections brought forward by Robinson: "When under fire, does he [the combat soldier] worry whether the man next to him is an adulterer, or merely whether he is brave and knows how to use his weapon? Almost certainly the later." This is not to say that soldiers do not abide by any moral standards, but it acknowledges a difference between the civilians and the military. Paul Robinson, "Ethics Training and Development in the Military," *Parameters* 37, no. 1 (Spring 2007): 23–47.

6 D. Baumann, "Military Ethics: A Task for Armies," *Military Medicine* 172 (Winter 2007): 34–8.

7 This tension has developed even within the Armed Forces when comparing reservists (part-time military) to regular Forces personnel: "Reservists may often approach military problems with a civilian skill set and a civilian set of priorities, often to the benefit of military missions. This is a symptom of a type of independence, however small, from doctrine that may define sets of Guard and Reserve soldiers and also separate them from their active peers ... So while active soldiers have imbued a certain 'warrior ethos' as part of the mentality of the regular soldier, it is not likely that there is the same saturation of that ethos in reservists. It is therefore less realistic for reservists to be expected to comply with or understand this standard. It is a potential source of friction when reserve units must interact with the regular military." M. Zelcer, "Ethics for the Weekends: The Case of Reservists," *Journal of Military Ethics* 11, no. 4 (2012): 338–9.

8 The Canadian Press, "Menard Fined, Busted Down a Rank for Afghan Sex Affair," http://www.ctvnews.ca/menard-fined-busted-down-a-rank-for-afghan-sex-affair-1.673264 (accessed 28 April 2015).

9 Canadian Forces, *Report of the Somalia Commission of Inquiry* (Ottawa: Minister of Public Works and Government Services Canada, 1997), http://www.forces.gc.ca/somalia/somaliae.html (accessed 28 May 2015).

See also Withers Study Group, "Balanced Excellence: Leading Canada's Armed Forces In the New Millenium" (Autumn 1998), http://www.rmc.ca/bg-cg/rep-rap/withers/index-eng.asp (accessed 28 April 2015).

10 For background information on the Tailhook scandal, see https://web.duke.edu/kenanethics/CaseStudies/Tailhook%26USNavy.pdf (accessed 28 April 2015).

11 R. Shenk, "Ethos at Sea," *Business Communication Quarterly* 58 (1995): 9.

12 R.H. Gimblett, "What the Mainguy Report Never Told Us: The Tradition of 'Mutiny' in the Royal Canadian Navy before 1949," *Canadian Military Journal* (2000): 85–92.

13 Ibid. Still today, ships typically deliver ethical annual reports only available on the DWAN (Defence Wide Area Network, Department of National Defence), on which a very clear Ethics plan is laid out, and where the criticisms are often the lack of systematic application of the plan and the application of double standards.

14 Kristen Everson, "HMCS *Whitehorse* Recall Prompted Navy Commander to Take Charge of PR Plan," *CBC News Politics* (18 November 2014), http://www.cbc.ca/news/politics/hmcs-whitehorse-recall-prompted-navy-commander-to-take-charge-of-pr-plan-1.2839408.

15 K. Mihelic, B. Lipicnik, and M. Tekavcic, "Ethical Leadership," *International Journal of Management and Information Systems* 14, no. 5 (2010): 31–41; E. Freeman and L. Stewart, *Developing Ethical Leadership* (Charlottesvilles, VA: Bridge Papers, 2006); Joanne B. Ciulla, "Integrating Leadership with Ethics: Is Good Leadership Contrary to Human Nature," in *Handbook on Responsible Leadership and Governance in Global Business*, ed. Jonathan P. Doh and Stephen A. Stumpf (Cheltanham, UK: Edward Elgar, 2005): 159–79; Michael E. Brown, Linda K. Trevino, and D.A. Harrison, "Ethical Leadership: A Social Learning Perspective for Construct Development and Testing," *Organizational Behavior and Human Decision Processes* (July 2005): 117–34.

16 Department of National Defence, *Leadership in the Canadian Forces: Doctrine* (Ottawa: Queen's Printer and Controller of Stationery, 2005), 7.

17 Russel Williams, former colonel of the CAF and serial killer, can be used as a recent and obvious example; see http://www.forces.gc.ca/en/news/article.page?doc=chief-of-the-defence-staff-statement-on-colonel-williams-guilty-plea/hnps1ugo (accessed 28 April 2015). He was released from the CAF as soon as he was found guilty.

18 L. Lessig, "'Institutional Corruption' Defined," *Journal Of Law, Medicine & Ethics* 41, no. 3 (2013): 553–5; V.M. Azarov and N.M. Burda, "Evaluating Soldiers' Moral and Psychological State," *Military Thought* 10, no. 3 (2001): 37–44.

19 Shenk, "Ethos at Sea," 5–11.
20 See, among others, S.E. French, *Code of the Warrior: The Values and Ideals of Warrior Cultures throughout History* (New York: Rowman & Littlefield, 2005).
21 M.N. Jensen, "Hard Moral Choices in the Military," *Journal of Military Ethics* 12, no. 4 (2013): 341–56; R. Moelker, "Virtue Ethics and Military Ethics," *Journal of Military Ethics* 6, no. 4 (2007): 257–8; M.M. Thompson, M.H. Thomson, and B.D. Adams, *Moral and Ethical Dilemmas in Canadian Forces Military Operations: Qualitative and Descriptive Analyses of Commanders' Operational Experiences* (Toronto: DRDC Toronto, TR 2008-183 Technical Report, 2008), 44; M.H. Thomson, B.D. Adams, C.D. Tario, A.L. Brown, and A. Morton, *The Impact of Moral Exemplar Training on Moral Judgment and Decision-Making in an Operational Context* (Toronto: DRDC Toronto, CR 2008-107, Contract Report, 2008), 90; M.H. Thomson and B.D. Adams, *Moral and Ethical Decision-Making in a Realistic Field Training Scenario* (Toronto: DRDC Toronto, CR 2007-012, Contract Report, 2007), 83; M.H. Thomson, B.D. Adams, C.D. Tario, and A.L. Brown, *Collaborative Team Decision-Making in a Realistic CF Training Scenario* (Toronto: DRDC Toronto, CR 2008-098, Contract Report, 2008), 104; M.H. Thomson, C.D.T. Hall, and B.D. Adams, *Current Canadian Forces Education and Training for Moral and Ethical Decision-Making in Operations* (Toronto: DRDC Toronto, CR 2009-043, Contract Report, 2010), 58; M. Schulzke, "Ethically Insoluble Dilemmas in War," *Journal of Military Ethics* 12, no. 2 (2013): 95–110.
22 M.N. Jensen, "Hard Moral Choices in the Military," 351.
23 M. Cook, *The Moral Warrior* (Albany: State University of New York Press, 2004), 123.
24 MS Finamore received both the Diamond Jubilee Medal for the actions that are related in the case study and the Chief of Defence Staff Commendation "for his exceptional leadership as medical technician onboard HMCS *Charlottetown* during NATO Operations in Libya, March to August 2011." See http://www.gg.ca/honour.aspx?id=223250&t=13&ln=finamore&lan=eng (accessed 28 April 2015) and http://publications.gc.ca/collections/collection_2014/mdn-dnd/D3-23-2013.pdf (accessed 28 May 2015).
25 Personal communication from MS Finamore to Dr Stéphanie Bélanger, 4 July 2014.
26 For an analysis of the importance and meaning of "doing their job," see S.A.H. Bélanger and M. Moore, "Public Opinion and Soldier Identity: Tensions and Resolutions," in *Beyond the Lines: Military and Veteran Health Research*, ed. A. Aiken and S.A.H. Bélanger (Montreal and Kingston: McGill-Queen's University Press, 2013), 103–13.

27 R.M. Scurfield and K.T. Platoni, eds., *War Trauma and Its Wake:
    Expanding the Circle of Healing* (New York: Routledge, 2012), 306;
    Robinson, "Ethics Training and Development in the Military"; T.
    Nadelson, *Trained to Kill: Soldiers at War* (Baltimore, MD: Johns
    Hopkins University Press, 2005).

2

Ethics of Command – Theory and Practice: An RCAF Perspective

JOE SHARPE

INTRODUCTION

This chapter focusses on the ethics of command of the RCAF, which can be traced back to the customs and traditions of the world's first independent air force, the Royal Air Force, many of which were perpetuated in the Canadian Air Force and RCAF between 1918 and 1968. After the Second World War, close co-operation with the United States Air Force, especially in the integrated North American Air Defence Command (as it was first called) command and control structure, brought an American influence to bear on the RCAF's ethics of command. The unification of the three Canadian services in 1968 was another major influence. After unification, the air environment of the Canadian Armed Forces carried on many of the customs and traditions of the RCAF, but new practices evolved as the integrated CAF command structure incorporated various elements of the former three services' command ethics. Arguably, the greatest influence on the ethics of command of today's RCAF was the events during and immediately after the Canadian armed services' "Decade of Darkness," the last decade of the twentieth century.[1]

This chapter will focus on some of the reforms and their outcomes that stem from the Somalia Commission (discussed elsewhere in this book), but more specifically as they apply to the RCAF. First, it examines the overall changes to the CAF's approach to command ethics as instituted by its senior leaders in this period, followed by a discussion of variations among the services in command ethics. The chapter concludes with an analysis of how a theoretical model linking the concepts of legality, professionalism, and ethics can be applied to military professional practice, using five scenarios as examples. This chapter is written from the perspective of practitioners of the profession of arms in Canada to reflect the challenges in applying some theoretical models in real-world situations. The concepts used here are those articulated by scholars and senior military professionals who have attempted to distill abstract concepts often found in the theoretical literature into guidelines that can be applied where ethical dilemmas occur in actual command situations.[2]

One of the difficulties in discussing the ethics of command is that the concepts of military culture, ethos, and ethics are closely linked, and are often used interchangeably in the academic literature and in official CAF publications.[3] One CAF strategic leader of the day, Vice-Admiral Larry Murray, observed that the situation in the 1990s was avoidable but came about not only because of the unethical and unprofessional conduct of a few soldiers, but because "as an institution we weren't listening,"[4] especially at the strategic level.

The use of the term 'institution' by Murray is revealing. In essence, it identifies that what happened in the Somalia inquiry, and subsequently, was not merely a problem with conduct at the tactical level but was present all across the Canadian Forces. That point was reinforced by an Air Force officer serving in a strategic leadership position at the time: "this wasn't an army problem. This was a Canadian Forces problem. It was an air force problem, it was a navy problem."[5] The majority of strategic leaders from the 1990s who were interviewed to identify leadership competencies important for CAF leaders to function successfully at the strategic level, felt that while the events that precipitated the Somalia incident may have begun with the army, there were professional and ethical lapses across the CAF as a whole that allowed the actions of a few at the tactical level to ignite a scandal that was able to seriously jeopardize the survival of the entire institution.[6]

A major distraction for the strategic leadership was the financial situation facing the CAF; it was acknowledged that "[i]t is difficult to put professional development in place if the military is underfunded."[7] At the time, the government was focused on reducing the national deficit and the Canadian Forces had undergone a series of debilitating budget cuts[8] that pressured many of the senior leaders to allocate a lot of time to protecting their services and managing the organization rather than leading the institution (or maintaining an awareness of what was happening in the field).

SERVICE VARIATIONS

Although the CAF has, at least technically, been a unified service for forty-five years, there continues to be an apparent association between service culture and the style and approach to leadership.

When it comes to personal ethics and behaviour, the influence of the group culture on an individual can be powerful. The RCAF puts great emphasis on technical leadership and professionalism in the air and on the ground for both air and ground crew, perhaps to the point of making technical leadership the most important aspect of RCAF leadership. This is a differentiating factor between the typical Air Force and Army officer with respect to leadership style. As Dr Allan English contends while discussing leadership differences in the Canadian Army, Navy, and Air Force: "Technical leadership is most clearly different from the traditional concept of army leadership in pilots who must ... be able to demonstrate an acceptable level of flying skill before they will be accepted as leaders."[9] Technical skill extends into the combat arena for the RCAF. As an example, for an Air Force pilot, a typical combat mission may result in the destruction of an unseen enemy, but may also result in possible harm to noncombatants and friendly forces if targeting is inaccurate. Indeed, the consequences of inaccurate weapons release in the NATO air campaign (Operation Allied Force) in March 1999 in Kosovo and the March 2011 Libyan air campaign (Operation Unified Protector) could have been far more severe from an international policy perspective than from a humanitarian one. The commander of the NATO military mission in Libya, Canadian Lieutenant-General Charles Bouchard, was particularly sensitive to the policy significance of targeting, noting that "it's not deciding what you are going to bomb, but why."[10]

Thus, an RCAF officer, even at junior ranks, may be called upon to make tactical decisions that have potentially very significant strategic consequences. In the kind of tactical situation where a single-seat fighter pilot may find himself operating, during an air-to-ground mission the release of a single bomb can be lethal to a large number of people. The final decision to launch a weapon is in the hands of the individual, and although the target selection has been done at an operational or even a strategic level, the responsibility for the final drop belongs in the cockpit. In an April 2002 incident in Afghanistan, four Canadian soldiers were killed when a United States Air Force fighter pilot mistakenly dropped a bomb on their training exercise location. The USAF pilot was found to have been derelict in carrying out his duty[11] but, as an individual, he never acknowledged his personal responsibility for his actions. Clearly, this pilot did not feel the restraint inherent in an "if you're not sure don't shoot" environment, and the results were tragic.

During the recent Libyan campaign, Lieutenant-General Bouchard considered the effect that target selection could have on world opinion and was very aware of the potential consequences of a targeting error. Knowing this, he nevertheless passed the final authority for weapons release to the aircraft pilot, while making the significance of that decision clear: "Let's not lose the hearts and minds ... I'll be damned if I have to stand up and apologise for shooting a bus load of people going to a wedding! If you're not sure, don't shoot."[12] An RCAF junior officer may have his or her finger on the trigger to launch a missile or release a bomb that could change the entire political course of a conflict. Similarly, he or she can be sent on a mission with the authority to release a weapon with the constraint that all the parameters must be right, including the potential for harm to noncombatants. This can and does create a difficult balance between being a warrior one minute and being sensitive to the ethical consequences of making a decision the next.

PIGEAU/MCCANN –
LEGALITY, PROFESSIONALISM, AND ETHICS

The Pigeau/McCann model[13] is a useful tool to illustrate the challenges involved with the ethics of command, especially when considering the unique challenges of strategic leadership and command where many of the less obvious ethical/legal conflicts occur. The portion of the Pigeau/McCann model that deals with the balanced command envelope (authority, responsibility, and competency)[14] is familiar to most CAF officers and is a significant aid to understanding the command environment. It is in Pigeau's definition of command as "the creative and purposeful exercise of legitimate authority to accomplish the mission legally, professionally and ethically"[15] that the ethical/legal conflict is most evident. This definition of command resonates with most military personnel and, indeed, with many civilians that are exposed to his approach. Pigeau illustrates his definition using a three-dimensional box that creates a volume referred to as the "total solution space" for the decision. This box holds all possible solutions ranging from legal to illegal along one axis, professional to unprofessional along the second axis, and ethical to unethical along the third. Inside this solution space is a smaller box with the 'acceptable' solution space constrained along the three axes of legality, professionalism, and ethicality.[16] The remainder of the potential solution space is out of bounds because command decisions or actions that lie in that area will be illegal, unprofessional, unethical, or some combination of the three.

Pigeau's method ascribes equal importance to all three dimensions, an approach that is excellent for teaching the concept but less practical in the real world of leadership and command. As a problem equally applicable at the tactical, operational, and strategic levels, the actual world of military decision-making can, at times, pose more complex scenarios. It is quite possible that a potential command decision may be professional and legal but unethical, or ethical and professional but illegal, with the major conflict being between the legality and the morality of a decision. The critical challenge to the commander then arises when it is not possible to find a decision that is both legal and ethical. The dilemma then becomes: do I follow the legal route at the expense of my ethical values, or do I do what is morally right but risk behaving illegally?

THE OCCASIONAL CONFLICT BETWEEN LEGAL AND ETHICAL

Fortunately for those with command responsibilities, doing the legal thing almost always aligns with doing the ethical thing. However, there is on occasion a natural tension between following orders and meeting ethical requirements, and on rare occasions the conflict between the two can be extreme.

> Military hierarchies sensibly insist upon obedience to orders and upon prompt, total discipline. Ethics, however, demurs, insisting upon conditional and contextual obedience to orders, which ought to be obeyed if lawful. So there is often, but not always, tension between the demands of military authority (or command) and the demands of ethical judgment (or conscience).[17]

It follows of course that the opposite is also true; a morally justifiable act may not be legal. Legal does not carry the connotation 'fair' or 'right,' so doing the right thing may indeed not be legal in some circumstances.

Nevertheless, there may come a time when a commander finds the two things are in conflict – the legal imperative (be it an order or legitimate direction or existing regulation) will push the commander in one direction while the ethical considerations will push in another. This conflict can occur at any level, but can be particularly challenging at the strategic level, where a wide range of specialist advisors exist to provide input to help the commander make a decision, and where the distance to the point at which the orders directly impact people is significantly greater.

The following scenarios illustrate some of the conflict issues that can arise.

Scenario 1 – Fighting the NDHQ Solution

Legalism (obeying orders and/or the Law) is sometimes of poor counsel in matters of ethical conduct. It does not follow that infractions against regulations or against the Law should be ignored.[18]

Michael Reid

The legalistic nature of the strategic level at NDHQ is well described in a Defence Research and Development Canada (DRDC) study of moral and ethical decision-making in CAF operations. The specific case from which this account is drawn occurred towards the end of the 1990s, and is not unique to this one situation. In this case, a United Nations Force Commander is quoted describing his consultation with NDHQ discussing Ottawa's very negative reaction to suggested Rules of Engagement that gave Canadian soldiers under UN command the right to use lethal force to protect any human being they were aware was being threatened. NDHQ was very reluctant to approve any such ROE, to the obvious disgust of the Force Commander:

The decision in Ottawa came from a legalistic point of view. It was just a few years after the Somalia crisis, so we had an NDHQ that was very gun shy, very nervous. The lawyers were almost in command of the CAF, and they would look at every word in the mandate and, if it was not legal, you could not do that and so on

... But there is what is legal and what is moral, and I knew that we could be on the high moral plane without being illegal. So then I debated with Ottawa on the principles and the values, the morality of it ... But, from a legalistic point of view, you don't give us the right to do so. I cannot live with that. Morally, I cannot live with that as a senior commander ... Legal or illegal in that circumstance, the right to use lethal force to protect any human being, I know that no one will ever tell you it is illegal to do so.[19]

The specific question of a commander's responsibility to ensure appropriate ROE for his subordinates, while a key command ethical responsibility, is not the major focus of this example; the tendency for legal advice to predominate at the strategic level is, along with the predicament it exacerbates for commanders in the field who are inclined to pursue the moral ahead of the legal. The focus on legal advice does not appear to have waned significantly at NDHQ. Describing a characteristic of Canadians during the Libyan air campaign, the NATO commander commented, "The Canadians were OK – but they drove me nuts with their lawyers and the targeting issues! ... and also they got really worried."[20]

The strategic-level commander cannot ignore the legal contribution any more than other advice he or she is offered, but as the commander he or she alone has the authority to make the decision, considering the direction suggested by the advice. The law, however, cannot be ignored, as succinctly stated in a thought-provoking discussion in the Canadian Military Journal: "illegality in and of itself does not render an act morally unjustifiable."[21] The advisor (be they legal, medical, or other) bears responsibility for the quality of the advice but not the outcome of the decision. In the end, if a commander makes a decision based on the input from an advisor, the commander alone is accountable for the outcome of the decision.

A dangerous trap for a commander when receiving advice that is potentially in conflict with the action believed to be appropriate is to go shopping for even more advice. The danger here is perhaps best stated by Sun Tzu: "the worst calamities that befall an army arise from hesitation."[22] A senior Air Force leader, who seldom hesitated himself, pointed out that an unwillingness to make decisions at NDHQ can have serious consequences; he identified decisiveness as a key strategic leadership competency:

> When [a specific individual] was Vice, decisions seemed to be difficult, and he was always looking for that higher order of confidence. And boy, it used to be frustrating ... You can't do that in the Vice's job, you really can't ... another one of those qualities, if I'm looking at a guy to be the Vice, you need a guy who is going to make those decisions.[23]

The major effect of a strategic-level leader interpreting advice as direction inevitably results in the creation of an ethical dilemma further down the chain, often producing enormous stresses for subordinate commanders who have less flexibility to deal with the decision.

Scenario 2 – Abandoning the Mission

Human beings generally know right from wrong, honor from shame, virtue from vice.[24]

J.H. Toner

Although not a Canadian example, the situation that occurred in Srebrenica in July 1994 during the Bosnian war illustrates the moral consequences of obeying orders at the operational/tactical level despite the ethical imperative. In this case, the actions of Lieutenant-Colonel Thom Karremans, the commander of the Dutch battalion soldiers assigned to the UN-protected enclave of Srebrenica, were in line with the legal direction he was given by higher UN command as well as the national policy of the Netherlands with respect to safeguarding the lives of Dutch soldiers. The event briefly: Lieutenant-Colonel Karremans' fear that his troops would be overpowered if he resisted the Serbian forces demanding the surrender of the Muslim enclave he was charged to protect caused him to submit without a struggle. In his defence, he had requested but not received UN air support, and felt he could not resist the capture of the enclave by the numerically superior Bosnian Serbs. Subsequently, the Bosnians transferred the women and children out of the protected zone and then systematically murdered the nearly 8,000 Muslim men and boys that were left. Karremans was promoted to colonel shortly after his return to the Netherlands.

For similar circumstances involving a Canadian general sheltering fleeing Serbs with a dramatically different outcome, the reader is referred to the testimony of Major-General Alain Forand in front of the Croatia Board of Inquiry.

A major ethical maxim that emerges from the above discussion: decisions have consequences. Even the 'correct' doctrinal decision, in keeping with national direction, can have a disastrous result. As a military commander, the responsibility for the consequences remains with the decision-maker, and those consequences cannot be ameliorated by pointing to doctrine, national direction, or advice.

Scenario 3 – "Mercy Killing"

Many choices in military ethics are defective precisely because airmen or soldiers forget or ignore the idea that, almost without exception, the end does not and cannot justify the means.[25]

J.H. Toner

A very clear conflict between what appeared to be a personal moral and ethical decision and an important legal restraint captured national attention in 2010 and placed an individual's decision up for national debate. It is clear from the discussion that ensued that both informed and merely interested public opinion was seriously split on this issue, which involved a purported battlefield 'mercy killing' in Afghanistan and the subsequent court-martial and conviction for disgraceful conduct of Captain Robert Semrau, the infantry officer involved. The range and intensity of opinion regarding this incident reflects the complexity of the ethical/legal conflict, and the potential for serious personal and institutional consequences. There was a large group of Canadians that supported Semrau's actions, including some prominent retired military leaders.

> Peter Worthington, columnist for the Toronto Sun ... described Semrau as "behaving honourably, humanely, decently," and Major-General (ret'd) Lewis MacKenzie, an experienced Canadian commander with many operational tours under his belt, was quoted in the press as declaring Semrau's actions "appropriate." In addition, over 8000 individuals had joined the Support the Freedom of Captain Robert Semrau Internet site as of 19 July 2010.[26]

The actual killing of the wounded Taliban fighter, assumed to be a mercy killing, cannot be justified by any ethical framework taught in the Canadian Armed Forces,[27] nor is it in any way supported by national or international law, including the law of armed conflict.

Even a result that is universally considered positive cannot be used to substantiate such a decision, a principle succinctly summarized by Dr Toner in the quotation above. Regardless, an action such as this is clearly supported by a large number of Canadians, even when the full details of the personal motivation are not known.

A USN Judge Advocate, Lieutenant Gabriel Bradley, says when describing the law, which he considers as a minimum standard for the conduct of war, that it "does an OK job of sorting out the aftermath of an incident and categorizing the participants as either guilty or not guilty. But the law often falls short as a catalyst for ethical behaviour, especially on the battlefield."[28]

At the individual level, decisions in situations such as this are deeply subjective, often drawing on personally held values and beliefs, but the reality of the law cannot be ignored. If an individual chooses to follow the ethical route, one could certainly argue that respect for the dignity of the person could involve alleviating suffering. Then, at the same time, one must accept the consequences of that decision, whether the consequences are deemed just or unjust by public opinion.

Scenario 4 – Air Force Targeting

I could see people taking over my targeting ... every bomb was a NATO bomb.[29]

Lieutenant-General G. Bouchard

Air power can be defined in a number of ways, but the common element is that it is force delivered from the air or from space with the intent of influencing the behaviour of people or the course of events on the ground. The fact that the deliverer is physically removed from the receiver illustrates the abiding challenge that targeting presents for an Air Force officer. Recent conflicts such as Iraq, Kosovo, Afghanistan, and Libya have demonstrated a range of such challenges.

The 1990 Gulf War placed exceptional stresses on the Air Force, which was still coming out of a Cold War posture and targeting mentality. In essence, targeting in this environment was a novel concern, and it was complicated by the lack of consensus within the Air Force about whether or not Canadian aircraft should even be involved in bombing.

Then we got to the point where now the Iraqis were in retreat and were Canadians going to bomb or were they not going to bomb? ... there wasn't one person that had the same opinion. Even within the headquarters in Winnipeg, there was a difference of opinion.[30]

In the end, the vast majority of CAF missions were not involved with delivering weapons against ground-based targets, and there were few ethical challenges that arose from targeting issues. Fortunately, by the time the next conflict involving the Air Force arose in Kosovo, the internal process had radically improved, as had the overall governance model of the CAF. The dramatic improvement was noted: "if you were somehow able to weigh these two and compare them as experiences, the bombing campaign out of Aviano was a no brainer compared to the dog's breakfast that was going on when the Gulf war was on."[31] The actual targeting issues during the air campaign in Kosovo proved to be more problematic. The targeting methodology was to select a combination of hard military targets and what was referred to as "dual-use" assets – that is, infrastructure that served the military but also provided essential services to the civilian population, such as the electrical power grid and oil facilities. The overall targeting approach was complicated by the rapidity with which information could transfer out of theatre and the impact that poor targeting selection and delivery errors could have on the support of the Western nations for the campaign. Vice-Admiral Cebrowski, the president of the US Navy War College (1998 to 2001), identified that the information age would have a direct effect on targeting: "our decision-making – our targeting decisions – will continue to be scrutinized in ever-increasing detail."[32]

The question of targeting civilian objectives as well as the issue of rebuilding essential civilian infrastructure after the conflict became a very real factor in the decision. In a report discussing the legal and ethical lessons from Kosovo, one author acknowledges that NATO targeted power facilities, but with caveats:

It is no secret that NATO targeted electrical power facilities. Such facilities are normally targeted during hostilities, because they do provide energy resources to military forces, and their destruction has a direct military advantage. Nevertheless, during

Kosovo, we were careful to avoid undue and prolonged power outages which would have a disproportionate effect on the civilian population ... There were some "hard kill" power grid attacks, and NATO did shut down the grid throughout Serbia at one point, but the outage was not permanent.[33]

The air campaign in Libya provides yet another example of the concern that commanders have for targeting in a modern conflict where the West continues to have an obligation to the population once the conflict ends. The thoughts of the commander of the NATO military mission in Libya reflect the increased focus on ethical targeting issues: "Shock and awe is not a good idea because you break a lot of things ... and we spend a lot of money re-building."[34] Unlike the use of air power in other campaigns and wars where the intent was to use the maximum force to achieve the maximum destruction in the shortest period of time, the commander of military operations in Libya had a different set of targeting priorities. "We worked very hard – we approached targeting differently. My weapon of choice was not kinetic ... we had a campaign that allowed us to do that."[35] Even when the kinetic approach was necessary, force was used judiciously, although it cost more in time. "[We proceeded] slow and deliberate ... [Senator John McCain] said we could have solved this problem a lot faster. I thought, yeah, but look at the mess we would have to clean up afterwards."[36] While not everyone agreed with the approach, it was effective: "Can you imagine how much china we would have [had] to fix [if we had used only kinetic means]?"[37]

At the operational and strategic levels, targeting philosophy has changed dramatically – and in the process it has become more aligned with ethical values.

Scenario 5 – Strategic Ethical Issues

You need a different skill set to survive in the NDHQ bureaucracy than you do in the field even a field command like the air command headquarters.[38]

Lieutenant-General G. Bouchard

While the leadership styles may vary at the strategic level, the ethics of command are the same. They are effectively the ethics of principle-guided leadership in a politically influenced environment. Decisions at this level are not simple; indeed, they can be very complex in a sphere where resource trade-offs may demand ethical and/or operational compromises. Such an example occurred in February 1999 when the Chief of Defence Staff, General Maurice Baril, made a decision to support the prime minister's reason for not personally attending King Hussein of Jordan's funeral, i.e., the Air Force could not provide him with an aircraft in time.[39] Despite the embarrassment of providing a blatantly false excuse (a journalist was able to access the RCAF log books to discover that the Air Force had flown the prime minister to a medical appointment in the United States at the time he was reportedly on a ski vacation),[40] Baril publicly stated that the Canadian Air Force had failed to be able to get the prime minister to Jordan on time. In this case, the CDS was making a decision that allegedly shaded the truth based on his assessment of benefit to the institution by sparing the prime minister political embarrassment. While that benefit may have been relatively short-lived (the financial cuts continued to impact the CAF after a short delay), the long-term impact on the CDS's reputation was not.

Another aspect of strategic command that reflects directly on ethics is the willingness to be accountable for the actions of subordinates, regardless of the level of personal knowledge of those actions. The sheer magnitude of the activities that are carried out on a regular basis under the responsibilities of a senior commander make it virtually impossible to be aware of everything; "You can find in any given day when you're in command there's a thousand things going on out there that you have no knowledge of, any one of which, if they blow up, you're going to wear."[41] Few will forget a previous CDS, Jean Boyle, who publicly blamed his subordinates' "lack of moral fibre" for an inaccurate answer he provided to the Somalia Inquiry.

Lack of awareness does not alter the responsibility of the commander; indeed, it increases the requirement for trust and the willingness to be held accountable. "You've got to hope that you've given the right guidance, you got to trust your people and you got to stand behind them. Then you've got to cross your fingers and hope nothing goes wrong. It's that bloody basic."[42]

The nature of serving Canada before self also shifts at the strategic level – whereas Allan English identifies loyalty[43] as being first to one's service, regiment, or branch, at the strategic level ethics demands that loyalty shifts away from the individual services and towards a joint institution with a full range of combatant capabilities – not always an easy or a successful transition. For some, it was seen as an increased loyalty, "[s]o our whole question of loyalty stepped up two notches higher than had ever been before."[44] It requires moving beyond narrow service interests to "creating the type of working environment and decision making environment wherein the right decisions were being made that should be able to explain to everybody, the Canadian public and the government."[45]

A previous Commander of Air Command, Kinsman, summed up the ethical motivation required of a good strategic leader in the CAF when he said, "The good strategic leader has to take gratification and motivation from the fact that what they are doing ultimately will benefit the organization, even if they are not around to see it anymore."[46]

CONCLUSION

The current ethical culture within which the men and women who make up the Canadian Forces operate had its roots in the Somalia scandal, an incident as much a result of institutional lapses as of individual misbehaviour. The original incident, a deplorable loss of discipline and order within the deployed Airborne Regiment, was exacerbated by the failures of senior leadership both before and after the incident. This was a senior leadership fixated on dealing with an exasperating succession of budget cuts that reduced strategic planning to a reactive exercise and encouraged serious inter- and intra-service rivalry for the shrinking financial base. Professional development struggled and serious morale issues flourished across the force.

It was into this formidable environment nearly twenty years ago that the CAF launched a renewed and invigorated professional development approach and a formal defence ethics programme. The intervening period has been characterized by intense operational activity and a much more positive financial environment for the military. Every indication, so far, is that the effect on morality and conduct has been universally positive, certainly at the tactical level.

The attainment of the same level of success at the strategic level is more difficult to assess, but looking at the key parameters of the efficacy of joint operations, the care and welfare of personnel (particularly the injured), and the effectiveness of acquiring essential equipment can provide a clue. Certainly throughout the involvement in combat operations in Afghanistan these three issues seemed to be doing reasonably well; however, with combat operations in Afghanistan ending and the operational intensity expected to remain relatively low into the future, the financial situation for the CAF is more problematic for the strategic leadership.

Vigilance will be required to ensure that strategic command attention is not diverted from these key issues.

NOTES

1 A. English and J. Westrop, *Canadian Air Force Leadership and Command: The Human Dimension of Expeditionary Air Force Operations* (Trenton, ON: CF Aerospace Warfare Centre, 2007), 4–112.

2 See for example A. English, *Understanding Military Culture: A Canadian Perspective* (Montreal and Kingston, ON: McGill-Queen's University Press, 2004); Ross Pigeau and Carol McCann, "What Is a Commander?" in *Generalship and the Art of the Admiral: Perspectives on Canadian Senior Military Leadership*, ed. Bernd Horn and Stephen J. Harris (St Catharines, ON: Vanwell Publishing, 2001), 80–3; Department of National Defence (DND), *The Fundamentals of Canadian Defence Ethics* (Ottawa: Defence Ethics Programme, January 2002), http://www.forces.gc.ca/assets/ FORCES_Internet/docs/en/about/fundamentals-fondements-eng.pdf (accessed 10 August 2014).

3 See for example DND, *Duty with Honour: The Profession of Arms in Canada* (Kingston, ON: CF Leadership Institute, 2003); DND, *Leadership in the Canadian Forces: Conceptual Foundations* (Kingston, ON: Canadian Defence Academy, 2005); DND, *The Fundamentals of Canadian Defence Ethics*. See also English, *Understanding Military Culture*, 60–1, and DND, *Ethics in the Canadian Forces: Making Tough Choices* (Kingston, ON: Canadian Defence Academy, 2006), 12.

4 Interview with Vice-Admiral Larry Murray conducted by the author on 21 March 2003. This unpublished interview was part of a series conducted by the author as part of a project for the Canadian Armed Forces Leadership Institute (CFLI) examining the strategic leadership competencies required by general and flag officers functioning at the strategic level at National Defence Headquarters. The results of the interviews are summarized in G.E. Sharpe and Allan English, "The Decade of Darkness – The Experience of the Senior Leadership of the Canadian Forces in the 1990s," unpublished paper written for the CFLI dated 24 February 2004. All subsequent interview citations refer to this series of interviews unless otherwise noted.

5 Interview with Lieutenant-General Dave Kinsman conducted by the author on 20 March 2003.

6 Sharpe and English, "The Decade of Darkness." A major focus of the discussion here was the impact, both short- and long-term, of the Somalia Inquiry on the senior leadership of the CAF, and a general sense of the ethical standards required of senior leaders in the Canadian Armed Forces.

7 Ibid., 5.

8 Interview with Lieutenant-General Al Dequettville by the author conducted on 10 March 2003. Referring to budget cuts, he said, "The reality was that we rolled into 1990 and I remember one point in there that in seven years we had eleven force development budget cutting exercises."

9 A. English, "The Masks of Command: Leadership Differences in the Canadian Army, Navy and Air Force," in *The Operational Art Canadian Perspectives: Leadership and Command*, ed. English (Kingston, ON: Canadian Defence Academy Press, 2006), 5.

10 Lieutenant-General Charlie Bouchard, unpublished interview conducted by the author and Brigadier-General (Ret'd) Terry Leversedge, 27 February 2012.

11 *CBC News Online*, "Friendly Fire, Friendly Fire Case: The Legal Saga," http://www.cbc.ca/news/background/friendlyfire/ (6 June 2005): "Schmidt faced two counts of dereliction of duty for not making sure he was dropping a bomb on the enemy and for disobeying air controllers' instructions to 'standby' while information was verified. The formal counts allege that he 'failed to comply with the applicable rules of engagement' and 'willfully failed to exercise appropriate flight discipline over his aircraft.'"

12 Lieutenant-General C. Bouchard, interview (27 February 2012).

13 A. English, *Command and Control of Canadian Aerospace Forces: Conceptual Foundations* (Trenton, ON: Canadian Forces Aerospace Warfare Centre, 2008), 9–13. This publication provides a good summary of the Pigeau/McCann model.

14 R. Pigeau and C. McCann, "Re-Conceptualizing Command and Control," *Canadian Military Journal* (Spring 2002): 53–64.

15 R. Pigeau and C. McCann, "Re-Conceptualizing Command and Control," presentation given to Command and Staff Course 31 (Canadian Forces College, 3 Sept. 2004); R. Pigeau and C. McCann, "Establishing Common Intent: The Key to Co-ordinated Military Action," in *The Operational Art Canadian Perspectives: Leadership and Command*, ed. A. English (Kingston, ON: Canadian Defence Academy Press, 2006), 92–5.

16 Pigeau and McCann, "Re-Conceptualizing Command and Control": "The will of Command has traditionally been bounded by certain principles. These guiding principles have taken three forms: military law, professional

standards, and ethical norms. Military law encompasses: 1 the explicit legal structure for the authority that the state gives to its military; in Canada, this authority is defined in the National Defence Act and is manifest in the military judicial system and the rules and regulations that derive from the NDA; 2 the international legal agreements that the state is party to. Militaries commonly view themselves as professionals with codes of conduct that guide self-regulation. These professional standards are a military's own mechanism for ensuring that a default level of expertise, identity and responsibility exists among its members. Finally, when neither laws nor professional principles are available, ethical norms are often the only recourse for determining acceptable behaviour. Ethical norms are an expression of a nation's values and beliefs – i.e., its culture."

17 J.H. Toner, "Military OR Ethics," *Air & Space Power Journal* (Summer 2003): 81.

18 M. Reid, "Where Ethics and Legality Collide," *Canadian Military Journal* 11, no. 3 (Summer 2011): 5.

19 "Moral and Ethical Decision Making in Canadian Forces Operations," DRDC Toronto no. CR 2006-013 (January 2006): 17.

20 Interview with Lieutenant-General Bouchard, 27 February 2012, conducted by the author and Brigadier-General (Ret'd) Terry Leversedge.

21 Reid, "Where Ethics and Legality Collide," 6.

22 S.F. Kaufman, *Sun Tzu, "The Art of War" – The Definitive Interpretation* (Boston: Tuttle Publishing, 2001).

23 Lieutenant-General O'Donnell, unpublished interview conducted by the author on 25 February 2003, discussing the strategic leadership competencies required for general officers functioning at the strategic level at NDHQ.

24 J.H. Toner, "Mistakes in Teaching Ethics," *Airpower Journal* (Summer 1998): 45.

25 Toner, "Military OR Ethics," 82.

26 P. Bradley, "Is Mercy Killing Justifiable?" *Canadian Military Journal* 1, no. 1 (Winter 2010): 8.

27 Ibid., 14.

28 Lieutenant (USN) Gabriel Bradley, "Honor, Not Law," *Armed Forces Journal* (March 2012): 1.

29 Lieutenant-General G. Bouchard, interview (27 February 2012).

30 Lieutenant-General D. Kinsman, interview (20 March 2003).

31 Ibid.

32 Vice-Admiral Cebrowski, "Kosovo, Legal and Ethical Lessons," Opening Remarks, "Challenges," *Law Studies* 78 (Newport, RI: Naval War College, 2002): 5.

33 Judith A. Miller, *Kosovo Legal and Ethical Lessons* – "Commentary,"
    109–10.

34 Lieutenant-General G. Bouchard, interview (27 February 2012).

35 Ibid.

36 Ibid.

37 Ibid.

38 Ibid.

39 Hansard no. 178 (10 Feb. 1999).

40 Ezra Levant, Ezra Levant Archives (1 February 2010), http://ezralevant.
    com/2010/02: "Under extreme political pressure, the air force released an
    unsigned press release, saying it had let down Chretien by not being ready.
    No mention was made of the Minnesota flight. And the next day, Gen.
    Maurice Baril, then the Chief of Defence Staff, held a press conference to
    personally accept the blame. Again, no mention of the Minnesota flight.
    But air force log books aren't subject to political cleanups: they show that
    Chretien wasn't in Vancouver on Feb. 8, 1999. At 7:55 a.m., he flew to
    Minnesota, and stayed there until 4:50 p.m., when he returned to Ottawa."

41 Lieutenant-General Al Dequettville, interview (10 March 2003).

42 Ibid.

43 English, "The Masks of Command," 26. "In each service there is a hier-
    archy of loyalties that influences how leadership can be exercised in each
    combat environment. In the Canadian navy and air force the loyalty hier-
    archy appears to be 1) service (navy or air force), 2) job/occupation (mari-
    time engineer, pilot, etc.), then 3) unit (ship or squadron). For the
    Canadian infantry, and to some degree the armoured corps, it seems to be
    1) regiment 2) branch (infantry or armoured), then 3) the army as a ser-
    vice. For other army branches, because of their relatively high technical
    leadership component, it may be: 1) job/branch 2) service 3) unit."

44 Lieutenant-General Kinsman, interview (20 March 2003).

45 Ibid.

46 Ibid.

3

Military Ethics and the Comprehensive Approach: Some Preliminary Observations[1]

PETER J. GIZEWSKI, HEATHER HRYCHUK, AND RICHARD DICKSON

INTRODUCTION

The need to practice a more coherent, holistic, and collaborative approach to the challenges of governance and security operations is becoming ever more recognized both in Canada and elsewhere. Numerous officials in Canada and a number of other states (e.g., the United States, the United Kingdom, and other NATO allies) are increasingly calling for the adoption of a more "Comprehensive Approach" (CA) to operations. Such an approach would see diplomatic, defence, development, and commercial resources aligned with those of non-governmental organizations, coordinated through an integrated campaign plan, and applied in areas of operations as needed. The result would be more effective responses to the security challenges confronted.

Thus far, advocates of the approach have largely focused on the practical benefits it promises – with emphasis placed on its capacity to aid in achieving mission goals in a complex and often multifaceted security environment. Yet, one area that has generally been neglected lies in the realm of military ethics. More precisely, little academic attention has been devoted to the potential opportunities and challenges that militaries may confront as they move to adopt and effectively implement (practice) a more collaborative, comprehensive approach to operations. Such neglect is unfortunate. Many of the practical challenges inherent in practising a CA often have ethical implications. More importantly, ethical decision-making not only represents a key component of the military profession, but is central to ensuring the credibility and legitimacy of military operations. As such, neglect of the ethical implications which a CA raises may well work to shortchange, if not undermine, the promise of the approach itself.

This chapter explores a number of these issues within the context of the Canadian military experience. Following a brief outline of the basic premises informing the CA, it identifies a number of potential implications that the approach raises for the practice of ethical decision-making – both in general and with reference to military operations. It then concludes with a discussion of those steps required to more fully ensure military practice of a Comprehensive Approach that is both ethically sound and, at the same time, operationally effective.

THE COMPREHENSIVE APPROACH: KEY ELEMENTS

The meaning ascribed to the term 'CA' varies.[2] While some see the approach as a means of interacting with a myriad of national and international entities to resolve security challenges, others have used the term primarily to refer to whole-government and/or inter-agency coordination. Still others have loosely employed it to refer to simple coordination mechanisms at the tactical level of operations.[3]

In general, however, a CA calls for bringing previously separate agencies into closer collaboration in achieving policy objectives. It entails developing a capacity to interact with such organizations and agencies in a cooperative, constructive manner, thus creating a competency that cuts across departments and dispenses with "stovepipes." In fact, the idea has roots in the private-sector management theory of re-engineering, and aims at streamlining processes from input to output in order to maximize efficiency and remove overlap and duplication. Such re-engineering seeks to create an end-to-end cross-departmental process, leading to an organization that runs more smoothly and efficiently.[4]

From a Canadian Armed Forces standpoint, such an approach involves:

• The adoption of a 'team' approach to develop an integrated campaign plan in order to realize its operational and strategic objectives in full-spectrum operations;

- The willingness to consider second- and third-order effects in its planning process;
- The ability to immediately plug into joint battle space operating systems to cooperate effectively;
- The ability to facilitate the building of inter-agency and multinational interoperability through collaborative planning mechanisms and protocols;
- The ability to connect non-governmental agencies with CAF operational architecture, and to act as a liaison to support these agencies in the execution of the mission;
- The ability to implement effective communication with joint and other multinational agencies (this would also include the ability to provide an efficient interface between conventional and special forces);
- The capacity to access key information in an efficient timely manner – so as to identify targets for attack and influence as well as determine the joint, inter-agency, multinational, and public resources required in operations; and
- The ability to clearly and effectively communicate mission goals, objectives, and actions to the public and members of the media *as required.*

With all actions based on agreed-upon principles and collaborative, cooperative processes, greater organizational efficiencies could be obtained, and traditional organizational "stovepipes" overcome through enhanced synergies. Information sharing between organizations would potentially be enhanced. Strategic framing of issues and campaign planning could be improved. Furthermore, the approach could well generate a greater degree of organizational awareness, interaction, integration, and coherence when addressing security threats. The overall results would be more effective responses to the security threats and challenges confronted.

THE "PROMISE" OF ETHICAL DECISION-MAKING

In fact, the approach has implications for decision-making not only in the security realm but in the field of ethics as well. As Peter Bradley notes, decisions have ethical implications if the choices available to a decision-maker possess the potential to harm or benefit people. Ethical decisions are those that lead to moral outcomes, satisfy the moral and professional obligations owed to stakeholders, and follow from moral motives rather than self-interest or non-moral influences.[5] The prospects that decisions having ethical implications will arise during military operations are clearly legion. Therefore, the ethical aspects of decision-making are important. In a world in which the legitimacy of one's actions is often the vital ground for both domestic and international support for policy, and in which decisions arrived at can have life and death consequences[6] (for both stakeholders and others), ethical behaviour clearly matters. Moreover, ethics and subscription to a code of ethical conduct go to the heart of the military identity – representing, in effect, a key component of military professionalism. As American ethicist and theologian H. Richard Niebuhr notes, "[t]he first question of ethics is not what should I do but rather what is going on?"[7]

In this regard, the very nature of a CA may work to more fully facilitate sound ethical decision-making in a variety of ways. In fact, it may work not only to help ensure more ethical outcomes, but also to create more ethically informed decision-makers. By increasing the capacity of militaries to more effectively interact with a host of other entities in an area of operations, including many individuals and organizations with their own unique skill sets and areas of expertise, a CA would facilitate increased awareness, and potentially better understanding, of both the operating environment and the players within it. Indeed, it would increase the character, amount, and quality of information upon which decisions could be based. As such, effective practice of a CA could raise the capacity of those practising it to gain a richer, more complete picture of "what is going on" – militarily, socially, culturally, economically, and/or politically – in an area of operations.

The fact that decision-making in a CA would often occur in contexts in which decision-makers and their actions would be under increased scrutiny – simply by virtue of the number of organizations and/or other entities involved at various points in the decision-making process – could serve as an additional support to ethical practice. By increasing the potential for the articulation and consideration of a range of ideas and viewpoints, both within the CAF and beyond it (through the involvement of other government departments, NGOs, private volunteer organizations, etc.), courses of action, key goals, and objectives may be more fully vetted, debated, monitored, and more consciously adjusted to ensure that the decisions arrived at and actions taken are not only operationally effective, but more ethically informed. Beyond this, and assuming that conduct of a CA were to eventually become an integral – and fully institutionalized – component of the policy-making process (i.e. informing not only the application of policy but its formulation as well), this could improve the chances that a number of key ethical issues would be considered and addressed well before any operational deployment took place. In turn, it would reduce the chances for a number of ethical dilemmas and challenges to arise during conduct of the operation or mission itself. At the very least, this would more fully ensure that decision-makers are better prepared to address such challenges if and when they are encountered.

In time, the approach could even play an important role in the ethical education and training of officers – most notably through the cataloguing and use of events from past operations that involve ethical dilemmas and challenges. Once recorded, such incidents could be used as teaching tools through which to convey key ethical issues, principles, and examples of past ethical best practice (i.e. lessons learned). They may even serve as a base upon which to develop scenarios involving key ethical dilemmas for critical discussion and analysis.[8] The result could well be a greater sensitivity to and appreciation of the ethical problems likely to arise in operations among those involved.

ETHICAL CHALLENGES / ETHICAL DANGERS

Nevertheless, ensuring that a CA in fact meets its full potential is by no means certain. Effective practice of such an approach is not simple. Interaction with a range of players, diverse perspectives, and new and varied sources of information can also complicate the decision-making process – raising as many challenges as it can potentially help address.

Developing the capacity to work with a range of organizations, each with its own culture, mindset, agendas, and goals, is no easy task. Such efforts often confront issues of cultural and professional bias, problems of information sharing, and constraints stemming from resource asymmetries between organizations. Absent effective practices and procedures capable of surmounting obstacles – such as communication between the multitude of players each with its own culture, mandate, and goals – which such an approach encourages, implementing a CA may not only be difficult, but could lead to ethical confusion or even paralysis as decision-makers wrestle with the often divergent viewpoints and perspectives that its practice can yield. In fact, rather than serving as an aid to ethical decision-making, the CA could result in a disunity of effort that would ultimately be self-defeating.

The ethical issues that can arise in the practice of a CA and the challenges they can raise for decision-makers are too numerous to be fully identified and examined here. No two military operations are identical and the circumstances giving rise to ethical issues are limitless. That said, a number of general examples are noteworthy in highlighting some of the key challenges that may arise. In fact, the very practice and institutionalization of the approach itself would tend to ensure that the issues and challenges these examples raise would likely be encountered by those practising it.

SELECT EXAMPLES

Ethics and Information Sharing

The practice of a CA is strongly premised on the likelihood, importance, and advantages of information sharing between parties. In a world in which security challenges are often multi-dimensional, the capacity to access information and analysis from a variety of sources – many with unique perspectives and areas of expertise – should help ensure more informed decision-making.

Certainly, over-classification of information can raise ethical dilemmas. In a collaborative environment, it can place CA partners at increased risk in the field. In conflict-torn regions such as Afghanistan, for instance, military dissemination of knowledge regarding locals suspected of possessing insurgent ties or taking part in other nefarious practices is often highly restricted. However, such information could well be crucial to civilian partners engaging in efforts to cultivate relations with local tribal leaders.[9] In such cases, constraints on information sharing may work to deny key players vital knowledge of potential risks and threats, reducing both their capacity to make informed decisions and, potentially, the security of both themselves and those they seek to influence.

Greater information sharing in military operations can nevertheless raise fundamental ethical questions. Military provision of information to NGOs and indigenous groups warning of impending military action or enemy attack offers a case in point. While such actions might reflect sound ethical practice in certain cases, the possibility of such conduct working to increase the chance of information leaks could clearly produce a less ethically satisfying result.

As but one example, NATO cooperation with Pakistan, a supposed ally in the War on Terror, resulted in information leaks and the promulgation of disinformation in the early days of war against the Taliban. Blamed on low-ranking Taliban sympathizers in the Pakistani Army and Inter-Services Intelligence, this resulted in numerous tactical challenges, including an incident in which US helicopters were subject to small-arms fire at the Dalbandin air base in Baluchistan.[10] By fighting a war out of Pakistan at the time, a task that required some information sharing with Pakistani authorities, the US found itself in the line of a strange variant of friendly fire. Were such information leaks to result in enemy attack and heavy casualties among soldiers, allies, and key partners, the outcome could well be even more counterproductive both strategically *and* ethically.

In short, rather than always facilitating ethical decision-making, the very character and practice of a CA could see ethical challenges multiply. Indeed, in a decision-making environment featuring multiple players and more agendas, fundamental ethical questions concerning not only what information should be shared, but when and with whom, may increase. Moreover, the capacity of decision-makers to effectively resolve such dilemmas may come under excessive strain.

Ethics of Association

Ethical challenges can also be encountered in a number of instances involving military association with other players. While on the whole encouraged under a CA, close association with certain groups within an area of operations may not only compromise the utility and effectiveness of such groups, but place them at increased risk of harm.

The experience of NGOs with a humanitarian focus bears out this point. While soldiers performing regular patrols in zones of conflict may have sources of information for aid workers on those sectors in which assistance is especially needed or in which specific community complaints have been raised, NGO receipt of such information is not always welcomed. Indeed, reliance on data provided by the military may run counter to NGOs' independence and to their neutrality in conducting their tasks.[11] The results may be ethically counterproductive – both for the NGOs themselves and for the local populations they seek to assist. Such associations may taint NGOs' relations with populations to a point where those in need come to associate all humanitarian aid with armed soldiers and thereby avoid approaching any NGO for assistance for fear of retribution from enemy combatants. They may also increase danger to humanitarian workers themselves – heightening risks that aid workers may be perceived as supporting military operations.[12]

Such possibilities appear well-founded. In Afghanistan, for example, reports indicate that armed insurgents have attacked aid workers despite their neutrality, as a tactic aimed at preventing development and increasing fear on all sides.[13] In fact, these problems and the rising dangers to NGO personnel resulting from them led to the temporary withdrawal of Médecins Sans Frontières from Afghanistan in 2004. The group articulated the reason behind the withdrawal when they criticized the American-led coalition force of using "troops to provide relief aid, confusing needed assistance with military and political objectives, [a] policy which blurs the lines between relief and military activity, [and] endanger[s] the lives of aid workers."[14]

Furthermore, such ethical challenges may not be solely confined to interacting with NGOs. Missions where coalition forces assist host nation officials may require military personnel to associate with officials who have less than reputable pasts, or who are accused of engaging in unethical behaviour. This may confront commanders, and individual soldiers, with issues of how to engage such officials to achieve mission objectives while at the same time not rewarding undesirable practices. At times, the course followed has been less than ethically satisfying. US military engagement with warlords in Afghanistan offers a case in point. A United States Senate Armed Services Committee inquiry uncovered evidence of cases where warlords associated with the private military company known as ArmorGroup worked with the Taliban, sold opium, and participated in activities that challenged coalition forces. According to the Committee's report, "warlords associated with ArmorGroup's security operations at Shindand engaged in murder, bribery, and anti-coalition activities ... Guards employed by ArmorGroup used drugs, threatened to attack Afghan Ministry of Defense personnel, attempted to leave their posts to seek revenge for an attack on the warlord to whom they were loyal, and knowingly provided sensitive security information to a Taliban-affiliated warlord."[15]

Such experiences underscore the fact that, while a CA is in part premised on the importance of engaging with other organizations to achieve more effective solutions to security issues, it confronts practitioners with the need to carefully weigh the ethical issues involved in any such engagement. In this regard, issues concerning the potential dangers of such association – both to organizational credibility and to the well-being of personnel – must be assessed against potential military benefits. So, too, must actions that may inadvertently serve to compromise such actors even further (e.g. military distribution of aid to indigenous groups in operational environments in which humanitarian organizations are known to perform a similar function).

Ethics of Employment and Appropriate Tasks

Ethical challenges are also likely to surround questions regarding the employment of military capabilities in operations involving a CA. Typical might be questions arising when choosing between the use of military resources for protecting NGO personnel vice their retention for other operations. However, the use of military capabilities *explicitly designed and intended* for more effective practice of a comprehensive approach may also create ethical challenges. The emerging capability known as Religious Leader Engagement offers a noteworthy case in point. Currently under development by the Canadian Army, RLE involves the use of military chaplains as a means of facilitating dialogue between indigenous faith-based leaders and groups in war-torn societies. Indeed, it promises to contribute to dialogue and relationship-building in societies where issues of religion are a key element of the culture.[16] Moreover, it eschews intelligence-gathering and the conduct of influence activity in support of military operations, largely so as not to taint the enterprise or place participants in harm's way. As such, its very nature reflects an acute sensitivity to the ethics of operating in conflict zones.

Even here, however, the ethical challenges surrounding employment may well be considerable. On the one hand, while the approach rejects both intelligence-gathering and influence activity as legitimate RLE activities, its conduct can easily be misinterpreted or misperceived as such.[17] Indeed, notions of what constitutes influence activity, while perhaps clear to Western militaries, may be far less so among indigenous groups in war-torn societies and failing states. On the other hand, even if misinterpretation is avoided, intentional distortion of RLE's true purpose cannot be ruled out. In societies ravaged by conflict, for instance, the enemy clearly gets a vote and can often wield considerable influence. In view of this, the ethical challenges confronting commanding officers as well as chaplains charged with the task of RLE can be considerable. Employed improperly or without careful consideration of how such engagement may be perceived, RLE may compromise the noncombatant immunity of chaplains as well as the safety and security of those indigenous religious leaders and groups involved in the enterprise. Rather than being a positive step toward conflict resolution, employment of RLE may make matters worse.

The military is not the only organization that risks raising such ethical issues. At times, civilian bureaucrats employ tactics and equipment mirroring those of the military when operating under a CA. For example, the United States sent its Drug Enforcement Agency's Foreign-Deployed Advisory and Support Teams to Afghanistan to assist in drug interdiction operations. On cursory examination, these civilian bureaucrats behave and function much like military units, distorting their standing under the Law of Armed Conflict and thus threatening to erode their rights and protections under the LOAC.

MAXIMIZING BENEFITS / MINIMIZING RISK

Certainly, few of the ethical benefits and challenges outlined above – or the many others that could presumably arise – are likely to be exclusive to military operations taking place within a CA context. Missions involving irregular warfare, counter-insurgency, stabilization, and reconstruction are – by their very nature – complex and ethically charged.[18] That said, the strong emphasis which pursuit of such an approach places on regularized and active interactions with a range of groups *does* suggest that such opportunities and challenges are more prone to arise in the context of CA practice than would otherwise be the case. Moreover, the fact that the approach has gained currency among an ever wider range of allied nations and international organizations can only further underline the likelihood of such occurrences.

Accordingly, efforts aimed at maximizing the CA's potential benefits for ethical decision-making and minimizing its dangers and challenges are ever more essential. In this regard, improvement of CA processes, practices, and procedure is imperative. Without a sound decision-making process, the risks of information overload, misinformation, political gridlock, and decision paralysis may well linger and increase, as will the problems that these obstacles can produce for effective and ethically sound decision-making.

At the same time, further development of the CA must occur *in tandem* with a sound programme of ethical training and education. No decision-making process, however well developed, can fully escape the fact that, ultimately, the ethical character of decisions made depends heavily on the degree of ethical grounding that those utilizing it bring to the table beforehand, as well as their skill and capacity to apply such knowledge when needed. Simply put, general solutions must involve *both* further development of the CA itself and continued ethical training and education of military personnel and their likely partners in CA operations. Both are needed to help ensure that conduct of operations is efficient, effective, *and* ethically sound.

ONGOING INITIATIVES

Notably, efforts in each of these areas are underway. With regard to the CA, recent years have witnessed a flurry of activity aimed not only at endorsement of CA philosophy, but at further development of CA-type processes, practices, and procedures.

For instance, the study *Sustaining Canada's Engagement in Acutely Fragile States and Conflict-Affected Situations* – a work jointly commissioned by the Department of Foreign Affairs and International Trade and the Canadian International Development Agency – has served to underline the need for organizations and agencies to work more regularly across organizational lines when involved in such missions.[19] The creation of the Stabilization and Reconstruction Task Force Advisory Board (at DFAIT) and the interdepartmental working group of the Chief of Force Development (within the Department of National Defence) has been similarly useful for CA development – with the former working to ensure greater collaboration and engagement in further conceptual development of the CA and supporting concepts, and the latter advocating greater inter-agency coordination in missions involving crisis-ridden, fragile states.

Training exercises involving inter-agency participation, such as the Maple Guardian series in support of Canada's mission in Afghanistan as well as the Arctic-focused Operation Nanook, have provided the Canadian military – along with their inter-agency partners – with enhanced opportunities for developing the skill sets necessary for working effectively in an inter-agency context. The most recent edition of the Army Leadership Training Manual stresses the importance of the concept and the need for Army commanders to work toward its effective practice.[20] Furthermore, research in areas such as inter-organizational trust-building and trust repair at DRDC Toronto is currently underway to help improve inter-agency collaboration in a CA context.[21]

Meanwhile, the Army Ethics Programme has endeavoured to offer additional guidance for ethical conduct and practise through its capstone doctrinal publication, *Duty with Discernment: CLS Guidance on Ethics in Operations*, with stated goals of "inculcating ethical awareness, reasoning, actions and leadership" in Canada's soldiers.[22] The AEP calls for all Army units to have an Ethics Plan (based on an ethical risk assessment) as well as a Unit Ethics Coordinator, and features enhanced ethics training – including the use of case study scenarios – for enhancing ethical awareness and skills among the troops.

FUTURE INITIATIVES

All such efforts aim to improve ethical decision-making in military operations. Such initiatives are aimed at further development of the CA, promising to help facilitate the creation of an environment more conducive to making ethically informed decisions on the one hand, while the development of ethical codes of conduct and training programs offers the prospect of ensuring a more ethically astute and aware soldier on the other.

Consideration might be given to the development of a more targeted "lessons learned" process – focussing *both* on the functioning of the CA as well as the ethical issues raised during the course of operations taking place within a CA context. As mentioned earlier, such an approach could facilitate the ethical education and training of leaders – serving as a catalogue of ethical dilemmas and challenges encountered in past operations and thus as a means through which to establish standards of best ethical practice. Through such study, participants could well develop greater sensitivity and appreciation of the ethical problems likely to arise in operations.

More proactive command involvement and mentoring in ethics could also yield benefits. Evidence indicates that loyalty to one's primary group can, at times, override ethical requirements and considerations.[23] Active command engagement with troops on ethical issues that may arise during the course of their service may provide a poten-tially useful means of altering such realities.

Beyond this, initiatives aimed at extending the practice of the CA to include policy formulation as well as operations in the field also demand serious consideration. Not only would a more institutional-ized and broadly based CA likely improve decision-making generally, but it would improve the prospects for enhanced ethical practice as well. More specifically, it would allow policy-makers and military officers greater opportunity to carefully consider potential ethical issues that could arise well before any operational deployment occurs. This could help to ensure that potential dilemmas may be better anticipated, and some ethical problems avoided entirely.

Finally, efforts must be made to monitor and assess the effective-ness of both the CA and the ethics programmes themselves. Such evaluation processes are important not only to ensure value for money, but more importantly, to see that those whose capabilities they are intended to serve receive the most effective guidance possible in support of their conduct as professionals.

CONCLUSION

Whether the creation of an environment more conducive to sound ethical decision-making will continue to progress is somewhat unclear. While efforts to improve the CA concept and provide ethical training to those charged with its practice are underway, additional research on the topics of the CA, ethics, and military professionalism is clearly indicated.

Efforts to ensure sound ethical reasoning and practice in military operations not only make good strategic sense, but also represent an essential component of the Canadian military profession. So too do initiatives aimed at further developing decision-making approaches that have the potential to facilitate good ethical practice (e.g. the CA). Viewed from this perspective, continued development of a CA is well worth supporting. While by no means a cure-all for the chal-lenges to ensuring better ethical reasoning in military operations, a CA, effectively practised, *can* serve as a critical tool for ensuring that decisions and actions are better informed – an important prerequi-site for sound ethical reasoning. Moreover, when combined with solid programmes of training and education in ethics, the impacts may well be mutually reinforcing. If these other aspects are neglected, however, the approach threatens to create as many problems as it solves, increasing the chances of gridlock, paralysis, and ethical uncertainty. Accordingly, efforts to maximize the potential of the CA and minimize the challenges it can produce are imperative.

NOTES

1 The authors wish to thank Lieutenant-Colonels Chris Rankin and Ron Bell of the Land Futures Unit, Canadian Army Land Warfare Centre; Dr Sarah Hill, Department of Military Psychology, Royal Military College of Canada; and Major Steele Lazerte, Canadian Doctrine and Training Centre, for providing useful comments on earlier versions of this chapter.

2 Literature on the Comprehensive Approach is extensive and growing. Useful discussions of the concept, its problems, and its prospects are available: C. DeConing and K. Friis, "Coherence and Coordination: The Limits of the Comprehensive Approach," *Journal of International Peacekeeping* 15 (2011): 243–72; M. Rostek and P. Gizewski, eds., *Security Operations in the 21st Century: Canadian Perspectives on the Comprehensive Approach* (Kingston, ON: McGill-Queen's University Press, 2011); P. Jakobsen, "NATO's Comprehensive Approach to Crisis Response Operations: A Work in Slow Progress," *DIIS Report 15* (Copenhagen: Danish Institute for International Studies, 2008); C. Schnaubelt, ed., *Towards a Comprehensive Approach: Strategic and Operational Challenges* (Rome: NATO Defence College, 2011); K. Rintasoski and M. Autti, eds., "Comprehensive Approach: Trends, Challenges, and Possibilities for Cooperation in Crisis Prevention and Management," based on *Comprehensive Approach Seminar* (Helsinki: Ministry of Defence, 17 June 2008); and C. Wendling, *The Comprehensive Approach to Civil-Military Crisis Management: A Critical Analysis and Perspective* (Paris: Institut de Recherche Strategique de l'Ecole Militaire, 2010).

3 Such variation in usage stems in part from the fact that development of the approach itself represents a work in progress and thus requires considerable dialogue within and between those organizations and agencies involved in its conduct. In general, usage that is broadly focused is often reflected in discussions and in works produced by international organizations such as the United Nations and NATO. In contrast, use within certain national organizations and agencies has been somewhat more restrictive, with some organizations (such as the US military) tending to limit the CA's meaning to interactions between various national and international agencies, vice organizations and individuals in the public sphere.

4 The mid-1990s saw a plethora of "re-engineering" projects in response to the dramatic budget cuts of the time. In Canada's case, the Department of National Defence and the Canadian Armed Forces undertook a re-engineering project – the Management Command and Control Re-engineering Project – which resulted in scattered "tactical" successes. The experience and knowledge gained from the successes and failures of past re-engineering projects may provide the CAF important experience and information in creating a comprehensive approach.

5 P. Bradley, "Just Following Orders Is Not Sufficient," *Canadian Army Journal* 14, no. 2 (Summer 2012): 45.

6 Decisions made in military operations can also fundamentally impact well-being – generating moral trauma, post-traumatic stress, and depression not only in those targeted by decisions but in those making them. See ibid., 45–6.

7 H.R. Niebuhr, *The Responsible Self: An Essay in Christian Moral Philosophy* (Westminster, UK: John Knox Press, 1999), 60.

8 In fact, a training course on ethical issues has already been developed by the CAF that takes this general approach (though differing in specifics), with a focus on decision-making within a comprehensive approach. See Canadian Forces Leadership Institute, *Ethics in the CF: Making Tough Choices: Instructors Manual* (Kingston, ON: Canadian Defence Academy and the Canadian Forces Leadership Institute, 2006).

9 In Afghanistan, such efforts at times took the form of a *shura* (Arabic for *consultation*).

10 There are competing accounts of this event. While initial reports cited enemy action, official US reports maintain the helicopter crash was not a result of enemy action. See J. Pomfret, "Taliban Says Its Forces Foiled U.S. Commandos," *The Washington Post* (21 October 2001), http://www.library.ohiou.edu/indopubs/2001/10/21/0014.html.

11 For a more detailed examination of this and related issues, see P. Gizewski, *Ensuring Effective Religious Leader Engagement: Thoughts on Its Place in CF Thinking* (DRDC-CORA LR 2012) 20 September 2012).

12 Some efforts have been made to overcome these security and neutrality challenges, namely the establishment of an NGO Safety Office. See H. Yalçinkaya, "The Nongovernmental Organizations–Military Security Collaboration Mechanism: Afghanistan NGO Safety Office," *Armed Forces & Society* 39, no. 33 (2013): 489–510.

13 For a general discussion of the problem, see N. Banerjee, "Comprehensive Approach and Fragile States; Non-Governmental Organizations Roles in Fragile Situations," in *Security Operations in the 21st Century: Canadian Perspectives on the Comprehensive Approach*, ed. M. Rostek and P.

Gizewski (Montreal and Kingston, ON: McGill-Queen's University Press, 2011), 54–5.

14 Marilyn McHarg and Kevin Coppick note that Médecins Sans Frontières "has found it harder to achieve … acceptance in countries where Western militaries are present … MSF claims of independence, no matter how true, are not perceived as such in these situations and are met with skepticism by forces opposed to Western militaries and by the Western military forces themselves. This perceived lack of independence and impartiality is exacerbated when militaries and governments seek integrated approaches, and non-governmental organizations join in and focus their efforts in the regions aligned with these militaries, or participate in state-building initiatives." See McHarg and Coppick, "We Share the Same Space, Not the Same Purpose: The Comprehensive Approach and Médecins sans Frontières," in *Security Operations in the 21st Century*, ed. Rostek and Gizewski, 69.

15 C. Gall, "Killings Drive Doctor Group to Leave Afghanistan," *The New York Times* (29 July 2004), http://www.nytimes.com/2004/07/29/world/killings-drive-doctor-group-to-leave-afghanistan.html.

16 Committee on Armed Services United States Senate, *Inquiry into the Role and Oversight of Private Security Contractors in Afghanistan* (28 September 2010), xi, 2, http://publicintelligence.net/senate-report-on-private-security-contractor-oversight-in-afghanistan/.

17 For an excellent discussion of the nature of and rationale for Religious Leader Engagement see S.K. Moore, *Military Chaplains as Agents of Peace: Religious Leader Engagement in Conflict and Post-Conflict Environments* (Lanham, MD: Lexington Books, 2013); S.K. Moore and S. Mansoor, "Religious Leader Engagement: An Emerging Aspect of the Comprehensive Approach," *The Three Swords Magazine* 24 (2013): 60–5.

18 Sergeant Jared Tracy, "Ethical Challenges in Stability Operations," *Military Review* 89, no. 1 (Winter 2009): 88–94.

19 Government of Canada, *Sustaining Canada's Engagement in Acutely Fragile States and Conflict-Affected Situations* (Ottawa: Government of Canada, July 2009).

20 B. Bentley and G. Scoppio, *Leading in Comprehensive Operations* (Kingston, ON: Canadian Forces Leadership Institute and the Canadian Defence Academy, September 2012).

21 See for instance M. Thompson, B.A. Adams, and W. Niven, "Trust in Military Teams," in *The Human Dimensions of Operations – A Personnel Research Perspective*, ed. G. Ivey, K. Sudom, W. Dean, and M. Tremblay (Kingston, ON: Canadian Defence Academy Press, 2014); R. Gill and M.

Thompson, "Interagency Collaboration and Trust: Insights for the Defence Team," in *The Defence Team: Military and Civilian Partnership in the Canadian Armed Forces and Department of National Defence*, ed. I. Goldenberg and A. Febbraro (Kingston, ON: Canadian Defence Academy Press, DRDC SL-2013-101, 2013); M. Thompson and A. Febbraro, "Trust in International Military Missions: Violations of Trust and Strategies for Repair," in *Trust in Military Teams*, ed. N. Stanton (Surrey, UK: Ashgate, 2011), 107–26; M. Thompson and R. Gill, "The Role of Trust in Whole of Government Missions," in *Mission Critical: Smaller Democracies' Role in Global Stability Operations*, ed. C. Leuprecht, J. Troy, and D. Last (Montreal and Kingston, ON: McGill-Queen's University Press, 2010), 225–44.

22 Department of National Defence, *Duty with Discernment: CCA Guidance on Ethics in Operations, Strategic Edition* (Ottawa: Department of National Defence, 2013).

23 Captain John Nelson Rickard, "Beyond Training: The Canadian Army and Creating Belief in Ethics Education" (Unpublished PhD dissertation, 2012), 6–7.

PART TWO

Ethics and Leadership: Tensions and Resolutions between Force Protection and Mission Success

4

Managing Ethical Risk in the Canadian Armed Forces

PETER BRADLEY AND SHAUN TYMCHUK

INTRODUCTION

Many of the nations that participated in the post-9/11 wars in Iraq and Afghanistan endured episodes of professional misconduct in which their soldiers violated the law of armed conflict or committed other forms of ethical failure. Indeed, the Canadian Armed Forces prosecuted two publicized cases of wrongdoing, with charges ranging in severity from fraternization to attempted murder.[1] While these incidents differed in the extent to which the transgressors violated moral standards of behaviour and caused harm to victims, in both cases the misconduct tarnished the reputation of Canada's Department of National Defence and the CAF, and diverted resources from other important work. These transgressions and others like them indicate that DND and the CAF are likely at risk for violations of this nature to occur again in the future. Consequently, individuals at all levels of the military hierarchy need to be able to anticipate ethical risk and take action to minimize its harm.

The aim of this chapter is to describe the problem ethical risk poses for military effectiveness and to suggest measures for managing this risk. The chapter has four parts. First, we show why it is important for uniformed and civilian members of the defence community to behave ethically. Second, we explain what we mean by the term "ethical risk" and a number of related concepts. Third, we focus on how to manage ethical risk, which involves two broad types of activities: those designed to prevent ethical failures from occurring, and those aimed at mitigating the harm after the fact. Fourth, we outline a three-stage model for assessing ethical threats at the societal, organizational, and individual levels, and show how surveys and organizational reporting measures can be used by military leaders in this assessment process to help identify where their organizations are ethically vulnerable.

WHY ETHICS IS IMPORTANT TO THE CAF

Most individuals understand why they need to be ethical. If they do not behave in an ethical manner, their social reputation will suffer, they may experience reprisals from other individuals, and, if their ethical transgressions violate the law, they can also be subject to legal sanctions. It is a similar story for organizations. In 2012, the Canadian meat-packing firm XL Foods shipped contaminated meat to grocery stores. What makes this episode relevant to our present discussion of ethical risk is that the company's directors had known for several weeks that their product was potentially harmful. Then, in what seems to be a monumental failure of leadership, the company's directors elected to remain silent in the face of the ensuing media maelstrom. The company lost millions of dollars, workers were laid off, and management of the company was taken over by a foreign firm.[2] That is what can happen in the private sector when a company has an ethical failure.

Similar things can happen in the public sector. Peter C. Newman described how two revered Canadian institutions were damaged by unethical behaviour when the Canadian Red Cross knowingly released tainted blood for use in blood transfusions in the 1990s and the soldiers of the CAF disgraced themselves by committing acts of torture and murder in Somalia in 1993.[3] The result was that two of the "nation's defining institutions first lost their credibility, then their authority and finally their followers,"[4] as discussed earlier in this book.

Prior to the 1990s, ethics was rarely discussed in Canadian defence circles, much less written about in military manuals and publications, so there may still be some in the military community who see ethics as a passing fad with little legitimate connection to the Canadian military ethos. In our view, there are a number of compelling reasons why ethical behaviour is indeed a critical component of Canadian military operations, which we present below in four steps. First, we highlight several developments that illustrate the significance of ethics in modern military affairs. Second, we suggest six practical reasons why military leaders need to ensure that their forces behave ethically. Third, we demonstrate how ethical competence is an essential element of the CAF's organizational effectiveness. Fourth, we show what can happen when a military unit does not live up to professional standards by recounting the moral failures of the Canadian Airborne Regiment in Somalia in 1993.

THE GROWING SIGNIFICANCE OF MILITARY ETHICS

To gain an appreciation of the growing importance of ethics in the military domain, one needs only to look at the resources being devoted to ethics instruction and the increased role for lawyers in the planning of military operations. Not too long ago, decisions about the use of force were made by military commanders and their operational staff, but that changed dramatically when the United States of America deployed over two hundred military lawyers to the First Gulf War in 1991 to vet every targeting decision.[5] Today, decisions concerning the use of armed force are normally taken at much higher levels in the military and political hierarchies, and always with the input of lawyers to ensure that national and international laws are followed.

WHY LEADERS NEED TO REINFORCE ETHICAL BEHAVIOUR

Canadian military leaders need to ensure that their troops behave ethically for six reasons. First, Canadian law and the international law of armed conflict require it. Second, some types of unethical behaviour can be very expensive. Third, unethical behaviour by soldiers can erode public confidence and support. Fourth, Canada's success in military missions requires that its forces work well with both allied forces and indigenous peoples in operational theatres, and unethical behaviour on the part of military personnel can undermine operational outcomes and damage the reputation of the CAF and the nation. Fifth, moral distress and psychological injury can incapacitate soldiers who participate in or even witness ethical violations.[6] Sixth, unethical behaviour by even a few soldiers can result in mission failure. We expand on each of these points below.

There have long been rules associated with the conduct of war, but the development of the Geneva Conventions and the inauguration of the International Criminal Court in the twentieth century brought a heightened emphasis on such rules, which ensured that the legal dimensions of warfare should be taken much more seriously than in earlier times. At home, the Canadian constitution and other domestic laws require that members of the CAF and DND behave professionally because Canada subscribes to the "rule of law" and Canadian soldiers must comply in their roles both as citizens of Canada and agents of their government. The example of Captain Robert Semrau, who fired two rounds into a wounded Taliban fighter in 2008, as explained in chapter 2 of this book, can illustrate this point.[7]

Certain categories of unethical behaviour can hurt organizational productivity, and some, such as theft, substance abuse, and workplace violence, can also incur financial costs. Studies in the US have estimated the cost of employee theft at $200 billion per year[8] and problem drinking at $170 billion.[9] To the best of our knowledge, DND and the CAF do not keep records on such losses, but based on data collected in civilian organizations, the costs might be substantial.

DND and the CAF are like many other large organizations in that they work more effectively when they have the trust, confidence, and good will of the public. Opinion polls conducted over the past six years consistently show that Canadian citizens are supportive of their military men and women,[10] and military leaders would be prudent to do what they can to maintain this support. When military forces are admired, recruiting is easier because young people are more inclined to sign up and parents are more likely to encourage their children to pursue a military career. Similarly, politicians will be more interested in associating with the military and more inclined to support military efforts. Furthermore, regular citizens and local businesses will look more favourably on men and women in uniform, and cordial relations are always more productive than disagreeable relations. In short, ethical behaviour increases public trust in the military and enhances the credibility of the CAF.

Ethics is an important ingredient in mission success. If the CAF's ethical integrity is questionable, other coalition nations may doubt Canada's ability to be a competent ally and may not want to partner with us in international operations. When Sub-Lieutenant Jeffrey Delisle was convicted in 2013 of selling secrets to the Russians, for example, there were some who thought his transgressions might make allies reluctant to share secrets with Canada in the future.[11] For a sense of how significant an impact ethics can have on international cooperation, consider the number of nations who joined with the United States against Saddam Hussein. Of the thirty-four nations that joined the US-led coalition for the First Gulf War (1990–91), which met the *jus ad bellum* criteria for a just war, twenty-one of these nations did not contribute to the 2003 invasion of Iraq, an invasion which did not meet the *jus ad bellum* criteria.[12]

Similarly, lapses in ethical conduct during international operations hamper productive working relations with local populations and can thwart mission success. The work of a military unit in a foreign country is easier when the population is obliging. Angry inhabitants can become uncooperative or hostile, requiring military leaders to devote more resources to force protection and other security tasks. In the recent war in Afghanistan, when coalition forces inadvertently killed, mistreated, or terrorized noncombatants, they actually encouraged ordinary law-abiding Afghans to support the insurgency.[13] In the words of American author and former Navy SEAL Dick Couch, "because an insurgency is a war for the people, our conduct and our ideas matter. The use of excessive force, violations of human rights, and abuse of civilians, even if they go unreported, cost us dearly in terms of achieving our goals and accomplishing our mission."[14] To some extent we witnessed this cost in the fall of 2012 when anger erupted in Pakistan over the US drone attacks that killed many noncombatant bystanders.[15] Although relations with noncombatants are recognized as critical to counter-insurgency efforts, good relations with local citizens have long been valued in military operations.

The Canadian Army of the Second World War certainly understood the importance of maintaining good relations with noncombatants. In July 1944, at the height of the desperate fighting to break out of the beaches at Normandy, the commander of 1st Canadian Army, Lieutenant-General H.D.G. Crerar, promptly directed educational and corrective action after receiving reports of 3rd Canadian Infantry Division soldiers looting and causing unwarranted damage to French civilian property. The tarnished reputation suffered by the division as a result of this unchecked misbehaviour contributed to Crerar's growing concern over the division commander's fitness to carry on. Writing to the commander of 2nd Canadian Corps (Lieutenant-General G.G. Simonds), Crerar asserted that "[i]t is a matter of national importance that the enviable record of behaviour of Cdn t[roo]ps, built up over these recent years, be jealously guarded."[16] Shortly afterwards, Simonds addressed the officers of 3rd Canadian Infantry Division and 2nd Canadian Armoured Brigade, stressing the national importance of discipline and attention to what he described as the moral dimension of the war. High standards of deportment and behaviour, according to Simonds,

> not only increase our own self-respect as a Nation, but also increase the respect for Canada from all other nations who have come to realize her greatness. The opinion formed of Canada and Canadians by peoples in Europe and in Britain will be based upon the impression created by the Canadian troops they see about them.[17]

Another reason for leaders to attend ethics is its impact on the physical well-being and mental health of military men and women. Research has shown that most violations are committed by otherwise good soldiers who are simply overpowered at the time by negative influences in their environment.[18] When they have occasion to reflect on their actions, or inactions in the case of witnesses who stand by, many develop stressful reactions or mental health disorders.[19] Others can have their career progressions blocked or delayed. Under the military justice system, ethical transgressors and their leaders often face stiff sentences for their misconduct, including financial penalties and dismissal from the military. The cumulative effect of this adverse impact can also extend to the military organization itself when eroding job satisfaction and weakened commitment to the military lead to increased numbers of personnel leaving the forces early, or reduced effort from remaining members. Research has also shown that job dissatisfaction can contribute to misbehaviour toward the organization.[20] Altogether, the potential impact of ethical transgressions on the health of individuals and the organization, in the form of lower force readiness, is serious. However, it is also avoidable if leaders take their ethical responsibilities seriously.

The possibility of mission failure has always been a concern in the military, but rarely has the difference between success and failure hinged on the actions of so few as it does today. At the turn of the twenty-first century, US Marine Corps General Charles Krulak coined the term "strategic corporal" to capture the importance of the individual soldier in modern military operations. His view was that with the omnipresent gaze of the media (and anyone with a cellphone), the actions of individual soldiers now had potentially strategic implications that were unheard of in earlier times.[21] As discussed in the first chapter of this book, a vivid example of this "strategic corporal" effect is captured in the description of the guards and interrogators who tortured detainees at the Abu Ghraib prison in Iraq as "the six guys who lost us the war."[22] Another instructive example of the damage that can be inflicted by the wrongdoing of a few soldiers may be found in the abuse of Iraqi looters by British soldiers in 2003 while securing the humanitarian aid depot known as Camp Bread Basket, near Basra. In sentencing two of the soldiers involved in what became dubbed as "Britain's Abu Ghraib," the presiding judge advocate stated "these acts have undoubtedly tarnished the international reputation of the British Army and to some extent the British nation too, and it will no doubt hamper the efforts of those who are now risking their lives striving to achieve stability in the Gulf region."[23] What this means, of course, is that shortcomings in the abilities, character, or training of individual members, which might have been managed in the past by strong leadership, can now pop up and be broadcast in the public and social media with devastating impact upon the reputation of the entire armed forces, the government, and the nation.[24]

ETHICAL COMPETENCE IS ESSENTIAL TO CAF ORGANIZATIONAL EFFECTIVENESS

According to CAF leadership doctrine, "effective leadership is about the creation, expression and preservation of values."[25] This doctrine identifies four categories of values that are essential to CAF success – Canadian values, legal values, ethical values, and military values. When one looks inside each category, however, ethical values are everywhere.[26] It seems clear, then, that ethics is deeply integrated into the CAF's vision of both effective leadership and organization success. The implication is that organizational success and the effectiveness of the CAF as a professional institution are now properly viewed as involving more than mission success, as witnessed in the 1993 Somalia mission of Canadian paratroopers described next.

ETHICAL FAILURE AT MULTIPLE LEVELS –
THE CANADIAN AIRBORNE REGIMENT IN SOMALIA

On the night of 16 March 1993, members of 2 Airborne Commando systematically tortured and beat to death a sixteen-year-old Somali named Shidane Abukar Arone, who had been caught sneaking into the Airborne camp near Belet Huen, Somalia. For over two hours, Master Corporal Clayton Matchee, a rebellious junior leader with a reputation as an intimidating bully, slowly pounded the life out of Arone, punching and kicking him, beating him with an iron bar, and burning the soles of his feet with a lit cigar. One of Matchee's subordinates, Corporal Kyle Brown, initially participated in the beating; then with growing unease, he stood by, unable to bring himself to stop the torture. At least eight other members of the Canadian task force dropped by at various times and witnessed the vicious abuse, but did nothing to stop it or report it.[27]

The murder of Shidane Arone came to be seen as "the defining moment of the Somalia mission if not for the very existence of the Canadian Airborne Regiment itself."[28] It was not, however, the first or the only instance of abuse and unnecessary killing by airborne troops during Operation Deliverance. On 4 March 1993, two unarmed Somali men were shot in the back by members of Captain Michel Rainville's airborne reconnaissance platoon as they attempted to flee the immediate vicinity of the Airborne camp. A medical officer in the Canadian contingent claimed that one of the two Somalis had been executed at close range as he lay wounded on ground. This was never proven, but doubts concerning the wisdom and morality of this episode persist.[29] To be sure, disciplinary problems had been brewing in the Airborne Regiment for years. Infantry regiments dumped their problem soldiers in the Airborne, resulting in a defiant minority that behaved more like a biker gang than professional soldiers.[30] But the disturbing lack of professional and ethical restraint that permitted this horrific and senseless crime to occur is directly attributable to the weak and ineffective unit leaders who failed to prepare the regiment for the Somalia mission, and then directed, condoned, or joined in the mistreatment of detainees: Lieutenant-Colonel Carol Mathieu (Commanding Officer of the Airborne Regiment), Major Anthony Seward (Officer Commanding, 2 Commando) and Captain Michael Sox (Matchee and Brown's platoon commander), all three of whom authorized and condoned the mistreatment of prisoners; Warrant

Officer Murphy (Matchee and Brown's platoon second-in-command), who joined in the abuse by kicking Arone in the head several times in the presence of Matchee; and Sergeant Mark Boland (Matchee and Brown's immediate supervisor), who failed to control his subordinates.[31] Ordinary Canadians expected better of their soldiers and were shocked and outraged, particularly when they saw the "trophy" photographs of Matchee and Brown posing with the bloodied and bruised Arone during the beating.[32] The violent excesses of the Airborne Regiment quickly overshadowed the operational success of Operation Deliverance, which had exceeded the regiment's mandate despite the exceptionally harsh and difficult conditions of Somalia. The humanitarian relief delivered; the security, governance, and public health improved; the schools, hospitals, bridges, roads, water wells, and electric generators built and restored; and the training of doctors, nurses, and police – all were forgotten or ignored by the Canadian public. The reputations of the entire mission, the Canadian Airborne Regiment, and the Army were tarnished by the atrocities committed by the uncontrolled few.[33] Equally damning, if not worse, in the eyes of Canadians and their political leaders was the ineffective, evasive, and deceptive response to these events by senior CAF leaders.[34]

The consequences of the Airborne Regiment's egregious misdeeds in Somalia and the prevarications by National Defence Headquarters in the aftermath provoked severe consequences for the individuals involved, for the Airborne Regiment, and for the CAF. Lieutenant-Colonel Mathieu was relieved of command in September 1993. Major Seward, Sergeant Boland, and Corporal Brown were sentenced by court-martial to imprisonment and subsequently dismissed from the CAF.[35] The government of Jean Chrétien disbanded the Canadian Airborne Regiment in 1995, an unprecedented move that sent a loud message to the CAF community that Canada's expectations of its military men and women should not be ignored.[36] The crisis created by the Somalia operation prompted two civil reviews of the CAF. The Minister of National Defence and the Commission of Inquiry into the Deployment of Canadian Forces to Somalia proposed more than two hundred recommendations for improvement, primarily in the areas of leadership and accountability, discipline, command and management, military justice, mission planning, and education and training.[37]

The importance of ethics, values, and ethos was a recurring theme of the reviews,[38] and the CAF was directed to integrate a formal statement of its values and beliefs into training programmes, professional development activities, and personnel performance assessments.[39] Finally, and perhaps most significantly, the cumulative ethical failures at the individual, unit, and institutional levels associated with the Somalia mission precipitated a profound crisis in confidence between the CAF and the society that it served, which required almost ten years of reform and exemplary performance to heal.[40]

DEFINING ETHICAL RISK

The CAF does not have an official definition of "ethical risk," but it has two definitions of "risk." Risk is defined in the CAF leadership manual, *Conceptual Foundations*, as "any circumstance which exposes a decision maker or course of action to some hazard which may produce either a negative effect or else prevent or impede the attainment of one or more objectives."[41] The CAF's doctrinal manual on operational risk management presents a slightly different definition of risk: "a possible loss or negative mission impact stated in terms of probability or severity."[42] Both definitions emphasize the potential for risk to negatively affect mission success, and the second definition introduces two important dimensions of risk, the likelihood (probability) that a risky event will occur and the expected impact (severity) the event will have, if and when it takes place.

For the purposes of ethical risk analysis, we subscribe to a broader definition of ethics which classifies all wrong behaviour as unethical, not just actions that are wrong because they harm others. We take this position because, as explained earlier in this chapter, serious wrongdoing of any nature can result in mission failure or crippling reputational damage to the CAF. For this reason, we suggest military commanders must avoid the harmful consequences of all wrongdoing in their units, not just harmful actions that violate ethical standards. Military commanders must also guard against actions that violate legal statutes and professional norms. Therefore, our broad definition of ethical risk analysis recognizes that ethics overlaps with the concepts of legality, professionalism, and morality, so that unethical behaviour can include actions that are illegal, unprofessional, or immoral. Ethics, legality, and professionalism each deal with right and wrong. Laws operate at the practical, societal level and ethics at the abstract, philosophical level. Very often that which is legal is also ethical; many illegal actions are also unethical. But there are important differences between ethics and the law as well:

Ethics may judge that some laws are immoral without denying that they are valid. For example, laws may permit slavery, — spousal abuse, racial discrimination, or sexual discrimination, but these are immoral practices. A Catholic or antiabortion advocate may believe that the laws permitting abortion are immoral.[43]

Following lawful orders, which is the legal course of action for soldiers, is also the ethical option most of the time, but not all laws are ethical and orders are not always lawful, so military personnel need to know how to determine when orders are lawful or unlawful, moral or immoral.

There are likely many ways to classify unethical actions, but one can get a good appreciation of the domain by focusing on the type of misbehaviour and the motives behind it. To this end, we present a categorization of wrongdoing by type in Table 4.1 and by motive in Table 4.2. Together, these tables present a comprehensive overview of the range of unethical behaviours one might experience in a military organization.

The model depicted in Table 4.1 lists seven types of wrongdoing identified by Near and colleagues based on their survey of 10,000 employees at a US military base, 3,000 of whom were military personnel.[44] We have added "other ethics violations" to cover wrongdoing not captured by the other categories. There may be occasions where it is useful to consider ethical risk from the perspective of the perpetrator's motivation, so we present a model of wrongdoing classified by motive in Table 4.2.

Based on the foregoing, we suggest the following definition of ethical risk for the military, which has four elements. First, ethical risk manifests in the form of a wrongdoing, which has ethical, moral, or legal overtones. Second, the wrongdoing is caused (intentionally or not) by agents of the military, namely anyone working for the military, whether they are soldiers, sailors, or air personnel in uniform, civilian employees of the military, or contractors who may have been temporarily hired for specific missions. Third, the wrongdoing has the potential to impact negatively on the force's ability to perform its mission, and by mission, we mean the full range of military activities conducted in operations, training, or the garrison. Fourth, ethical risk can be reduced before the wrongdoing occurs and mitigated, to some extent, afterwards.

Table 4.1 Types of wrongdoing

Wrongdoing type	Specific examples
Stealing	Stealing funds Stealing property, materiel Accepting favours, bribes, kickbacks Giving unfair advantage to contractors Abuse of office
Waste	Managing a program badly Wasting organizational assets
Mismanagement	Covering up poor performance Making false reports or projections of performance
Safety violations	Using unsafe or noncompliant products Unsafe working conditions
Sexual harassment	Unwelcome sexual advances Requests for sexual favours Verbal or physical contact of a sexual nature
Unfair discrimination	Discrimination based on factors that are not job-related, including discrimination on those bases protected by *The Canadian Charter of Rights and Freedoms* (e.g., race, sex, religion)[1]
Violations of the law	Laws of war Rules of engagement Queen's Regulations and Orders Relevant military regulations
Other ethics violations	Misconduct which violates professional military standards but is not covered by the other categories (e.g., rampant careerism).

1 *The Canadian Charter of Rights and Freedoms*, http://publications.gc.ca/collections/Collection/CH37-4-3-2002E.pdf (accessed 23 July 2014).
Source: Adapted from J.P. Near, Michael T. Rehg, James R. Van Scotter, and Marcia P. Miceli, "Does Type of Wrongdoing Affect the Whistle-Blowing Process?" *Business Ethics Quarterly* 14 (2004): 226–7.

MANAGING ETHICAL RISK

Managing ethical risk is about reducing the probability, frequency, scope, and costs of ethical failure.[45] It is also about anticipating, preventing, mitigating, and surviving ethical failures.[46] A robust ethical risk management programme will focus on two areas: (1) preventing ethical failures before they happen and (2) responding to ethical failures after they occur to mitigate their harm and ensure they do not happen again.

Table 4.2 Wrongdoing categorized by motive

Motive	Examples
To benefit the perpetrator	Actions targeting work (distorting data) Actions targeting the organization's property, resources (stealing, sharing secrets) Actions targeting other members (harassing co-workers)
To benefit the perpetrator's organization	Falsifying records
To inflict damage in order to hurt the organization or people	Damaging organizational equipment Hurting co-workers or other organizational stakeholders

Source: Adapted from Y. Vardi and E. Weitz, *Misbehaviour in Organizations: Theory, Research and Management* (Mahwah, NJ: Lawrence Erlbaum Associates, 2004), 33–4.

PREVENTING ETHICAL VIOLATIONS

Robert Chandler, author of the *Ethical Conduct Audit*, suggests the following tactics for preventing ethical misconduct:

- Set and maintain integrity goals at the strategic level;
- Demonstrate top management's commitment to integrity;
- Monitor and audit conduct (formal and informal);
- Tie performance rewards system to integrity conduct;
- Distribute written rules, policies, and procedures;
- Reinforce written rules, policies, and procedures;
- Train employees to recognize and make ethical decisions;
- Establish a Corporate Ethics Officer/Team;
- Designate an Ethical Compliance Manager;
- Install surveillance and evaluative processes and foster collaborative participation;
- Maintain "whistle-blower" channels and policies;
- Ensure a supportive climate for ethical conduct;
- Reward acts of integrity and ethical decisions;
- Abide by and enforce disciplinary policy consistently and fairly;
- Offer Organizational Transformation training and development programmes; and
- Immediately respond to misconduct; follow procedures consistently and fairly.[47]

While written for civilian business organizations, many of the interventions listed above can be applied to the military environment. Indeed, some of them are already well established in the CAF (e.g., distribute written rules, policies, and procedures), while others are less so (e.g., maintain whistle-blower channels).

Social psychologists such as Philip Zimbardo tell us that unethical behaviour is caused by external influences in the environment (such as leaders, peers, unit norms, and the nature of the work) and internal qualities of the individual actor;[48] therefore interventions to minimize the impact of ethical violations should focus on both. The objective here is to produce what Richard Gabriel describes as "ethical soldiers":

> To be an ethical soldier, to act ethically, and to exercise ethical judgment, the soldier must know *why* certain things are right and wrong, *why* he or she clings to certain values, and *why* he or she chooses to do one thing over another. In the complex societies that modern military professionals serve, the soldier must have firm ethical moorings. If not, the soldier risks being overwhelmed by the strong social, cultural, and organizational forces of the society that restrict the soldier's intellect and freedom, reducing the warrior to an instrumentality of another's will. Under these conditions, the soldier may seek to escape from ethical responsibility because it is too difficult to deal with, seeking safety in the command to follow orders, and will become a danger to himself/herself and to his/her profession. To prevent this, the military professional must be an ethical soldier.[49]

The path to creating ethical soldiers begins with ethical leaders who can build ethical units founded on the concept of shared ethos.[50] The military has several tools at its disposal for creating ethical units, including ethics (professional) codes and regulations, selection, socialization, and training.

Codes

Peruse the website or promotional material of any large organization and you are likely to find an ethics code or a similar list of encouraged or prohibited behaviours; but there is some doubt about the effectiveness of these codes. They are less effective in organizations where the behaviours needed to survive in the organization are different from those espoused in the code.[51] That said, there is evidence that codes can have an effect.[52] They are most effective when reinforced on the job by organizational leaders and in training courses by instructional staff.[53] The actions of individuals in the workplace are governed by two motives that occasionally conflict: self-interest and the desire to do what is right.[54] Written codes are useful because they help all members understand what is right; ethics codes emphasize professional responsibilities and the sort of behaviour the organization expects from its members. DND and the CAF jointly endorse a *Code of Values and Ethics*,[55] and the CAF has a code of conduct.[56] For the Canadian Army, *Duty with Discernment* goes beyond the above-mentioned codes to describe in detail the ethical obligations of Army personnel in operations.[57] There are no studies on the effectiveness of ethics codes in the military, but a study of civilian financial managers in the developing world found that codes of ethics were indeed linked with reduced wrongdoing, but not with reporting wrongdoing.[58] Research has shown that many military personnel are reluctant to report wrongdoing,[59] so the CAF recently reminded its members of their duty to report wrongdoing and issued guidance on how to do so.[60]

Enforcing Codes and Regulations

Codes and regulations by themselves will not lead to ethical behaviour, but must be supported with the use of rewards, sanctions, and control measures. Organizations are usually more adept at punishing unethical behaviour than rewarding ethical behaviour. Because the CAF has many mechanisms in place for rewarding exemplary actions, it should be relatively easy to find a way to acknowledge exceptionally ethical behaviour. For example, the CAF could establish an honour similar to the Golden Whistle Award presented by the Ottawa-based discussion group "Peace, Order and Good Government." To view some of the morally noteworthy actions recognized by this group, see the website of Canadians for Accountability.[61]

Recruiting and Selection

Unethical behaviour could be prevented to some degree by strengthening CAF selection standards, but the potential gains would likely be minimal because the CAF already has a rigorous screening procedure that includes reference checks and running recruits' names through law enforcement databases to screen out undesirable applicants. The field of honesty and integrity testing could yield additional benefit in this area, for studies indicate that these tests can predict counterproductive behaviours such as theft,[62] substance abuse,[63] and absenteeism.[64] But there are shortcomings associated with these tests. Because the tests are relatively transparent, dishonest individuals can easily fake their responses.[65] As with all predictive tests, there is a margin of error with these measures, meaning that some of the recruits who fail the tests could have actually gone on to serve successfully in the military, had they been enrolled. Perhaps the biggest problem with adding more tests to CAF selection procedures is the length of time it would take to administer the measures. Screening procedures at CAF recruiting centres are already lengthy, and additional tests would be viewed as burdensome unless their predictive contribution were significant.

Ethics Training

Most of the countries in the Western world provide ethics instruction to their military personnel.[66] As a rule, militaries tend to devote a lot of resources to training on a wide range of subjects, and, considering how the importance of ethics has soared in recent years, it is not surprising that military ethics instruction has grown as well. What is perhaps more surprising is that there is little evidence that this instruction is effective. To date, there has been only one published study on the effectiveness of military ethics training. Using scripted instructional materials and movie vignettes, leaders in a US Army Stryker Brigade in Iraq delivered battlefield ethics training to 3,500 of the brigade's soldiers. After the training, a smaller group of soldiers completed a survey from which researchers determined that the instruction had contributed to lower levels of battlefield ethics violations and increased willingness to report wrongdoing.[67] This success was likely due to two reasons: the training was delivered by unit leaders, and those leaders employed instructional materials tailored to the ethical risks faced in their operating environment. Other research with civilian subjects shows that university-level education can enhance moral awareness,[68] judgment,[69] and behaviour,[70] but not moral motivation. It is not clear if ethics training of relatively short duration will be effective, however, as one civilian study showed that programmes of less than three weeks were unable to raise levels of moral judgment.[71]

A new "Defence Ethics Plan," signed by the Deputy Minister and the Chief of the Defence Staff in June 2012, may stimulate ethics training in the Canadian military.[72] This plan requires the Royal Canadian Navy, Canadian Army, and Royal Canadian Air Force to submit reports twice a year on ethics training activities they have conducted, resources they have devoted to ethics training, and related activities conducted by leaders to promote ethics (e.g. speeches, letters, etc.). It is too early to measure the impact of this initiative, but it has the potential to raise the profile of ethics training in the Canadian defence community.

A recent issue of the *Canadian Army Journal* includes an outline for a five-module ethics instruction programme that units could adapt for their ethics training needs.[73] Each module represents two to three hours of instruction that could be conducted by unit leaders. Module I begins with the ethical and legal foundations of military service in Canada. Module II covers the personal and environmental influences that typically lead to unethical behaviour. Module III focuses on specific ethical problems soldiers are likely to face on operations. This module would have to be modified for particular missions and updated regularly, and there is a potential role here for ethics specialists to assist in the development of quality mission-specific training, as many unit leaders may have neither the time nor the expertise to produce instructional materials. Module IV instructs soldiers on how to conduct an ethical analysis. Simply following rules is not sufficient, as Barry Schwartz shows in his TED lecture.[74] Rules have to be bent or broken sometimes in order to do the right thing.[75] This module would help soldiers develop the wisdom to know when such rule-breaking is appropriate. Many of the teaching points of this module would be based on the four-stage decision-making model promoted by the Canadian Army Ethics Programme (perception, judgment, action, learning).[76] Module V shows soldiers how to take proper ethical action. We suspect that, in some cases, soldiers take no action because they do not know what to do. This module would help in this regard by showing them what to do when they witness ethical violations.

Ethics training is often presented as separate activities, but some researchers have suggested that ethics instruction in professional schools (for physicians, accountants, lawyers, engineers, etc.) is more effective when it is integrated with professional training rather than taught as separate courses; unfortunately there are no conclusive studies to support this assertion.[77] CAF professional courses for mid- and senior-grade personnel have adopted this approach by embedding ethics modules within course curricula. We believe that providing ethics training in the form of stand-alone courses delivered by civilian experts or others from outside the professional community will simply reinforce the notion that ethics is not a core military competency. Having it taught by organizational leaders demonstrates that ethics is an integral element of military activity and provides CAF leaders with an opportunity to serve as ethical role models.

Socialization

While soldiers can learn a great deal from formal training sessions, one should not underestimate the impact of informal, vicarious learning. Research has shown that the ethical attitudes and behaviour of individuals are shaped by co-workers and immediate supervisors.[78] One study into the effectiveness of ethics codes found that informal social influences within the organization, such as managerial example and organizational norms, had a greater impact on the ethical attitudes of employees than formal training methods.[79] Several other studies in business ethics indicate that codes of conduct and training by themselves are insufficient. Determined ethical leadership beginning at the top, a supportive organizational climate, and the integration of ethical objectives and considerations into everyday work are also essential to achieve ethical institutional performance.[80] Canada's Chief of the Defence Staff elaborated similar themes in a 2009 interview with the *Journal of the Defence Ethics Programme*.[81] Further evidence of the importance of vicarious learning within the military sphere may be gleaned from the abundant supply of memoirs and other first-hand accounts that extol the importance of informal instruction and example from unit mates and superiors. Consider, for example, Air Commodore Leonard Birchall's inspirational and practical example of selfless leadership during three and a half years of confinement in Japanese prisoner-of-war camps during the Second World War,[82] and Colonel Ian Hope's passionate and compelling call for "the strongest moral presence and commitment" as the bases for combat leadership.[83]

Assessing Ethical Risk

As discussed in chapter 4 of this book, in order to prevent ethical failures before they occur and to be prepared to respond effectively to ethical violations, leaders need to have a sense of the risks facing the organization and the ability of their unit to face these threats (i.e., their unit's vulnerabilities).[84] This due diligence is best achieved with an extensive programme of assessment, measurement, and analysis, which we will address later in this chapter.

Responding to Ethical Violations

When an organization has experienced a serious ethical violation, it needs to mitigate the harm and provide remedy decisively and quickly.[85] US business practice takes a carrot and stick approach toward encouraging ethical performance. US federal law holds senior corporate leaders personally responsible for the accuracy of quarterly financial reports, while a growing number of firms have come to the conclusion that ethical behaviour provides a financially measureable competitive advantage.[86] Consequently, to fulfill legal and moral responsibilities, and to further their own interests, organizations need to respond to ethical misdeeds in ways that will, *inter alia*, preserve their ethical integrity and reputation, demonstrate that unethical conduct is not tolerated, minimize the costs of the unethical actions, restore the damage done, and provide assistance to the victims and perpetrators. The most effective organizational responses will build on the four themes we describe next.

Understanding and Learning

Investigations of ethical misconduct fundamentally seek to understand the root causes of ethical risk within the organization, so that effective remediation can occur. Depending on the nature of the violation, the investigation may take various forms (e.g., summary investigation or board of inquiry within the CAF context). Regardless of the specific situation, all investigations of ethical misconduct should proceed without delay to avoid any perception of cover-up or lack of interest within the organization. The completed investigation should inform decision-making on any remedial action required, such as enhanced controls or disciplinary action. Stripped of personal details, the results of the investigation should also be shared extensively, both to demonstrate commitment to ethical performance and compliance, and to further ethics training and education.[87]

Communication

Proactive, complete, and candid communication with both internal and external audiences is essential when serious ethical breaches come to light.[88] Without compromising national security, personal privacy, an ongoing investigation, or a matter before the courts, the requirement is to explain the nature of the crisis and the organizational response with maximum openness and transparency. Military personnel and the Canadian public expect senior leaders, as stewards of the military profession, to speak for the institution in dire situations, and to do so in an honest and forthright manner. Anything less will fail to satisfy the inevitable thirst for information and risk further damage to the reputation of the organization.[89] As Stephen Skyvington, president of PoliTrain Inc., says, "silence, as everyone in my business [public relations] understands, just doesn't cut it. Silence is not an answer. Silence is not a message. Silence is an admission of guilt."[90] As noted earlier in the paper, inadequate communication by senior leaders fuelled the ethical disaster that wracked the CAF in the aftermath of the Airborne Regiment's wrongdoing in Somalia.[91] Systemic reform followed, but as we will point out later in the chapter, an organizational reflex of secrecy and denial continues to hamper open and transparent communication in the CAF.[92]

Punishment

Prompt and fair sanctions must be the inescapable consequence of serious violations of an organization's ethical code of conduct.[93] The *DND and CF Code of Values and Ethics* states that CAF members who fail in their ethical obligations may be subject to change of duties, disciplinary action under the National Defence Act, or administrative action including release from the CAF.[94] As discussed earlier, in sentencing Captain Semrau following his conviction on the charge of disgraceful conduct, the presiding military judge stated that it was necessary to send a clear message to all concerned that such behaviour is unacceptable and will not be tolerated.[95]

Follow-up and Monitoring

A number of issues must be attended to before the response can be considered complete. Harm caused by the ethical misconduct should be put right. Vigilance must be exercised to counter any reprisals against persons who disclosed the wrongdoing, which are prohibited by the *DND and CF Code of Values and Ethics*.[96] At the same time, whistle-blowers must be managed in a way that promotes legitimate whistle-blowing and discourages frivolous accusations (which is, admittedly, easier to say than to do). Measures to rehabilitate offenders (e.g., training, counselling, probation) or, in extreme cases, to release them from the CAF must be set in motion. Finally, the effectiveness of pertinent policies, practices, and procedures, including training, must be evaluated and refined as necessary.[97]

ASSESSING ETHICAL RISK

The idea behind ethical risk analysis is to identify threats and vulnerabilities so that they can be eliminated or their risk reduced before they lead to ethical failure. Unfortunately, ethical risk analysis may not be well understood in the CAF, and therefore may not be viewed as an important aspect of mission planning. The *Chief of the Defence Staff Guidance to Commanding Officers* directs Commanding Officers to manage ethical risk, but does not provide any advice on how to do it.[98] The CAEP recommends that COs assess unit ethical risk prior to assuming command, after taking command, and when warned for an operational mission; however, the methods suggested for this do not make use of established CAF operational planning and risk management procedures.[99] This gap between precept and process might cause some commanders to overlook ethical risk analysis in their mission planning or to treat it as a lower-priority activity. There is clearly a need to incorporate ethical risk in CAF doctrine and procedures for operational planning and risk management, but that is a subject for another time. For the present, we will provide some practical suggestions on how to assess ethical risk.

Ethical risk analysis involves two basic processes. The first is conceptual in nature, aimed at speculating where the threats and vulnerabilities are, and the second involves the use of surveys and other measures to collect hard data for evaluating the probability and severity of these risks.

A CONCEPTUAL FRAMEWORK FOR ANALYZING ETHICAL RISK

Ethical threats are context-dependent, meaning that they will vary according to environmental characteristics such as geography, type of military operations, intensity of combat, type of work one is engaged in, and so on. For example, many of the ethical threats facing military personnel who work in logistics are different from those facing medical staff. In a similar vein, the risk of military personnel committing drug-related offences will be higher in a drug-producing region or in operations where soldiers have easy access to the local population. At the same time, there are threats and vulnerabilities that are ubiquitous, such as the influence of charismatic, immoral peers and leaders.

We recommend analyzing ethical threats and vulnerabilities at three levels – the environment, the organization, and the individual – in order to capture all potential risks. There are unique risks at each of these levels, but some risks affect several levels with slightly different implications depending on the level observed. For example, the tendency of the national government towards secrecy with respect to its ongoing programmes[100] might encourage military officers with careerist motives to suppress negative information that they have a duty to report.

Environment

The search for environmental factors that influence ethical attitudes begins with the social and political norms that shape society. In the case of Canada, a democratic and ethnically diverse nation, perceptions about right and wrong are based on the rule of law, social justice, and fair play. Research in the US shows that public perception about the government's use of military force hinges on the probability that the mission will succeed and the justice (rightness or wrongness) of the cause.[101] Although research of this nature has not been conducted in Canada, the results would likely be similar, as support for Canada's involvement in the Afghanistan war was strong in the early days when the cause was perceived as noble, but declined later when casualties rose and war-weary Canadians became increasingly pessimistic about the success of the mission.[102] Social and political motives to maintain public support for military initiatives can contribute to unethical outcomes, either separately or working in combination. These influences are pervasive and sometimes subtle, so much so that individuals are often unaware of their impact.

The fortunes of political leaders in democratic nations turn on the support they receive from their electorate, so they tend to emphasize the positive and downplay the negative, a practice that is apparent to all, but especially to senior government officials and military officers who work closely with politicians. One potentially harmful consequence of this influence can be reluctance on the part of some senior military leaders to communicate frankly about military affairs. We are not talking here about military secrets that should be kept from potential enemies. Secrecy, beyond what is required for legitimate security purposes, can lead to immoral consequences. High-level decisions impact on many stakeholders, and sometimes there are strong pressures to act in a particular way that will benefit some stakeholders over others. Transparency ensures that decision-makers will consider the implications for all who may be affected. But when there is a lack of transparency, decision-makers are more susceptible to decision-making biases such as justification, self-deception, and groupthink, and more likely to choose options that are self-serving. Canada's Afghan detainee scandal may provide an instructive example of the ethical problems associated with secrecy and denial. Professor Stephen Saideman, who observed CAF efforts in Afghanistan to prevent the abuse of detainees while simultaneously demonizing whistle-blowers in Ottawa, has criticized the CAF for a lack of openness and a dangerous habit of denying the existence of problems.[103]

The CAF response to press reports alleging that Commanding Officers told their subordinates to ignore incidents of sexual abuse of boys by Afghan army and police personnel provides another instructive example of problems that may result from an organizational reflex of secrecy and denial, and insufficient attention to assessing ethical risk. Public trust in the CAF was shaken by these allegations, particularly the suggestion that Canadian Army leaders were aware of the problem in 2007, almost a year before it became public knowledge.[104] The situation worsened in May 2009 when release of the findings of a military police investigation into the allegations provoked charges of cover-up and calls for an independent inquiry.[105] Further public allegations of cover-up and inaction by the CAF in September 2009 prompted the Army to finally make known the extensive improvements that had been made to its training to prepare soldiers for the ethical challenges that they would face in Afghanistan.[106]

There are many interests, motives, and agendas present in the socio-political realm of senior military decision-makers that can sway individuals to make unethical choices. CAF leadership doctrine emphasizes the importance of transparency and openness to align organizational culture with ethos and promote collaborative civil-military relations.[107] The same doctrine advises senior military officers to view themselves as stewards of the Canadian military profession,[108] so it is their responsibility to educate themselves about these issues and how they may impact on the CAF's ability to do its job.

Another environmental-level ethical risk stems from the desire within the political-military sphere to minimize the danger facing one's soldiers in operations. Political leaders wish to avoid friendly force casualties because such losses erode public support for military missions. Military leaders wish to avoid casualties because they value their soldiers as well as the continued support of political leaders and the public. In the Western world, this has led to what Martin Shaw calls "risk-transfer war," a style of fighting that relies on precision weapons to transfer the risk of personal injury and death from one's own soldiers to enemy combatants and noncombatants, and media management to control the message conveyed to the public.[109] Transferring the risk in this way can lead to the disproportionate and indiscriminate use of force, thereby violating two important just war principles (proportionality and discrimination), and media management can lead to the withholding of information that should be made public.

In addition to the social and political influences described above, there is also the experience of combat itself, because, in the words of Chris Hedges, former war correspondent and author, "war exposes the capacity of evil that lurks not far below the surface within all of us."[110] Stephen Shi, lawyer and former US Marine infantry officer, used the term "centrifugal effect of combat" to capture the idea that combat can push the behaviour of soldiers to the outer limits of legal and ethical acceptance, and sometimes beyond.[111] Several recent studies provide empirical evidence that combat exposure can lead to ethical wrongdoing by soldiers.[112] Soldiers in combat may experience such intense levels of pressure that some of them will lose their moral compass and commit horrible acts, as we have observed repeatedly, so unit leaders taking soldiers into operations need to recognize the inherent ethical risks associated with combat.

Organization

There are many ethical risks in military organizations, particularly with respect to organizational culture.[113] Organizational culture refers to the spirit of an organization[114] and encompasses the "assumptions, values and beliefs shared by organizational members."[115] Linda Trevino, a scholar who studies ethics in organizations, suggests that four aspects of an organization's culture can impact on the ethical functioning of its members and can help to produce sound ethical behaviour or unethical actions. First, there are the unit's norms, which are rules within an organization, many of them informal and not written down, that guide the social behaviour of unit members. Second are the unit's leaders, who have the ability to influence the perceptions and actions of other unit members.[116] Third is the extent to which unit members obey authority figures and comply with unit regulations. Responsible obedience is required here, not blind obedience, because passive subordinates conforming to or colluding with bad leaders can create unethical units.[117] Fourth, there is the extent to which a unit holds its members accountable for their actions. Those units that promote accountability are more likely to have soldiers who behave ethically than units that fail to punish unethical behaviour or neglect to reward morally superior actions.[118]

Careerism is an aspect of military culture associated with ethical risk. Defined here as "the compromising of some moral principle or principles in order to advance one's career goals,"[119] careerism is the antithesis of professionalism and a potential lead-in to unethical behaviour.[120] Nascent careerism is rife in the military because most individuals wish to be promoted. With promotion comes increased status and pay, and a larger pension when one retires. On the positive side, the prospect of promotion can encourage people to work hard and seek greater responsibility, thereby contributing to the organization. But careerism can also entice individuals to avoid their professional responsibilities by playing it safe, creating no waves, and being politically correct.[121] When seen in this light, careerism is a manifestation of "risk aversion," a behaviour generally disparaged in military circles. At its worst, careerism can also lead service members to curry favour with their superiors by engaging in a range of unethical behaviours such as complying with ethically ambiguous orders, keeping problems quiet, failing to voice dissent when the situation calls for it, and basically going along to get ahead.[122] As already discussed, the Report of the Somalia Inquiry gives a thorough account of careerist behaviours related to the selection and screening of personnel for the Canadian Airborne Regiment, actions that no doubt contributed to the Regiment's ethical failures in Somalia in 1993.[123]

Competition is another element of military culture which can lead to ethical risk. Competition among individuals, units, or organizations that is not kept in check can result in an unhealthy lack of cooperation, which in turn can lead to neglect of some stakeholders' interests and ultimately cause ethical failures. On reading about the disagreement around the proper management of detainees in Afghanistan,[124] one wonders if perhaps competition between military officers and officials from the Department of Foreign Affairs or other components of Canada's Afghanistan effort may have contributed in some way to the development of unsatisfactory detainee handling procedures, which resulted in scandal.

R.A. Cooke has identified fourteen internal characteristics that suggest an organization is at ethical risk.[125] According to Cooke, organizations are at ethical risk when they emphasize short-term gains over long-term goals, experience regular violations of professional codes, desire to fix ethical problems with simple solutions, avoid taking an ethical stand when costs are involved, send ethical problems to the legal department, view ethics as a public relations tool, have unfair performance-appraisal procedures, and provide no avenues for internal whistle-blowing.[126]

Military leaders cannot take corrective action if they do not know what needs to be fixed, so an important aspect of a unit's ethical culture (called its ethical climate by some) is the effectiveness of the unit's system for reporting ethical failures to the chain of command. Usually, there are few problems in this area if the misconduct is witnessed by a leader, but it is less certain that a soldier who is not in a leadership position will report any misconduct he or she observes. Studies of US marines and soldiers have shown that many would not report unit members who had committed ethics violations on the battlefield.[127] Such results have many implications, not the least of which is that unit leaders must be alert if they are to have a good appreciation of the ethical climate in their units.

Reporting misconduct may also be a problem at the institutional level of the CAF. Given that an important function of the Canadian military ethos is to "create and shape the desired military culture of the Canadian Forces,"[128] the CAF may have difficulty building a desirable culture if a sizeable portion of its unprofessional behaviour goes unreported. This is where internal whistle-blowing mechanisms can play an important role. The Canadian Army had such a mechanism in place in the early 2000s, called the Lamplighter programme, where soldiers could bypass their chain of command to report breaches of ethics directly to the Army Ethics Officer, who would then bring the violations to appropriate authorities for corrective action. There was never any public statement within (or outside) the Army on the effectiveness of Lamplighter, but it was replaced in 2013 with a new process more aligned with government-wide reporting policy.[129]

CAF leadership doctrine states that the institution must be a learning organization, one that openly encourages the debate of new ideas, critically examines its successes and failures on an ongoing basis, and learns from experience.[130] Although CAF leadership doctrine does not emphasize the close relationship between organizational learning and ethics, this theme is explicit in the Government of Canada's Management Accountability Framework, which guides CAF management practices.[131] Given the importance that ethics has in the learning organization construct, there are several recent developments in the Canadian military community that seem regrettable.

The Semrau case raised many legal and ethical lessons which could be used in training, but what seemed to be missing most at the end of this episode was a strong statement from Army leadership labelling Captain Semrau's actions as both illegal and unprofessional conduct utterly inconsistent with the Canadian military ethos. During the sentencing stage of the trial, an Army brigadier-general condemned Semrau's actions in clear language, but his statement was not widely carried in the media and may have been missed by many Army personnel. By contrast, the commander of the British Army addressed the press following the conclusion of legal proceedings against British soldiers who abused Iraqi civilians, saying that the incidents were "in direct contradiction to the core values and standards of the British Army."[132]

Another regrettable event, whose impact will be felt across the CAF, is the recent decision to discontinue the Officer Professional Military Education Programme.[133] The rationale behind this decision was not publicized; perhaps financial or time constraints were involved. The OPME Programme consisted of a half-dozen courses (four of which were university-level courses in history, politics, and military leadership and ethics) that had to be completed by junior officers to advance in rank. The OPME courses involved open discussion and critical exchange on complex issues facing military professionals. The details of the new programme are vague at this time

(2013), but it appears that the former active-learning programme, which included an evaluation component based on written exams and papers demanding critical thought and analysis, will be replaced with passive-learning training delivered via computer-based courses, perhaps the type in which students work their way through a series of slides towards a multiple-choice exam at the end. Early indications seem to be pointing to a new programme that will fall short of the learning organization standard for ethics.

A third regrettable element is the lack of opportunities for Army personnel to have a public dialogue on ethics issues. To its credit, the CAF experimented with ethics conferences and symposia in the recent past, but these efforts have not been sustained. About a half-dozen annual ethics conferences – called the Canadian Conference on Ethical Leadership – were held between 1996 and 2006, but they have not been offered since. Similarly, an ethics symposium for general officers ran for several years in the early 2000s, but this activity appears to have been discontinued as well. Equally disappointing is the fact that some of the proceedings of these events were not saved.[134] On a more encouraging note, the Army worked with Queen's University to host a conference on the subject of ethical warriors in June 2013.[135]

Individual

While the environmental and organizational influences can sometimes seem abstract and difficult to pinpoint with accuracy, they ultimately manifest themselves in the concrete and plainly observable actions of individuals. The success or failure of military units depends on the actions of its members, and any system relying on human performance is bound to have failures, as we so frequently observe in newspaper reports and newscasts. At the individual level of analysis, ethical risks appear in the form of cognitive, motivational, and physical limitations of individual military members. For greater precision in analyzing these limitations, we can view ethical competence as consisting of four dimensions: moral awareness, moral judgment, moral motivation, and moral action.[136] Moral awareness, which is also called moral sensitivity and moral perception by some, refers to the individual's ability to perceive the moral ramifications of a situation. Individuals with low awareness are less able to grasp the ethical demands of a particular event and may therefore be more likely to make unethical choices. Moral judgment, which is also called moral reasoning ability, refers to the ability to analyze the moral implications of a particular situation to identify the most moral course of action. As with the other moral competencies, individuals will vary in moral judgment ability. According to Kohlberg, an early researcher in this field,[137] some individuals at the lower end of the moral development scale will decide what is right on the basis of self-interest. Most individuals operate a little higher on the scale and make decisions based on normative influences such as rules, regulations, and the opinions of others (most military personnel function at this level). A smaller group performs at the highest level of moral judgment and makes their moral choices on the basis of ethical principles. Moral reasoning capacity is related to general intelligence, and, like awareness, can be improved with education and training. Moral motivation is like moral courage or will. Individuals with strong moral motivation are able to subordinate their self-interest to moral or professional principles. Moral action (also called implementation by some researchers) refers to the ability to apply the three moral components of awareness, judgment, and motivation together to generate an overt, ethical act.

Three points warrant emphasis here. First, all four of the above-mentioned moral components can be viewed as abilities, so some people will be stronger in these capacities than others. Second, research has shown that moral awareness and judgment are most responsive to ethics instruction, but there are also several studies showing that actual behaviour can be improved with moral training.[138] It is still not known how best to raise levels of moral motivation, but we would like to suggest that training, along with a strong ethical example from unit peers and leaders, would have a positive impact that has yet to be assessed. Third, all of these moral competencies are vulnerable to decision-making errors and biases, so training interventions should devote some time to instructing individuals how to manage such threats to sound decision-making.

In addition to the moral capacities discussed above, personal disposition, attitudes, and affect (emotion) also impact on ethical functioning. Research has shown that empathy, ego strength, and locus of control are related to unethical behaviour.[139] Individuals who are low on empathy are more likely to overlook the interests of others and more likely to participate in harmful acts against others.[140] This is a potential problem in cohesive military units, where it is not uncommon to disdain members of out-groups. What may start as simple dismissal or rejection of an out-group can escalate into abuse in the absence of strong discipline or leadership. Ego strength is a strong antidote to unethical influences,[141] because it enables individuals to self-regulate and resist harmful impulses. Locus of control also has an impact on moral behaviour.[142] Individuals with an external locus of control believe that what they do has little impact on eventual outcomes, so they are more susceptible to unethical influences than individuals with an internal locus of control who believe that their actions can affect outcomes in some way. Leaders need to recognize that it is relatively easy for junior soldiers to adopt an external locus of control, believing that their efforts are insignificant and have little impact on the end-state. Ethics training can address this by encouraging everyone in the unit to take responsibility for the unit's reputation, which, in turn, will promote professionalism within the unit.

Studies show that some job-related attitudes are associated with organizational misbehaviour. In particular, individuals who are dissatisfied with their jobs and/or have low levels of commitment to their organization are more likely to engage in workplace misconduct.[143] We also know, from both academic studies and practical military experiences, such as the My Lai massacre in 1968[144] and the Somalia scandal in 1993,[145] that emotions such as anger, fright, and rage can explode in the protracted stress of combat. The overpowering urge for revenge can be a particularly potent trigger of immoral battlefield behaviour, and the death of comrades has frequently provoked a killing rampage in the heat of combat and, on occasion, against enemy soldiers trying to surrender.[146] For example, in the bloody carnage of First World War trench combat, infantry soldiers of the Canadian Expeditionary Force often found it difficult to accept the surrender of Germans who, moments before, had been killing their comrades.[147] Revenge also figured prominently in the desperate struggle between the 3rd Canadian Infantry Division and the German 12th ss Panzer Division around Caen, Normandy, in June and early July 1944.[148] More recently, journalistic accounts suggest that many Canadian soldiers in Afghanistan experienced a desire to avenge the deaths of their comrades.[149]

MEASURING ETHICAL RISK WITH SURVEYS

The CAF has a number of tools that could be used in assessing ethical risk. These include the ethical climate surveys conducted periodically by the Defence Ethics Programme; the Human Dimensions of Operations surveys administered regularly to deployed CAF units; the Unit Morale Profile; an HDO survey administered to non-deployed units; three other measures originally developed for evaluating the CAEP; and additional data that the CAF collects as part of its regular reporting system.

DEP Surveys

Since its launch in 1997, the DEP has surveyed the ethical climate of the CAF four times, in 1999,[150] 2003,[151] 2007,[152] and 2010.[153]

There are several ways in which the results from the DEP surveys can aid in assessing ethical risk. First, the surveys capture a measure of ethical climate by asking respondents their perceptions of their workplace 'right now' on a list of ethics dimensions, including rules, self-interest, job completion, supervisor expectations, co-worker behaviour, organizational fairness, and several other categories. Low scores on any of these would suggest to leaders which potential risk areas require more scrutiny. Second, the surveys measure individual values by asking respondents how things 'should be' on the same list of ethics dimensions. This allows researchers to calculate difference scores between respondents' ratings of 'should be' and 'right now.' Those ethics dimensions with high differences between 'should be' and 'right now' are potential risk areas. Third, the DEP surveys include several moral dilemmas with accompanying questions, the responses to which yield insights into how the respondents analyze ethical problems. For example, the results of the 2010 survey revealed that junior personnel were more inclined to employ either a care-based or self-interested approach to ethical dilemmas (recall that self-interested decision-making indicates a low level of moral development) and that DND civilians were more likely to use a rules-based approach.[154] Such information is useful in developing ethics training programmes. Fourth, the DEP surveys include questions about ethics training and the respondents' knowledge of the DEP, which can alert leaders to training deficiencies. In this regard, results of the 2010 survey showed that forty percent of the respondents had not participated in ethics training in the previous three years.[155]

HDO Surveys

The HDO Project is a series of studies launched in 1996 to examine leadership and morale in CAF units deployed in the Balkans[156] and later expanded to measure important operational concepts such as stress, battlefield ethics, and unit climate in other operational the-atres. HDO survey results provided valuable insights into the ethical attitudes and opinions within deployed units in the Army, but these results were rarely distributed beyond senior Army leaders, so their utility was limited. Since the termination of combat operations in Afghanistan, the HDO surveys have been discontinued.

Unit Morale Profile

Where the HDO surveys measured attitudes and opinions of deployed soldiers, the Unit Morale Profile (UMP) measures many similar con-cepts in non-deployed units throughout the CAF. There are two ver-sions of the UMP, both of which may have utility in assessing ethical risk. The original UMP (called v1.0 by researchers) measures those elements that affect the morale of service members (trust, leadership, ethical climate, support given to family, etc.) and others that are in turn affected by morale (ethical attitudes, psychological distress, deployment readiness, commitment to unit, etc.).[157] A recently devel-oped version of the UMP (v2.0) measures aspects of the workplace environment that contribute to psychological distress.[158]

CAEP Surveys

There are three measures, initially developed for evaluating the CAEP, that could also assist in assessing ethical risk – the Commanding Officer Survey, the Unit Ethics Coordinator Survey, and the General Survey. The Commanding Officer Survey was designed to gather information from COs on the relevance of the CAEP website, the CO's ethics plan for their unit, ethics training in the unit, and ethical problems in the Army. Similarly, the Unit Ethics Coordinator Survey was developed to gather data from unit ethics coordinators on the unit's ethics plan, ethics training in the unit, problems with ethics training, and satisfaction in their role as ethics coordinator. The General Survey was designed to be completed by everyone else in the Army and includes questions which measure knowledge about the CAEP, its website, ethical decision-making and the CAEP decision model, attitudes and motivation towards Army ethics, knowledge about Army ethics, unit ethics training, and ethical climate.[159] Plans are still underway to administer the CAEP surveys.

Survey Shortfalls

The above-mentioned surveys provide a sound basis on which to build an ethical risk assessment plan, but there are two areas in which changes are needed to make them optimal risk assessment measures. First, the personal identification items have to be amended so that survey responses can be grouped by units. At present, perhaps in the interests of encouraging honest responses, the DEP surveys do not ask respondents to identify their home unit. As a result, research staff cannot determine how unit results compare with responses from other units or with the units' own responses on previous surveys, a significant problem if one's goal is to pinpoint ethical risk and/or track the risk over time. Some versions of the HDO survey asked respondents for identifying information on their parent unit, down to sub-unit level in some cases, making HDO results from these surveys more amenable to precise analyses.

The second area in which the surveys should be modified to make them better ethical risk assessment tools is the type of questions asked. At present, most of the ethics questions of these surveys are aimed at capturing respondents' attitudes about ethics issues and their impressions of the ethical climate in their unit, but more specific questions are needed to gain a realistic picture of the type of wrongdoing that occurs in military units. Surveys should include questions on actual misconduct such as: What types of ethics violations occur most frequently in your unit? Have you ever been pressured by a superior or peer to commit an ethical violation? Have you ever not reported an ethics violation you witnessed? Have you ever witnessed a unit comrade: torture anyone, mistreat a detainee, mistreat a non-combatant, steal personal property, damage personal property, violate rules of engagement, abuse subordinates? Armed with this kind of information, leaders would be better prepared to manage ethical crises when they occur and better able to tailor unit training to help their subordinates cope with the ethical challenges in their unit.

Judge Advocate General Report

Another source of information which could be useful in ethical risk analysis is the *Annual Report of the Judge Advocate General to the Minister of National Defence on the Administration of Military*

Justice in the Canadian Forces, which gives an overview of the summary trials and courts-martial conducted in the Army.[160] This report includes descriptions of the different type of offences heard (e.g., absence without leave) and the numbers of summary trials and courts-martial for each offence type.

Other Assessment Tools

To help with the task of identifying ethical risks in the Army and regularly updating this list, Army officers on career courses (e.g., captains on the Army Operations Course, majors on Joint Command and Staff Programme, and colonels on the National Security Programme) could be asked to complete the following request: "Provide three ethical threats that CAF units like your current (or most recent) unit face and for each threat please provide a brief assessment of its likelihood and impact."[161] Similar questions could be included in surveys conducted by the DEP and AEP to identify potential risks in operations, training, and garrison life. In addition, focus groups could be conducted periodically with individuals throughout the chain of command to identify ethical risks. By regularly collecting ethical risk scenarios in this way, the scenarios could be arranged by occupation, unit type, or type of operation and made available to unit COs and CAF schools for use in ethics training.

CONCLUSION

Ethical risk is rarely discussed in the military, so our intent with this chapter was to start a discussion on this topic by emphasizing the importance of ethical risk analysis and providing a framework for assessing ethical threats and vulnerabilities. We began by demonstrating why it is important for military personnel and civilian defence employees to behave ethically and showing just how many different types of unethical behaviour might possibly occur in military units. Next we provided a definition of ethical risk, which has been lacking in CAF doctrine. Then we described how assessing ethical risk is best done by considering threats over three levels of analysis – the societal level, the organizational level, and the individual level – and showed how surveys and other organizational reporting measures could be employed to evaluate ethical threats and vulnerabilities.

Military units are human systems, and all human systems experience moral failures from time to time. Thus, it is incumbent on leaders throughout the military community to prepare for these failures by educating themselves on the threats and vulnerabilities within their units and developing mechanisms for managing the ethical risk. This chapter is an initial step in developing a more comprehensive approach to anticipating and managing ethical risk.

NOTES

1 Brigadier-General Daniel Ménard pleaded guilty to engaging in sexual relations with a female subordinate in Kandahar in 2010, while he was serving as the commander of the CAF Task Force in Afghanistan. See René Bruemmer, "Revelation of Affair Ruined His Life: Disgraced General," *Postmedia News* (21 July 2011), http://news.nationalpost. com/2011/07/21/life-ruined-by-affair-disclosure-disgraced-general/, and CAF news release dated 23 November 2010, http://www.forces.gc.ca/en/ news/article.page?doc=brigadier-general-menard-to-face-court-martial/ hnps1uyk. Captain Robert Semrau was arrested on 31 December 2008 and charged with second-degree murder for shooting an unarmed and wounded insurgent while serving in Afghanistan as commander of an Operational Mentor Liaison Team. A military court subsequently found Captain Semrau guilty of disgraceful conduct (and not guilty of second-degree murder, attempted murder, or negligent performance of a military duty). See CAF news release dated 5 October 2010, http://www.forces. gc.ca/en/news/article.page?doc=captain-semrau-sentenced-following-court-martial-proceedings/hnps1ux3; and M. Friscolanti, "A Soldier's Choice," *Maclean's Magazine* (24 May 2010): 20–5.
2 A. Picard, "Despite E. Coli Scandal, It's Business as Usual for XL Foods," *The Globe and Mail* (16 October 2012), http://www.theglobeandmail. com/news/national/despite-e-coli-scandal-its-business-as-usual-for-xl-foods/article4617285/; R. D'Aliesio, J. Wingrove, and A. Mehler Paperny, "Brazilian-Owned Firm Takes Control of XL Foods Plant," *The Globe and Mail* (17 October 2012), http://www.theglobeandmail.com/news/national/ brazil-owned-firm-takes-control-of-xl-foods-plant/article4619806/.
3 P. C. Newman, *The Canadian Revolution 1985–1995: From Deference to Defiance* (Toronto: Viking, 1995), 80–90.
4 General Rick Hillier, *A Soldier First: Bullets, Bureaucrats and the Politics of War* (Toronto: Harper Collins, 2009), 107–31.

5 M. Byers, *War Law: Understanding International Law and Armed Conflict* (Vancouver, BC: Douglas & McIntyre, 2005), 119–21.

6 S. Maguen and B. Litz, *Moral Injury in the Context of War* (2011), http://www.ptsd.va.gov/professional/co-occurring/moral_injury_at_war.asp (accessed 23 July 2014); H. Hendin and A. Pollinger Haas, *Wounds of War: The Psychological Aftermath of Combat in Vietnam* (New York: Basic Books, 1984), 11; J. Shay, *Achilles in Vietnam: Combat Trauma and the Undoing of Character* (New York: Scribner, 1994), 20.

7 *R. v. Capt. R.A. Semrau*, http://www.jmc-cmj.forces.gc.ca/en/2010/semrau.page (accessed 23 July 2014); see also *R. v. Semrau*, 2010 CM 4010, *Reasons for Sentence*, para. 36, http://www.jmc-cmj.forces.gc.ca/assets/CMJ_Internet/docs/en/2010cm4010.pdf (accessed 23 July 2014).

8 J. Greenberg, "The Steal Motive: Managing the Social Determinants of Employee Theft," in *Antisocial Behaviour in Organizations*, ed. R.A. Ciacalone and J. Greenberg (Thousand Oaks, CA: Sage Publications, 1997), 85–107.

9 T.W. Mangione, J. Howland, and M. Lee, *New Perspectives for Worksite Alcohol Strategies: Results From a Corporate Drinking Study* (Boston: JSI Research and Training, 1998).

10 Canadian Opinion Research Archive, "Canadian Public Opinion Trends," http://www.queensu.ca/cora/_trends/armed_forces.htm (accessed 23 July 2014); Ipsos Reid Corporation, "Qualitative & Quantitative Research: Views of the Canadian Forces – 2010 Tracking Study," March 2010, http://epe.lac-bac.gc.ca/100/200/301/pwgsc-tpsgc/por-ef/national_defence/2010/078-09/summary.pdf (accessed 23 July 2014); Lee Berthiaume, "Declining Visibility in the Canadian Forces," *Postmedia News* (18 September 2012), http://o.canada.com/news/0919-military-visibility/.

11 Murray Brewster, "Jeffrey Delisle, Navy Spy, Removed from Canadian Military," *Canadian Press* (13 February 2013), http://www.huffingtonpost.ca/2013/02/13/jeffrey-delisle-spy-removed-canadian-military_n_2680436.html.

12 J. Lorenz, "The Coalition of the Willing," http://www.stanford.edu/class/e297a/The%20Coalition%20of%20the%20Willing.htm (accessed 23 July 2014).

13 M. Vernon, "Tracking Down the Taliban, but at What Cost?" http://lonewolfcommunications.wordpress.com/category/afghanistan/ (accessed 23 July 2014).

14 D. Couch, *A Tactical Ethic: Moral Conduct in the Insurgent Battlespace* (Annapolis: Naval Institute Press, 2010), 8.

15 International Human Rights And Conflict Resolution Clinic (Stanford Law School) and Global Justice Clinic (NYU School of Law), *Living

Under Drones: Death, Injury, and Trauma to Civilians From US Drone Practices in Pakistan (September 2012), http://www.livingunderdrones.org/report/ (accessed 23 July 2014). For more on the ethical challenges of drones see B.O. Martins, "Legal, Ethical, and Political Issues in Use of Drones – Analysis," *Eurasia Review* (11 March 2013).

16 Crerar to GOC 2 Cdn Corps (13 July 1944), Library and Archives Canada, H.D.G. Crerar Papers, MG 30, E157, 7. The authors are grateful to Capt. J.N. Rickard for this reference. See also Dominick Graham, *The Price of Command: A Biography of General Guy Simonds* (Toronto: Stoddart, 1993), 144; and John A. English, *The Canadian Army and the Normandy Campaign: A Study of Failure in High Command* (New York: Praeger, 1991), 261n34. For a more detailed description of the looting and vandalism carried out by British and Canadian troops in northwest Europe in 1944–45 and efforts to control it, see Sean Longden, *To the Victor the Spoils: D-Day to VE Day, the Reality Behind the Heroism* (Gloucestershire, UK: Arris, 2004), 229–48. Concerning the misbehaviour of Canadian troops in Italy toward the local population and efforts to control it, see Jeffrey A. Keshen, *Saints, Sinners and Soldiers: Canada's Second World War* (Vancouver, BC: UBC Press, 2004), 245–6, 248–9.

17 T. Copp, "General Simonds Speaks: Canadian Battle Doctrine in Normandy," *Canadian Military History* 8, no. 2 (Spring 1999): 74–5.

18 P. Zimbardo, *The Lucifer Effect: Understanding How Good People Turn Evil* (New York: Random House, 2007).

19 B.T. Litz, N. Stein, E. Delaney, L. Lebowitz, W.P. Nash, C. Silva, and S. Maguen, "Moral Injury and Moral Repair in War Veterans: A Preliminary Model and Intervention Strategy," *Clinical Psychology Review* 29 (2009): 700.

20 Y. Vardi and E. Weitz, *Misbehaviour in Organizations: Theory, Research and Management* (Mahwah, NJ: Lawrence Erlbaum Associates, 2004), 257.

21 General Charles C. Krulak, "The Strategic Corporal: Leadership in the Three Block War," *Marines Magazine* (January 1999), http://www.au.af.mil/au/awc/awcgate/usmc/strategic_corporal.htm (accessed 23 July 2014).

22 D. Streatfeild, *Brainwash: The Secret History of Mind Control* (New York: Thomas Dunne Books, 2007), 378.

23 "Soldiers Guilty of 'Revolting' Iraqi Abuse," *Daily Mail (MailOnline)* (23 February 2005), http://www.dailymail.co.uk/news/article-338973/Soldiers-guilty-revolting-Iraqi-abuse.html.

24 "Shock and Shame: Abuse in Iraq," *The Guardian* (20 January 2005), http://www.guardian.co.uk/uk/2005/jan/20/military.iraq1.

25 *Leadership in the Canadian Forces: Conceptual Foundations* (Kingston, ON: Canadian Defence Academy, 2005), 16–34, http://publications.gc.ca/

collections/collection_2013/dn-nd/D2-313-2-2005-eng.pdf (accessed 23 July 2014).

26 *Conceptual Foundations*, 21–3.

27 D. Bercuson, *Significant Incident: Canada's Army, the Airborne, and the Murder in Somalia* (Toronto: McClelland and Stewart, 1996), 8–13.

28 Lieutenant-Colonel Bernd Horn, *Bastard Sons: An Examination of Canada's Airborne Experience 1942–1995* (St Catharines, ON: Vanwell Publishing, 2001): 197.

29 See Horn, *Bastard Sons*, 197; Bercuson, *Significant Incident*, 236–8; and the Report of the Commission of Inquiry into the Deployment of Canadian Forces to Somalia, *Dishonoured Legacy: The Lessons of the Somalia Affair* 5 (Ottawa: Public Works and Government Services Canada, 1997), 1059, 1130–2, 1136–7, 1146–50.

30 For a description of the long-standing command climate problems within the Canadian Airborne Regiment and 2 Airborne Commando and the underlying reasons for them, see Horn, *Bastard Sons*, 193–5, 232–3, and Bercuson, *Significant Incident*, 201–5.

31 Bercuson, *Significant Incident*, 6–11; Peter Worthington and Kyle Brown, *Scapegoat: How the Army Betrayed Kyle Brown* (Toronto: Seal Books, 1997), 124–5.

32 Hillier, *A Soldier First*, 125; Peter Desbarats, *Somalia Cover-up: A Commissioner's Journal* (Toronto: McClelland and Stewart), 3, 21.

33 Horn, *Bastard Sons*, 198–201, 218; Katie Domansky, "The Canadian Forces in Somalia: An Operational Assessment," *Canadian Army Journal* 14, no. 1 (Spring 2012): 101–21; Grant Dawson, *Here Is Hell: Canada's Engagement in Somalia* (Vancouver, BC: UBC Press, 2007), 158–9; Hillier, *A Soldier First*, 127–8.

34 Horn, *Bastard Sons*, 226–7; *Dishonoured Legacy* 4 (2008): 1041–54.

35 Master-Corporal Matchee was arrested and placed in close custody on 18 March 1993. The following day he was found hanging in his cell and was subsequently declared unfit to stand trial as a result of brain damage.

36 For a detailed review of the events that led to the disbandment of the Canadian Airborne Regiment, see Horn, *Bastard Sons*, 217–48.

37 Major Robert Near, "Divining the Message: An Analysis of the MND and Somalia Commission Reports," in *Contemporary Issues in Officership: A Canadian Perspective*, ed. Bernd Horn (Toronto: Canadian Institute of Strategic Studies, 2000), 65; David J. Bercuson, "Up From the Ashes: The Re-Professionalization of the Canadian Forces After the Somalia Affair," *Canadian Military Journal* 9, no. 3 (2009): 35–8; D.L. Bland, *National*

Defence Headquarters: Centre for Decision – A Study Prepared for the Commission of Inquiry into the Deployment of Canadian Forces to Somalia (Ottawa: DND, 1997), 51–2.

38 See the report from the Minister of National Defence, Douglas Young, *Report to the Prime Minister on the Leadership and Management of the Canadian Forces* (25 March 1997), 11–19; *Dishonoured Legacy*, Executive Summary, ES-52, ES-54, ES-61.

39 *Report to the Prime Minister on the Leadership and Management of the Canadian Forces*, http://publications.gc.ca/collections/collection_2013/ dn-nd/D2-313-5-2007-eng.pdf (accessed 28 May 2015), 14.

40 Hillier, *A Soldier First*, 126–8, 256–7.

41 *Conceptual Foundations*, 132.

42 *Risk Management for CF Operations*, Joint Doctrine Manual B-GJ-005-502/FP-000 (2007): 1–2.

43 L.P. Pojman, *Ethics: Discovering Right and Wrong, 6th ed.* (Belmont, CA: Thomson Wadsworth, 2009), 4.

44 J.P. Near, Michael T. Rehg, James R. Van Scotter, and Marcia P. Miceli, "Does Type of Wrongdoing Affect the Whistle-Blowing Process?" *Business Ethics Quarterly* 14 (2004): 226–7.

45 Vardi and Weitz, *Misbehaviour in Organizations*, 252.

46 R.C. Chandler, "Avoiding Ethical Misconduct Disasters," *Graziadio Business Review* 8, no. 3 (2005), http://gbr.pepperdine.edu/?p=2314 (accessed 23 July 2014).

47 Ibid., 6.

48 Zimbardo, *The Lucifer Effect*, 5.

49 R.A. Gabriel, *The Warrior's Way: A Treatise on Military Ethics* (Kingston, ON: Canadian Defence Academy Press, 2007), 1.

50 S.J.-R. Blanc, "The Effect of Combat Exposure on Soldiers' Ethical Attitudes: Preliminary Model and Mitigation Strategy" (Halifax, NS: PhD dissertation, St Mary's University, November 2012), http://library2.smu. ca/bitstream/handle/01/24802/blanc_sebastien_j_r_PHD_2012.pdf? sequence=1 (accessed 23 July 2014).

51 J. Dobson, "Why Ethics Codes Don't Work," *Financial Analysts Journal* 59, no. 6 (2003): 33.

52 LRN (formerly Legal Research Network), "The Impact of Codes of Conduct on Corporate Culture," 2006, http://www.ethics.org/files/u5/ LRNImpactofCodesofConduct.pdf (accessed 23 July 2014); L.K. Trevino, G.R. Weaver, and S. Reynolds, "Behavioural Ethics in Organizations: A Review," *Journal of Management* 32, no. 6 (2006): 951–90.

53 A.M. Adam and Dalia Rachman-Moore, "The Methods Used to Implement an Ethical Code of Conduct and Employee Attitudes," *Journal of Business Ethics* 54 (2004): 239.

54 J. Haidt, "The New Synthesis in Moral Psychology," *Science* 316 (2007): 998.

55 *DND and CF Code of Values and Ethics* (18 July 2012), http://www. forces.gc.ca/en/about/code-of-values-and-ethics.page. Some context for the specific values and expected behaviours included in the *DND and CF Code of Values and Ethics* (e.g., stewardship and excellence) may be traced to the *Values and Ethics Code for the Public Sector* that became effective on 2 April 2012: http://www.tbs-sct.gc.ca/pol/doc-eng.aspx?id=25049& section=text.

56 *Code of Conduct for CF Personnel* (B-GG-005-027/AF-023), n.d.

57 R.J. Walker, *Duty With Discernment: CLS Guidance on Ethics in Operations, Strategic Edition* (Ottawa: Directorate of Army Public Affairs, 2009) (B-GL-347-001/FP-000), 5–6.

58 J.O. Okpara, "Can Corporate Ethical Codes of Conduct Influence Behaviour? An Exploratory Study of Financial Managers in a Developing Economy," paper presented at the Academy of Business and Administrative Sciences, Brussels, 11 July 2003.

59 Mental Health Advisory Team (MHAT) IV Operation Iraqi Freedom 05-07, Final Report (17 November 2006), http://i.a.cnn.net/cnn/2007/images/05 /04/mhat.iv.report.pdf.

60 Internal CAF communication CANFORGEN 056/13 CDS 024/13 051659Z April 2013 entitled "INTERIM GUIDANCE CANADIAN FORCES DIS- CLOSURE PROCESS."

61 *Canadians for Accountability*, http://canadians4accountability.org/golden- whistle-award/#2012 (accessed 23 July 2014).

62 J.E.Wanek, "Integrity and Honesty Testing: What Do We Know and How Do We Use It?" *International Review of Selection and Assessment* 7, no. 4 (1999): 183–95.

63 D.S. Ones, C. Viswesvaran, and F.L. Schmidt, "Comprehensive Meta- Analysis of Integrity Test Validities: Findings and Implications for Personnel Selection and Theories of Performance," *Journal of Applied Psychology Monograph* (1993): 78, 679–703.

64 D.S. Ones, Chockalingam Viswesvaran, and Frank L. Schmidt, "Personality and Absenteeism: A Meta-Analysis of Integrity Tests," *European Journal of Personality* 17 (2003): S19–S38.

65 G.M. Alliger and S.A. Dwight, "A Meta-Analytic Investigation of the Susceptibility of Integrity Tests to Faking and Coaching," *Educational and Psychological Measurement* 60, no. 1 (2000): 59–72.

66 See, for example, P. Robinson, N. de Lee, and D. Carrick, eds., *Ethics Education in the Military* (Aldershot, UK: Ashgate, 2008), 224.

67 C.H. Warner, G.N. Appenzeller, A. Mobbs, J.R. Parker, C.M. Warner, T. Grieger, and C.W. Hoge, "Effectiveness of Battlefield-Ethics Training during Combat Deployment: A Programme Assessment," *The Lancet* (3 September 2011): 915–24.

68 M.J. Bebeau, "The Defining Issues Test and the Four Component Model: Contributions to Professional Education," *Journal of Moral Education* 31, no. 3 (2002): 271–95; K.L. Dean and J.M. Beggs, "University Professors and Teaching Ethics: Conceptualizations and Expectations," *Journal of Management Education* 30, no. 1 (2006): 15–43.

69 A. Colby, "Fostering the Moral and Civic Development of College Students," in *Handbook of Moral and Character Education*, ed. Larry P. Nucci and Darcia Narvaez (New York and London: Routledge, 2008), 400; E.T. Pascarella and P.T. Terenzini, *How College Affects Students: Findings and Insights from Twenty Years of Research* (San Francisco, CA: Jossey-Bass, 1991); E.T. Pascarella and P.T. Terenzini, *How College Affects Students: A Third Decade of Research* (San Francisco, CA: Jossey-Bass, 2005), 2.

70 Pascarella and Terenzini, *How College Affects Students* and *A Third Decade*.

71 A. Schlaefli, J. Rest, and S. Thoma, "Does Moral Education Improve Moral Judgment? A Meta-Analysis of Intervention Studies Using the Defining Issues Test," *Review of Educational Research* 55, no. 3 (1985): 342–7.

72 The Defence Ethics Plan is not in the public domain, but one of its elements is: the Defence Integrity Framework is posted at http://www.forces.gc.ca/en/about/defence-integrity-framework.page (accessed 23 July 2014).

73 J.P. Bradley, "Just Following Orders Is Not Sufficient: Soldiers Need to Know How to Make Ethical Decisions," *Canadian Army Journal* 14, no. 2 (Summer 2012): 45–52, http://www.army.forces.gc.ca/assets/ARMY_Internet/docs/en/canadian-army-journal/CAJ_Vol14.2_07_e.pdf (accessed 23 July 2014).

74 B. Schwartz, "Our Loss of Wisdom," http://www.youtube.com/watch?v=lA-zdh_bQBo (accessed 23 July 2014).

75 M.J. Orsiel, *Obeying Orders: Atrocity, Military Discipline and the Law of War* (New Brunswick, NJ: Transaction Publishers, 1999), 6.

76 Canadian Army Ethics Programme (CAEP), Unit Ethics Coordinator Course, Teaching Point: "Decision Making Based on Army Ethos – Global Model."

77 T.G. Ryan and Jeremy Bisson, "Can Ethics Be Taught?" *International Journal of Business and Social Science* 2, no. 12 (2011): 46–7.

78 G.R. Weaver, L.K. Trevino, and B. Agle, "Somebody I Look Up To: Ethical Role Models in Organizations," *Organizational Dynamics* 34, no. 4 (2005): 314.

79 Adam and Rachman-Moore, "Methods Used," 225.

80 L. Sharp Paine, "Managing for Organizational Integrity," *Harvard Business Review* (March–April 1994): 106, quoted in *Ethics in Finance, 2nd ed.*, ed. John R. Boatright (Malden, MA: Blackwell Publishing, 2008), 26; Lynn Sharp Paine, *Cases in Leadership, Ethics, and Organizational Integrity: A Strategic Perspective* (Boston, MA: Irwin McGraw-Hill, 1997), x; L.E. Sekerka, "Organizational Ethics Education and Training: A Review of Best Practices and Their Application," *International Journal of Training and Development* 1, 3, no. 2 (2009): 78–9.

81 "CDS on Ethical Leadership: General Walt Natynczyk Shares His Thoughts on Ethics," *Journal of the Defence Ethics Programme* 2, no. 1 (December 2009), http://www.forces.gc.ca/en/about-reports-pubs-ethics/2009-journal-defence-ethics-programme.page (accessed 23 July 2014).

82 Air Commodore Leonard Birchall, "Leadership," speech given at the CF School of Aerospace Studies, Winnipeg (17 September 1997), reproduced in *The Canadian Air Force Journal* 2, no. 1 (Winter 2009): 28–40, http://airforceapp.forces.gc.ca/CFAWC/eLibrary/Journal/Vol2-2009/Iss1-Winter/Sections/06-Leadership-A_Speech_By_Air_Commodore_Leonard_Birchall_e.pdf.

83 Lieutenant-Colonel Ian Hope, *Dancing with the Dushman: Command Imperatives for the Counter-Insurgency Fight in Afghanistan* (Kingston, ON: Canadian Defence Academy Press, 2008), 20–2, 152–5.

84 Chandler, "Avoiding Ethical Misconduct Disasters," 1.

85 Ibid., 2, 5; *DND and CF Code of Values and Ethics*, para. 28, 29.

86 LRN, "Ethics and Compliance Risk Management: Improving Business Performance and Fostering a Strong Ethical Culture through a Sustainable Process" (2007), 12, 15, http://www.ethics.org/files/u5/LRNRiskManagement.pdf (accessed 23 July 2014).

87 LRN, "Ethics and Compliance Risk Management," 9, 13.

88 O.C. Ferrell and Linda Ferrell, "Ethical Disaster Recovery Model For Marketing" abstract, http://www.sbaer.uca.edu/research/mma/2003/papers/30.pdf (accessed 23 July 2014); Chandler, "Avoiding Ethical Misconduct Disasters," 2.

89 LRN, "Ethics and Compliance Risk Management," 9.

90 S. Skyvington, "I Like Rob Ford, but It's Over," *The Kingston Whig-Standard* (28 May 2013).

91 N. Hannaford, "The Military and the Media in Canada since 1992," *Security and Defense Studies Review* 1 (Winter 2001): 204–7; Carol Off, "Winning the Public Trust," in *From the Outside Looking In: Media and Defence Analyst Perspectives on Canadian Military Leadership*, ed. Bernd Horn (Kingston, ON: Canadian Defence Academy Press, 2005), 92.

92 L. Gordon, "Let Canadians Decide," in *Generalship and the Art of the Admiral*, ed. Bernd Horn and Stephen J. Harris (St Catharines, ON: Vanwell Publishing, 2001), 323–8; Sharon Hobson, "The Information Gap: Why the Canadian Public Doesn't Know More About Its Military" (Calgary, AB: Canadian Defence & Foreign Affairs Institute, 2007), 16–17.

93 Chandler, "Avoiding Ethical Misconduct Disasters," 7–8; Richard M. Steinberg and Robert J. Faulk, "Internal Control – A Question of Integrity, Ethics and Competence," *Journal of Corporate Accounting and Finance* (Summer 1991): 406; Mary-Jo Kranacher, "Fraud Mitigation," *The CPA Journal* (January 2009): 80.

94 *DND and CF Code of Values and Ethics*, para. 7.

95 *R. v. Semrau*, 2010 CM 4010, *Reasons for Sentence*, para. 52.

96 *DND and CF Code of Values and Ethics*, para. 28.

97 LRN, "Ethics and Compliance Risk Management," 3.

98 *CDS Guidance to COs*, ch. 3, "Defence Ethics and Senior Leadership," para. 302.2. The current version of this document is no longer available on the DND public website, but the 2011 version may be viewed at http://www.docstoc.com/docs/97958723/CDS-Guidance-to-COs_2011 (accessed 24 July 2014).

99 AEP para. 5.b. (3), Annex B (Supplement to ch. 3 of CDS *Guidance to COs*: Commanding Officer's Unit Ethics Plan), para. S-304.4, S-305.2, S-305.7, S-307.1. There is also a job aide provided to assist in development of a unit ethics plan, which includes in its steps the identification of ethical risks. These documents are no longer available on the DND public website.

100 P. Wells, "What Harper Is Hiding," *Maclean's Magazine* (15 April 2013): 18–19.

101 C. Gelpi, P.D. Feaver, and Jason Reifler, *Paying the Human Causes of War* (Princeton, NJ: Princeton University Press, 2009), 20.

102 CBC News, "Public Support for Afghan Mission Lowest Ever: Poll" (5 September 2008), http://www.cbc.ca/news/canada/public-support-for-afghan-mission-lowest-ever-poll-1.707644; Stephen M. Saideman, *Afghanistan as a Test of Canadian Politics: What Did We Learn from the Experience?* The Afghanistan Papers, no. 10 (Waterloo, ON: The Centre for

International Governance Innovation [CIGI], May 2012), 13–14, http://
www.cigionline.org/sites/default/files/Afghanistan_Paper_10.pdf (accessed
24 July 2014); J. Kirton and J. Guebert, "Two Solitudes, One War: Public
Opinion, National Unity and Canada's War in Afghanistan" (paper for
a conference on "Quebec and War," Université de Québec à Montréal
[UQAM], Montreal, October 5–6, 2007), 28, http://www.g8.utoronto.ca/
scholar/kirton2007/kirton-afghanistan-071008.pdf.

103 S. Saideman, "The Canadian Forces Have a Dangerous Habit of Denial,"
The Globe and Mail (15 January 2013), http://www.
theglobeandmail.com/commentary/the-canadian-forces-have-a-dangerous-
habit-of-denial/article7353925/.

104 R. Westhead, "Don't Look, Don't Tell, Troops Told; Civilian Sex Assaults
by Afghan Soldiers Ignored, Military Chaplain Says," *The Toronto Star*
(16 June 2008), http://www.thestar.com/news/2008/06/
16/dont_look_dont_tell_troops_told.html.

105 Canadian Forces Provost Marshal Backgrounder, "CFNIS Investigation
Into Alleged Sexual Abuse" (12 May 2009), http://media3.marketwire.
com/docs/bga.pdf; Mike Blanchfield, "Military 'Washing Its Hands' of
Afghan Abuse Charges: Critic," *Canwest News Service* (12 May 2009),
http://www.canada.com/news/Military+washing+hands+Afghan+abuse+ch
arges+Critic/1588348/story.html; montrealsimon, "Canada and the Raped
Boys of Afghanistan" (13 May 2009), http://montrealsimon.blogspot.
ca/2009/05/canada-and-raped-boys-of-afghanistan.html.

106 D. Pugliese, "Sex Abuse and Silence Exposed: DND Brass Told of Rape of
Boys by Afghan Allies," *The Ottawa Citizen* (21 September 2009), http://
www.ottawacitizen.com/news/abuse+silence+exposed/2010032/story.html.

107 *Leadership in the Canadian Forces: Leading People* (Kingston, ON:
Canadian Defence Academy, 2007), 21, http://publications.gc.ca/
collections/collection_2013/dn-nd/D2-313-3-2007-eng.pdf (accessed
24 July 2014); *Duty With Honour: The Profession of Arms in Canada*
(Kingston, ON: Canadian Defence Academy, 2009), 68, 75, http://
www.21armystuff.30wl.com/pd/Duty-with-Honour-The-Profession-of-
Arms-in-Canada-2009-e.pdf (accessed 24 July 2014); *Leadership in the
Canadian Forces: Doctrine* (Kingston, ON: Canadian Defence Academy,
2005), 13, http://publications.gc.ca/collections/collection_2013/dn-nd/D2-
313-1-2005-eng.pdf (accessed 24 July 2014).

108 *Leadership in the Canadian Forces: Doctrine*, 38.

109 M. Shaw, *The New Western Way of War: Risk-Transfer War and Its Crisis
in Iraq* (Cambridge: Polity Press, 2005), 1–2.

110 C. Hedges, *War Is a Force That Gives Us Meaning* (New York: Anchor Books, 2002), 3.

111 J. Stephen Shi, "usmc Law of War Training Program and Irregular Warfare," presented at the International Symposium for Military Ethics in San Diego, ca, 28 January 2010.

112 US Department of the Army, Office of the Surgeon, Multinational Force – Iraq and Office of the Surgeon General, US Army Medical Command, Mental Health Advisory Team (mhat-iv), *Operation Iraqi Freedom 05-06 Final Report* (17 November 2006), http://armymedicine.mil/documents/mhat-iv-report-17nov06-full-report.pdf; US Department of the Army, Office of the Surgeon, Multinational Force – Iraq and Office of the Surgeon General, US Army Medical Command, Mental Health Advisory Team (mhat-v), *Operation Iraqi Freedom 06-07 Final Report* (14 February 2008), http://armymedicine.mil/pages/mental-health-advisory-team-v-information-.aspx; C.A. Castro and D. McGurk, "Battlefield Ethics," *Traumatology* 17 (2007): 8–13; J.E. Wilk, P.D. Bliese, J.L. Thomas, M.D. Wood, D. McGurk, C.A. Castro, and C.W. Hoge, "Unethical Battlefield Conduct Reported by Soldiers Serving in the Iraq War," *The Journal of Nervous and Mental Disease* 201, no. 4 (2013): 259–65.

113 Some authors distinguish between the concepts of organizational culture and organizational climate. We use the terms interchangeably.

114 Edgar Schein, *The Corporate Culture Survival Guide* (San Francisco, ca: Jossey-Bass, 1999).

115 L.K. Trevino, "Ethical Decision Making in Organizations: A Person-Situation Interactionist Model," *Academy of Management Review* 11, no. 3 (1986): 611.

116 Weaver, Trevino, and Agle, "Somebody I Look Up To," 314.

117 A. Padilla, R. Hogan, and R.B. Kaiser, "The Toxic Triangle: Destructive Leaders, Susceptible Followers, and Conducive Environments," *The Leadership Quarterly* 18 (2007): 182–3.

118 For those interested in seeing more examples of how these four elements of organizational culture can lead to unethical consequences in a military unit, one of us has written on how they likely contributed to the ethical failings of the Canadian Airborne Regiment in Somalia in 1993: J.P. Bradley, "Why People Make the Wrong Choices: The Psychology of Ethical Failure," in *The Moral Dimension of Asymmetrical Warfare: Counter-Terrorism, Democratic Values and Military Ethics*, ed. Th.A. van Baarda and D.E.M. Verweij (Leiden, Netherlands: Martinus Nijhoff Publishers, 2009), 217–311.

119 J.C. Ficarrotta, "Careerism in the Military Services: An Analysis of Its Nature, Why It Is Wrong, and What Might Be Done About It," in Ficarrotta, *Kantian Thinking about Military Ethics* (Surrey, UK: Ashgate, 2010), 31–42.

120 Major Michael L. Mosier, USAF, "Getting a Grip on Careerism," *Airpower Journal* (Summer 1988), http://www.airpower.maxwell.af.mil/ airchronicles/apj/apj88/sum88/mosier.html (accessed 24 July 2014).

121 G.I. Wilson, "Careerism," in *The Pentagon Labyrinth: 10 Short Essays to Help You Through It*, ed. Winslow T. Wheeler (Washington, DC: Center for Defense Information, 2011), 44–5, http://dnipogo.org/labyrinth/ (accessed 24 July 2014).

122 Ibid., 54. See also Chris Hedges, "The Careerists," posted on *Truthdig* (23 July 2012), http://www.truthdig.com/report/item/the_careerists_ 20120723/; and Lecture at the US Military Academy by Secretary of Defense Robert M. Gates (21 April 2008), http://www.defense.gov/ speeches/speech.aspx?speechid=1233.

123 *Report of the Somalia Commission of Inquiry*, ch. 20, "Personnel Selection and Screening," 501–41.

124 J. Gross Stein and E. Lang, *The Unexpected War: Canada in Kandahar* (Toronto: Viking, 2007), 246–58; Murray Brewster, *The Savage War: The Untold Battles of Afghanistan* (Mississauga, ON: John Wiley and Sons, 2011), 63–8; Graeme Smith, *The Dogs Are Eating Them Now: Our War in Afghanistan* (Toronto: Alfred A. Knopf, 2013), 127–54.

125 R.A. Cooke, "Danger Signs of Unethical Behaviour: How to Determine if Your Firm Is at Ethical Risk," *Journal of Business Ethics* 10 (1991): 249–53.

126 Ibid., 251–2.

127 US Department of the Army, Office of the Surgeon, Multinational Force – Iraq and Office of the Surgeon General, US Army Medical Command, Mental Health Advisory Team (MHAT-IV), *Operation Iraqi Freedom 05-06 Final Report* (17 November 2006).

128 *Duty with Honour*, 26.

129 Internal CAF communication CANFORGEN 056/13 CDS 024/13 051659Z April 2013 entitled "INTERIM GUIDANCE CANADIAN FORCES DIS-CLOSURE PROCESS."

130 *Duty With Honour*, 68; *Conceptual Foundations*, 93, 131; *Leadership in the Canadian Forces: Doctrine*, 13, 31. Note also that the Canadian Public Service describes the learning organization as "a self-reflective organiza-tion. It not only seeks to achieve results, but also seeks to understand how it achieves results. It actively seeks to learn from its successes and failures. It asks itself difficult questions, can discuss its weaknesses openly, and has

the courage to correct itself. It regularly challenges its basic assumptions about how things are done. In sum, it seeks to overcome what [Chris] Argyris calls their organizational defence patterns – routine excuses, knee-jerk reflexes and 'skilled incompetence." See "A Primer on the Learning Organization" (February 2007), http://www.tbs-sct.gc.ca/dev/dwnld/lapn-eng.pdf (accessed 24 July 2014).

131 Treasury Board of Canada Secretariat, "Management Accountability Framework," http://www.tbs-sct.gc.ca/maf-crg/index-eng.asp (accessed 24 July 2014).

132 BBC News, "Army Chief's Statement in Full" (25 February 2005), http://news.bbc.co.uk/2/hi/uk_news/4299725.stm (accessed 24 July 2014).

133 The OPME Programme ceased to be delivered on 30 April 2013 (para. 2 of the internal Canadian Forces General (CANFORGEN) message 218/12 dated 011212Z November 2012). See also CANFORGEN 067/13 CMP 032/13 151356Z April 2013 message entitled "UPDATE-CANADIAN ARMED FORCES JUNIOR OFFICER DEVELOPMENT (CAFJOD) PROGRAMME."

134 The proceedings of the first four ethics conference conducted by the CF (1996–99) are no longer accessible on the Defence Ethics Programme website. Similarly, proceedings of the conferences held at the Royal Military College of Canada (RMC) on 7–9 November 2001 and 16–18 October 2005 are not readily accessible. Proceedings of the seventh conference, held at RMC on 28–29 November 2006, are available in print; see *Proceedings from the 7th Canadian Conference on Ethical Leadership* (2 vols.) (Kingston, ON: Canadian Defence Academy Press, 2008).

135 Kingston Conference on International Security, "Ethical Warriors: The Profession of Arms in Contemporary Perspective" (Kingston, ON: 10–12 June 2013), http://www.queensu.ca/kcis/index.html.

136 Adapted from Rest's four-component model of morality. See J. Rest, *Moral Development* (New York: Praeger Publishers, 1986); also D. Narvaez and J.R. Rest, "The Four Components of Acting Morally," in *Moral Development: An Introduction*, ed. W.M. Kurtines and J.L. Gewertz (Boston, MA: Allyn and Bacon,1995).

137 L. Kohlberg, "Moral Stages and Moralization: The Cognitive-Developmental Approach," in *Moral Development and Behaviour: Theory, Research and Social Issues*, ed. T. Lickona (New York: Holt, Rinehart, and Winston, 1976), 34–5.

138 E.P. Waples, A.L. Antes, S.T. Murphy, S. Connelly, and M.D. Mumford, "A Meta-Analytic Investigation of Business Ethics Instruction," *Journal of Business Ethics* 87 (2008): 139.

139 L.K. Trevino, "Ethical Decision Making in Organizations," 603.

140 N. Eisenberg, "Emotion, Regulation, and Moral Development," *Annual Review of Psychology* 51 (2000): 665–97.

141 L.K. Trevino, "Ethical Decision Making in Organizations," 603.

142 A. Forte, "Locus of Control and the Moral Reasoning of Managers," *Journal of Business Ethics* 58 (2005): 65–77.

143 Vardi and Weitz, *Misbehaviour in Organizations*, 133.

144 M. Bilton and K. Sim, *Four Hours in My Lai* (London: Viking, 1992).

145 Horn, *Bastard Sons*, 197; Bercuson, "Up From the Ashes," 236–8.

146 J. Ellis, *The Sharp End of War: The Fighting Man of World War II* (London: David and Charles, 1980), 317–19; Tim Cook, "The Politics of Surrender: Canadian Soldiers and the Killing of Prisoners in the Great War," *The Journal of Military History* 70, no. 3 (July 2006): 650–4.

147 M. Cook, *The Moral Warrior* (Albany: State University of New York Press, 2004), 644; see also W.R. Bird, *Ghosts Have Warm Hands* (Toronto: Clarke, Irwin & Company, 1968), 161, 173–4, 202–3.

148 R.H. Roy, *1944: The Canadians in Normandy* (Toronto: Macmillan of Canada, 1984), 47–9; Alexander McKee, *Caen: Anvil of Victory* (London: Pan Books, 1964), 211–19.

149 C. Blatchford, *Fifteen Days: Stories of Bravery, Friendship, Life and Death from Inside the New Canadian Army* (Toronto: Anchor Canada, 2007), 104–10; Brewster, *The Savage War*, 64; Smith, *The Dogs Are Eating Them Now*, 73, 90.

150 V. Catano, K. Kelloway, and J.E. Adams-Roy, *Measuring Ethical Values in the Department of National Defence: Results of the 1999 Research* (Ottawa: Directorate Human Resources Research and Evaluation, Sponsor Research Report 00-1, July 2000).

151 S. Dursun, R.O. Morrow, D.L.J. Beauchamp, *2003 Defence Ethics Survey Report* (Ottawa: Directorate Human Resources Research and Evaluation, Sponsor Research Report 2004-18, February 2005).

152 K. Fraser, *2007 Defence Ethics Survey Analysis* (Ottawa: Defence Research and Development Canada [DRDC] Centre for Operational Research and Analysis [CORA] and Director-General Military Personnel Research and Analysis [DGMPRA], DRDC CORA TN 2008-016, August 2008).

153 D.L. Messervey, G.T. Howell, T. Gou, and M. Yelle, *2010 Defence Ethics Survey Report* (Ottawa: DRDC and DGMPRA, DGMPRA TM 2011-037, December 2011). Copies of these reports are available at http://www. forces.gc.ca/en/about/defence-ethics.page.

154 Ibid., 35.

155 Ibid., 40.

156 Internal CAF document by H.J. McQuaig Edge, TM 2013-03, *TFI-10 Strategic Analysis: The Human Dimensions of Operations Project* (2013).

157 H.J. McCuaig Edge, *Psychometric Analysis of the Unit Morale Profile: English 2012 Trial Version*, Technical Memorandum submitted for publication (Ottawa: Defence Research and Development Canada, 2013).

158 S. Blanc, personal communication, 17 December 2013.

159 J.P. Bradley, D.F. O'Keefe, A.T. MacIntyre, J.D.Lagacé-Roy, and B.A. Ball, *Measuring the Effectiveness of the Army Ethics Program: Army Ethics Program Evaluation Project, Year-End Report for Fiscal Year 2007/08* (Kingston, ON: Royal Military College of Canada, 2008).

160 This report is available online at http://www.forces.gc.ca/en/about-reports-pubs-military-law/index.page (accessed 23 July 2014).

161 Adapted from George A. Neufeld, "Managing Reputation Risk: How to Avoid Being Dragged Through the Mud," *Risk Management Magazine* (September 2007): 40.

5

Antecedents of Ethical Leadership: Can We Predict Who Might Be an Ethical Leader?

DAMIAN O'KEEFE, VICTOR M. CATANO,
E. KEVIN KELLOWAY, DANIELLE CHARBONNEAU,
AND ALLISTER MACINTYRE

INTRODUCTION

While this book has made quite a few references to ethical leadership, this chapter aims at addressing the concept from a very original angle: its predictability. There are several examples in recent history of unethical or criminal behaviour on the part of corporate, municipal, and military leaders. We are familiar with the cases of investment scandals in the United States and Canada, as well as recent unethical behaviour and corruption charges against several Canadian civic officials. From a military perspective, unethical behaviour by military leaders could have a disastrous impact on the operations and morale of the unit. (In)famous instances of unethical military behaviour include the torture and death of a civilian detainee by Canadian soldiers in Somalia, and the mistreatment of prisoners by US soldiers at Abu Ghraib and Guantanamo Bay, which leaves one wondering about the ethicality of some of the leaders in these organizations. There are a few studies that have examined the ethical dimensions of leader behaviour (i.e., the moral person) and followers' expectations that leaders behave ethically. Indeed, some researchers suggest that the leader is the single most important determinant in shaping an organization's ethical climate, and has a significant impact on the ethical behaviour of organizational members.[1] However, there is little research that has tried to predict the propensity to be an ethical leader. In other words, is it possible to develop a selection system to identify ethical leadership potential?

Brown, Trevino, and Harrison defined ethical leadership as "the demonstration of normatively appropriate conduct through personal actions and interpersonal relationships, and the promotion of such conduct to followers through two-way communication, reinforcement, and decision-making," and postulated that leaders influence the ethical conduct of followers via modelling.[2] Ethical leadership encompasses both the personal ethical conduct of the leader, and the leader's explicit expectations that followers will behave ethically.

Most strikingly, extant research has focused on the consequences of ethical leadership and has largely ignored the potential antecedents of ethical leadership. Little work has been conducted to determine if it is possible to develop personnel selection or training systems that can identify and train leaders who have the propensity to be ethical. Brown and Trevino advanced a number of propositions that considered individual and contextual influences on ethical leadership, but many of these have yet to be investigated.[3] In this chapter, we provide conceptual postulations of situational and individual antecedents, which we hope will stimulate future lines of research on ethical leadership.

ETHICAL LEADERSHIP

Using the social learning approach, Brown et al. explored ethical leadership from the perspective of organization members, and argued that leaders are models for ethical conduct.[4] As such, they become the targets for emulation from their followers, influence ethics-related outcomes, and engage in and reinforce ethical behaviour. Such behaviour involves honesty, integrity, and the fair treatment of others. Leaders develop a more ethical climate through multiple means, including their own behaviour and the use of rewards for the ethical behaviour of their followers.[5] Although supervisors should serve as a key source of ethical guidance for employees, it is only in the past few years that empirical research has focused on the ethical dimension of leadership. In the past, ethical leadership behaviour was discussed within leadership models, particularly the idealized influence component of the transformational leadership model.[6]

Ethical leadership is related to the recently developed concept of authentic leadership, which involves self-regulation, self-awareness, internalized moral perspectives (i.e., consistency between values and behaviours), balanced processing (i.e., analyzing information before making a decision), and relational transparency on the part of leaders that influences positive development.[7] However, one subtle difference between these leadership concepts is that, while authentic leadership appears to focus on the leader's personal development, ethical leadership places equal importance on both the personal ethical conduct of the leader, and the leader's expectations that followers will behave ethically.

Ethical leadership is useful in predicting trust in the leader, interactional justice (i.e., being treated with dignity and respect), perceived effectiveness of leaders, and followers' job satisfaction and dedication.[8] Moreover, measures of ethical leadership predicted these relations over and above that accounted for by transformational leadership, suggesting that the ethical leadership construct is distinct from transformational leadership. Ethical leadership is also related to job task significance, autonomy, and organizational citizenship behaviour,[9] self-efficacy and job performance,[10] workplace deviance,[11] ethical climate and employee misconduct,[12] affective commitment,[13] and job-related affective well-being.[14] All of these studies on ethical leadership have focused on outcomes, with little attention paid to the individual and situational antecedents of ethical leadership.

Brown and Trevino considered individual and contextual influences on ethical leadership.[15] In their paper, they proposed several individual influences on ethical leadership, which include occupational personality constructs, such as agreeableness (positive relationship), conscientiousness (positive relationship) and neuroticism (negative relationship), as well as Machiavellianism (negative relationship), moral reasoning (positive relationship), and locus of control (positive relationship). Situational influences include role modelling and ethical context (positive relationship). To date, most research has focused on outcomes of ethical leadership; thus, Brown and Mitchell argue that there is much to be learned about its antecedents as well.[16]

PROPOSED MODEL OF ANTECEDENTS OF ETHICAL LEADERSHIP

Our proposed model of antecedents of ethical leadership (see Figure 5.1) advocates the use of individual (personal) and situational factors that predict who might be an ethical leader. We propose that individual antecedents of ethical leadership include occupational personality, values, psychological capital, and moral reasoning. Situational antecedents of ethical leadership include perceptions of organizational ethical climate, and organizational justice. We also think that personal and situational factors may interact when predicting ethical leadership. Finally, we discuss the role that moral licensing may play in predicting ethical leadership. The remainder of this chapter puts forward the theoretical and empirical justification for our proposed model.

INDIVIDUAL ANTECEDENTS OF ETHICAL LEADERSHIP

Occupational Personality

In recent years, the 'Big Five' factor structure of personality, more than any other structure, has profoundly influenced the study of individual differences in the workplace.[17] These broad domains incorporate hundreds of traits into five categories: neuroticism, or emotional instability as opposed to adjustment; extroversion, described by a need for stimulation, activity, assertiveness, and quantity plus intensity of interpersonal interaction; openness or intellect, represented by flexibility of thought and openness to feelings, experiences, and new ideas; agreeableness, represented by a compassionate rather than antagonistic interpersonal orientation; and conscientiousness, or degree of organization, persistence, and motivation in goal-directed behaviour.[18]

Meta-analytic research by Barrick and colleagues shows links between the five factors and several organizational outcomes.[19] Conscientiousness has the most consistent association with job performance and academic achievement.[20] Neuroticism has a strong association with teamwork, and extroversion is positively associated with training and managerial performance.[21] Openness has a strong association with training performance[22] and academic achievement,[23] and agreeableness predicts both positive relations with others and job performance,[24] as well as academic achievement.[25]

Meta-analytic research investigating the link between the Big Five factors and transformational leadership (TL) shows that extroversion, openness, and agreeableness correlate significantly with TL. Specifically, the ethical dimension of TL (i.e., idealized influence) is related to extroversion, openness, and agreeableness.[26] Just a few studies have investigated the link between the Big Five and ethical leadership. Walumbwa and Schaubroeck found that agreeableness and conscientiousness (and none of the other three factors) were positively related to ethical leadership;[27] these results were replicated by Kalshoven, Den Hartog, and De Hoogh.[28]

We propose that agreeableness and conscientiousness should be positively related with ethical leadership, and that neuroticism should be negatively related with ethical leadership. This is because agreeableness deals with altruism and cooperation, conscientiousness deals with self-discipline and order, and neuroticism deals with vulnerability to stress, all of which are characteristics of ethical leaders.[29]

Values

Schwartz and Bilsky developed a universal model of human values, defined as concepts or beliefs that pertain to desirable end states or behaviours.[30] Values are thought to be trans-situational beliefs that serve as guiding principles for people to use to evaluate and behave in the world. Schwartz postulated ten types of values:[31] achievement (pursuit of personal success through demonstrating competence according to social standards); benevolence (concern for and enhancement of the welfare of others in one's life); conformity (restraint of actions and impulses that are likely to upset others or violate social expectations and norms); hedonism (personal pleasure and gratification); power (dominance over others); self-direction (independent thought); security (safety and stability); stimulation (excitement and challenge); tradition (moderation and preservation); and universalism (concern for and protection of the welfare of all people and nature). There is a link between Schwartz's values in general and transformational leadership,[32] and between the individual values of achievement, benevolence, self-direction, and universalism and transformational leadership,[33] but there is little research investigating the link between values and ethical leadership.

We propose that the values of achievement, benevolence, conformity, and universalism are related to ethical leadership. Ethical leadership is the demonstration of ethical behaviour, which should therefore be related to the restraint of actions that violate social norms (conformity), as well as the pursuit of personal success (achievement). Moreover, ethical leadership also involves the expectations of ethical behaviour among followers, which should be related to concern for the others in one's life (benevolence) and the welfare of others (universalism).

Psychological Capital

The concept of 'psychological capital' emerged from positive psychology (the study and application of positively oriented human resource strengths)[34] and is defined in terms of four positive psychological capacities: confidence, hope, optimism, and resilience.[35] These four capacities are similar to the four states used by Stajkovic in his description of core confidence for work motivation.[36] Confidence is defined as one's conviction about his/her abilities, which is similar to self-efficacy (the perception of "how well one can execute courses of action required to deal with prospective situations").[37] Hope is a positive motivational state that involves goal-orientation and a plan to accomplish the goal. Optimism is a positive attribution about succeeding now and in the future, and resilience is defined as one's ability to 'bounce back' from adversity.[38]

Although psychological capital is a relatively new construct, research studies have found it predictive of self-reported actual job performance[39] as rated by supervisors,[40] job satisfaction,[41] affective commitment,[42] and citizenship behaviour.[43] More relevant to ethical leadership, psychological capital predicted trust in management,[44] authentic leadership,[45] and transformational leadership.[46] No research has examined the relationship between psychological capital and ethical leadership. We propose that psychological capital should be positively related to ethical leadership because confident, positively motivated, optimistic, and resilient leaders should have the motivation and personal drive to behave in an ethical manner and expect ethical behaviour from followers.

Moral Reasoning

Moral reasoning refers to the degree to which people think about and reason what is right in a given situation. Researchers use Kohlberg's model of moral development to explain differences in the process that people use to determine right and wrong in making judgments. Kohlberg and Hersh described moral development in terms of three broad levels, each comprising two stages.[47] In the first level (pre-conventional), moral decision-making is based on a punishment and obedience orientation (Stage One), and the hedonistic satisfaction of one's own needs (Stage Two). In the second level (conventional), moral decision-making is based on the need to "live up to" the expectations of others (e.g., family, peer group, nation), and comprises the "Good-boy/nice-girl orientation" (Stage Three), and the "Law and Order orientation" (Stage Four). The third level of Kohlberg's moral development is the post-conventional level, which involves morality based on abstract principles. Stage Five in this level is the "Social Contract" and is based on the principle of utilitarianism, and Stage Six is the orientation of universal ethical principles.

Interestingly, there is little empirical research investigating the link between moral reasoning and leadership. One study found that leaders who score higher in moral reasoning were rated higher in transformational leadership by followers compared to leaders who scored lower in moral reasoning, but there is no research that has examined the relationship between ethical leadership and moral reasoning.[48] We propose that ethical leadership will be significantly and positively related to moral reasoning, because ethical leaders are described as having integrity (i.e., the unconditional and principle-based approach to doing the right thing), which is indicative of someone who is functioning at the post-conventional level of Kohlberg's model of moral development.

SITUATIONAL ANTECEDENTS OF ETHICAL LEADERSHIP

Among the situational antecedents of ethical leadership proposed by Brown and Trevino,[49] we propose that organizational ethical climate as it relates to caring, rules, and independence should influence ethical leadership. In addition, we propose that perceptions of organizational justice, as it is related to procedural and distributive justice, should also be an antecedent of ethical leadership.

Ethical Climate

Ethical climate is the "general and pervasive characteristics of organizations, affecting a broad range of decisions" that people use to determine if a decision is right or wrong,[50] which has a profound impact on the ethical behaviour of workers.[51] Schneider hypothesized that ethical climate has an organizational basis, and that groups within organizations develop a unique approach and set of rules with regard to decision-making.[52] When group members know these rules well enough, the rules become part of the work climate or the psychological life of the organization, as discussed in the previous chapter.

Climate is similar to culture; however, unlike culture, which is associated with beliefs and values, climate is usually defined as perceived attitudes towards specific aspects of organizational behaviour, such as safety, service, or ethical issues.[53] Organizations with clear ethical norms and strong ethical climates report fewer serious ethical problems, and are more likely to deal with ethical issues when they arise, compared with organizations that have weaker ethical climates.[54] Indeed, in a study of Canadian Armed Forces personnel, O'Keefe found that people who perceived the climate of their organization to be weak were more likely to act in a discriminatory and self-serving manner.[55]

Victor and Cullen developed an ethical assessment measure.[56] Although they initially hypothesized it as a nine-dimensional construct, statistical analyses yielded five climate types (Caring, Law and Code, Rules, Instrumental, and Independence), each representing a distinct theoretical type of climate. Caring is a measure of how much respondents believe that people in their immediate work unit value other members. Law and Code assesses the degree to which respondents comply with the law and professional standards. Rules assesses the degree to which respondents perceive that people in their immediate work unit emphasize following rules and regulations. Instrumental is the degree to which employees look out for their own self-interest. Independence is the degree to which people believe that those in their immediate work unit value independent thought and action (e.g., following one's personal sense of right and wrong), and would be expected to be guided by their personal moral beliefs.

Several studies report a significant relation between ethical climate and maladaptive practice at work, such as organizational misbehaviour (OMB) intentions, which is defined as intentional acts that violate formal core organizational rules.[57] For example, one study using a sample from a metal-products company reported that the ethical climate factors of Rules, Caring, and Instrumental significantly predicted OMB, with Rules having the largest impact on behaviour.[58] In other words, people who perceived that the ethical climate as it related to Rules (i.e., emphasis placed on following rules and regulations) was weak were more inclined to misbehave.

We propose that ethical climate as it relates to Caring, Rules, and Independence (i.e., personal morality) will be positively correlated with ethical leadership. This is because organizations that promote a caring environment encourage organizational members to follow strong morals, and organizations that emphasize the importance of adhering to laws and rules would create an environment where leaders would not only display ethical behaviour, but promote ethical behaviour from followers.

Organizational Justice

Organizational justice is people's perception of fairness in organizations and consists of three factors: distributive justice, procedural justice, and interactional justice. Distributive justice is the degree to which one expects his/her profits or outcomes to be proportionate to his/her investments.[59] Procedural justice is the degree to which people feel as if the procedures used in decision-making are fair.[60] Interactional justice deals with the quality of interpersonal treatment people receive as procedures are enacted, and is divided into two distinct factors: interpersonal justice, which refers to perceptions of respect and propriety in one's treatment, and informational justice, which refers to the perceptions of the adequacy of the explanations given for that treatment, in terms of their timeliness, specificity, and truthfulness.[61]

There are significant relationships between organizational justice and several outcomes. Folger and Konovsky reported, using data from a survey of reactions to pay raise decisions of 217 first-line employees in a manufacturing plant, that distributive justice accounted for more satisfaction with pay than did procedural justice, but that procedural justice accounted for more organizational commitment and trust in supervisors, compared with distributive justice (commitment and trust, respectively).[62] McFarlin and Sweeney reported that distributive justice was related to personal outcomes such as pay satisfaction and job satisfaction, and that procedural justice was related to organizational outcomes, such as organizational commitment.[63] Skarlicki and Folger reported significant correlation coefficients between organizational retaliation behaviour (ORB) and distributive justice, but higher correlations between ORB, procedural justice, and interactional justice.[64] Interestingly, however, only a few studies have investigated the link between organizational justice and leadership.

Meta-analytic research reports significant correlations between agent-reference evaluation of authority (i.e., followers' immediate supervisor) and distributive justice, procedural justice, interpersonal justice, and informational justice.[65] Bennett, Duffy, Henle, and Lambert found that a supervisor's rating of procedural justice was negatively correlated with followers' ratings of abusive behaviour by supervisors, suggesting that supervisors who perceived organizational procedures to be fair were more inclined to treat followers fairly.[66] Wiesenfeld, Brockner, and Thibault, in a study that investigated managers' behaviours following a layoff, reported a significant positive relationship between managers' perception of the fairness of layoff procedures and their self-reported propensity to engage in effective managerial behaviour as it pertained to leading, guiding, and supporting followers.[67] This result suggests that managers who perceive that organizational procedures are fair are more motivated to use effective managerial practices.

We propose that distributive and procedural justice would be significantly and positively correlated with ethical leadership. This is because leaders who feel that they belong to an organization that enacts organizational policies and procedures fairly, and ensures that employees are rewarded accordingly for strong performance, should be motivated to act fairly in their own role as leaders. As such, leaders should be motivated to act in accordance with their perceptions of their organization, thus resulting in strong ethical behaviour and high expectations of ethical behaviour from followers because there are organizational policies in place to reward such behaviour.

PERSONAL AND SITUATIONAL FACTOR INTERACTION IN PREDICTING ETHICAL LEADERSHIP

So far, we have argued that personal and situational factors might play a direct role in predicting whether one might be an ethical leader. While this may be the case, the relationship between personal and situational factors and ethical leadership might be a little more complicated, and indeed these aspects may influence each other. For example, the personality factor of agreeableness may predict ethical leadership in an organization that promotes a caring environment, but not in an organization whose workers feel that it is not concerned with their welfare.

The idea that personal and situational factors interact in predicting behaviour is not new. Mischel postulated the cognitive social learning approach to explain behaviour,[68] and argued that relatively stable personal variables interact with situational characteristics to

Figure 5.1 Predictors of ethical leadership

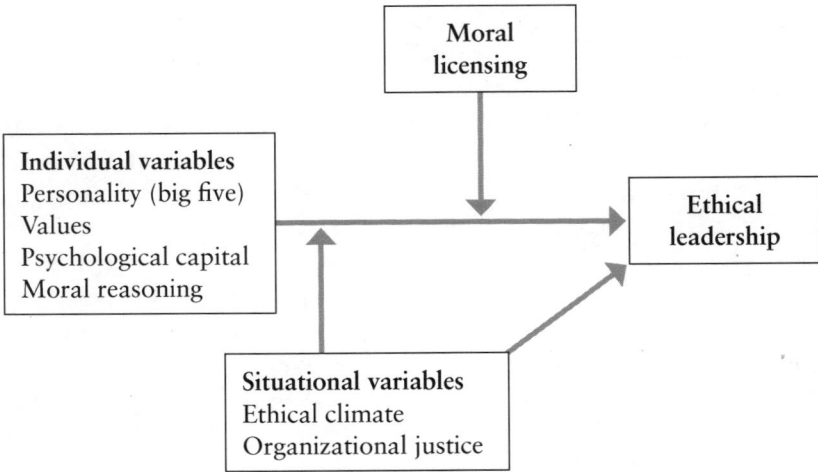

generate stable but discriminative patterns of behaviour.[69] According to Mischel, an individual's level of cognitive social competence reflects the degree to which he/she can attend to[70] and process information in a manner that permits it to be integrated with an existing cognitive structure, and then to generate adaptive and skilful behaviours that will be beneficial for him/her.[71]

We propose an interactionist model of antecedents of ethical leadership that advocates for an interaction between personal and situational factors when predicting ethical leadership.

There is some evidence to support this assertion. Trevino postulated an interactionist model of ethical decision-making in organizations, and argued that decision-making can be explained in terms of an interaction between moral cognition (i.e., stage of moral development based on Kohlberg's model) and situational components.[72] In her model, Trevino argued that situational factors such as organizational culture (e.g., normative structure, reference to others, obedience to authority, and responsibility for consequences) could moderate the cognition-to-behaviour relation, such that when culture is weak, the relation between the stage of moral development and ethical behaviour should be significant and positive. Barnett and Vaicys found such an interaction and reported that perceived climate did not have a direct effect on behavioural intentions, but moderated the relation between ethical judgment and behavioural intentions.[73] Specifically, when the perception of the ethical climate was weak, as ethical judgment (i.e., ratings of ethicality of behaviour) increased, unethical behavioural intentions (e.g., questionable selling practices) decreased. In contrast, when the perception of ethical climate was strong, the relation between ethical judgment and unethical behavioural intentions was non-significant.

Using a sample of 364 Canadian Army personnel, O'Keefe showed that the perceptions of organizational ethical climate moderated the relationship between the personality variables of social dominance orientation (degree to which one desires hierarchy among social groups) and right-wing authoritarianism (degree to which one is submissive to authority, aggressive towards out-groups, and socially conventional), and self-reported discriminatory behaviour.[74] The nature of the interaction was such that respondents who scored lower in SDO and RWA and perceived a strong ethical climate reported fewer instances of discriminatory behaviour, compared with three other groups: people who were lower in SDO and RWA but perceived a weak ethical climate, and people who were higher in SDO and RWA and perceived either a weak or a strong ethical climate. These results suggest that perceptions of the ethical climate of an organization can influence how frequently people engage in unethical behaviour. Although no research shows the interactive effects of personal and situational factors when predicting ethical leadership, we postulate that such an effect may exist.

We propose that although personal and situational variables may have a direct impact on ethical leadership, they also may interact when predicting ethical leadership. For example, perhaps perceptions of organizational justice or the organizational ethical climate might moderate the relationship between personal variables such as personality, values, and psychological capital and ethical leadership. Specifically, we propose that among leaders who feel they belong to an organization that enacts organizational procedures fairly and rewards employees for strong performance, or who feel they are part of an organization that promotes a caring environment, personal variables such as personality, values, and psychological capital would predict ethical leadership. This is because organizations that have fair and just procedures and a strong ethical climate might encourage leaders to have concern for and enhance the welfare of others, to pursue a positive motivational state that involves goal orientation about succeeding now and in the future, and provide strong moral guidance under stressful conditions. In contrast, for leaders who perceive that their organization is not fair, or does not care about the welfare of workers, personal variables such as personality, values, or psychological capital would not predict ethical leadership, because leaders would have little situational incentive to be ethical.

THE ROLE OF MORAL LICENSING ON PREDICTING ETHICAL LEADERSHIP

Another factor that may influence one's propensity to be an ethical leader is moral licensing. Moral licensing is the concept that previous moral behaviour may provide individuals with moral credentials, which could lead them to relax their strivings towards morality and engage in less moral behaviour.[75] That is, moral licensing occurs when past moral behaviour provides justification for acting immorally without feeling immoral.[76] This phenomenon has been reported in studies dealing with prejudicial behaviour,[77] environmentally friendly actions and donations to charity,[78] self-indulgence,[79] and prosocial behaviour.[80] In these studies, individuals who had reported that they engaged in more virtuous behaviours previously were more likely to engage in less virtuous behaviour, compared with people who reported engaging in less virtuous previous behaviour.

Merritt and colleagues postulated that one factor that could be relevant in moral licensing is whether subsequent moral behaviour is a blatant transgression or an ambiguous behaviour.[81] They argued that perhaps past moral behaviour provides moral licensing for ambiguous moral behaviour but not for blatant moral transgressions. For example, individuals who have established high moral credentials may not openly discriminate against specific groups of people (i.e., blatant transgression), but may not intervene when they observe discrimination against specific groups of people (i.e., ambiguous moral transgression). In an operational environment, one could argue that ethical military leaders would never allow troops under their command to mistreat detainees (i.e., blatant transgression), regardless of how high their moral credentials may be. In contrast, perhaps these same leaders might not intervene in a situation where there is suspicion (but no proof) that an ally nation is mistreating detainees (i.e., ambiguous moral transgression).

As discussed, the idea of moral licensing suggests that "ethicality" is a resource that could deplete with repeated use. In the case of ethical leadership, perhaps when leaders self-report past moral behaviour indicative of strong ethical leadership, they may then develop moral credentials and a strong feeling of moral self-regard, thus allowing them to engage in less ethical leadership than they would otherwise allow themselves to engage in. The concept of moral licensing is especially relevant to military leaders, who are often placed in situations (frequently ambiguous ones) where they must make ethical decisions repeatedly. This repeated requirement to act ethically may provide leaders with moral credentials to the point that they feel they could engage in less moral behaviour and still be ethical, regardless of their personal dispositions (e.g., personality, values, psychological capital).

To this end, we propose that moral licensing might moderate the relationship between personal variables (e.g., personality, values) and ethical leadership. The nature of this moderation is such that among leaders who report higher moral credentials (i.e., having engaged in moral behaviour in the past), the relationship between occupational personality (i.e., agreeableness, conscientiousness, and neuroticism) and human values (i.e., achievement, benevolence, conformity, and universalism) and ethical leadership will be lower, compared with the relationship between occupational personality and values and ethical leadership for leaders who report lower moral credentials.

DISCUSSION AND CONCLUSION

Research on ethical leadership has highlighted the important impact that the ethicality of leaders has on the ethical behaviour of followers, with some researchers suggesting that the leader is the single most important determinant of an organization's ethical climate.[82] However, until recently the critical role that leaders play in shaping and transmitting an ethical climate has been ignored.

In this chapter, we have proposed a model of antecedents of ethical leadership that advocates the use of individual and situational factors that predict who might be an ethical leader. Specifically, we propose that individual antecedents of ethical leadership include: the occupational personality factors of agreeableness, conscientiousness, and neuroticism; psychological capital; the human values of achievement, benevolence, and conformity; and finally, moral reasoning. Situational antecedents of ethical leadership include: ethical climate as it relates to caring, rules, and independence (i.e., personal morality); and organizational justice, particularly procedural and distributive justice. We also propose that personal and situational variables will interact in predicting ethical leadership, such that personal variables should predict ethical leadership in situations of strong organizational justice and ethical climate, but not where those factors are weak. Finally, we propose that moral licensing will moderate the relationship between leaders' personalities and values and ethical leadership, such that leaders with higher moral credentials may engage in less ethical leadership behaviour compared with leaders with lower credentials.

We believe that ethical leaders: display a positive motivational state that involves goal orientation and a positive attribution about succeeding now and in the future; are altruistic and cooperative; and have an innate ability to provide strong moral guidance under stressful situations. We also believe that ethical leaders display a pursuit of personal success through demonstrating competence according to social standards; have concern for the welfare of others and nature; and exhibit restraint of actions and impulses that are likely to upset others or violate social expectations and norms. Moreover, we believe that leaders who feel that they belong to an organization that enacts organizational policies and procedures fairly, and who promote a caring environment, encourage organizational members to follow strong morals, and emphasize the importance of adhering to laws and rules, would create an environment where such leaders would not only display ethical behaviour, but promote ethical behaviour from followers. Finally, we believe that leaders who engage in moral behaviour build moral credentials, which could lead to moral licensing that might in turn lead to less moral behaviour, particularly in ambiguous situations.

Ethical leadership is an important component of organizations, particularly military organizations. Ethical leaders are required for the success of operations and the morale of their units. Unfortunately, ethical leadership has not been studied extensively, although it has immense practical value. We have proposed a comprehensive model based on existing literature that outlines the antecedents of ethical literature. The next step in this process is to test this model in a military environment.

NOTES

1 M.J. Neubert et al., "The Virtuous Influence of Ethical Leadership Behaviour: Evidence from the Field," *Journal of Business Ethics* 90, no. 2

(2009): 313–26; M. Schminke, M.L. Ambrose, and D.O. Neubaum, "The Effects of Leader Moral Development on Ethical Climate and Employee Attitudes," *Organizational Behaviour and Human Decision Processes* 97 (2005): 135–51; R. Stringer, *Leadership and Organizational Climate* (Upper Saddle River, NJ: Pearson Education, 2002).

2 M.E. Brown, L.K. Trevino, and D.A. Harrison, "Ethical Leadership: A Social Learning Perspective for Construct Development and Testing," *Organizational Behaviour and Human Decision Processes* 97 (2005): 120.

3 M.E. Brown and L.K. Trevino, "Ethical Leadership: A Review and Future Directions," *The Leadership Quarterly* 17 (2006): 595–616.

4 Brown, Trevino, and Harrison, "Ethical Leadership," 117–34.

5 R.R. Sims and J. Brinkman, "Leaders as Moral Role Models: The Case of John Gutfreund at Salomon Brothers," *Journal of Business Ethics* 35, no. 4 (2002): 327–39.

6 See, for example: B.M. Bass, *Leadership and Performance beyond Expectations* (New York: Free Press, 1985); B.M. Bass and P. Steidlmeier, "Ethics, Character, and Authentic Transformational Leadership Behaviour," *Leadership Quarterly* 10 (1999): 181–217.

7 B.J. Avolio and W.L. Gardner, "Authentic Leadership Development: Getting to the Root of Positive Forms of Leadership," *The Leadership Quarterly* 16 (2005): 315–38; F.O. Walumbwa et al., "Authentic Leadership: Development and Validation of a Theory-Based Measure," *Journal of Management* 34, no. 1 (2008): 89–126.

8 Brown, Trevino, and Harrison, "Ethical Leadership," 117–34.

9 R.F. Piccolo et al., "The Relationship Between Ethical Leadership and Core Job Characteristics," *Journal of Organizational Behaviour* 31 (2010): 259–78.

10 F.O. Walumbwa et al., "Linking Ethical Leadership to Employee Performance: The Roles of Leader-Member Exchange, Self-Efficacy, and Organizational Identification," *Organizational Behaviour and Human Decision Processes* 115 (2011): 4–24.

11 J.B. Avey, M.E. Palanski, and F.O. Walumbwa, "When Leadership Goes Unnoticed: The Moderating Role of Follower Self-Esteem on the Relationship Between Ethical Leadership and Follower Behaviour," *Journal of Business Ethics* 98 (2011): 573–82.

12 D.M. Mayer, M. Kuenzi, and R.L. Greenbaum, "Examining the Link Between Ethical Leadership and Employee Misconduct: The Mediating Role of Ethical Climate," *Journal of Business Ethics* 95 (2011): 7–16.

13 M.J. Neubert et al., "The Virtuous Influence of Ethical Leadership Behaviour: Evidence from the Field," *Journal of Business Ethics* 90, no. 2 (2009): 313–26.

14 K. Kalshoven and C.T. Boon, "Ethical Leadership, Employee Well-Being, and Helping: The Moderating Role of Human Resource Management," *Journal of Personnel Psychology* 11, no. 1 (2012): 60–8.

15 Brown and Trevino, "Ethical Leadership: A Review and Future Directions," 595–616.

16 M.E. Brown and M.S. Mitchell, "Ethical and Unethical Leadership: Exploring New Avenues for Future Research," *Business Ethics Quarterly* 20 (2010): 583–616.

17 M.R. Barrick, M.K. Mount, and T.A. Judge, "Personality and Performance at the Beginning of the New Millennium: What Do We Know and Where Do We Go Next?" *International Journal of Selection and Assessment* 9 (2001): 9–30; L.R. Goldberg, "The Structure of Phenotypic Personality Traits," *American Psychologist* 48 (1993): 26–34; A.E. Poropat, "A Meta-Analysis of the Five-Factor Model of Personality and Academic Performance," *Psychological Bulletin* 135, no. 2 (2009): 322–38.

18 T.S. Bateman and J.M. Crant, "The Proactive Component of Organizational Behaviour: A Measure and Correlates," *Journal of Organizational Behaviour* 14 (1993): 103–18.

19 Barrick, Mount, and Judge, "Personality and Performance," 9–30.

20 Poropat, "A Meta-Analysis," 322–38.

21 Barrick, Mount, and Judge, "Personality and Performance," 9–30.

22 Ibid.

23 Poropat, "A Meta-Analysis," 322–38.

24 Barrick, Mount, and Judge, "Personality and Performance," 9–30.

25 Poropat, "A Meta-Analysis," 322–38.

26 T.A. Judge and J.E. Bono, "Five-Factor Model of Personality and Transformational Leadership," *Journal of Applied Psychology* 85, no. 5 (2000): 751–65.

27 F.O. Walumbwa and J. Schaubroeck, "Leader Personality Traits and Employee Voice Behaviour: Mediating Roles of Ethical Leadership and Work Group Psychological Safety," *Journal of Applied Psychology* 94 (2009): 1275–86.

28 K. Kalshoven, D.N. Den Hartog, and A.H.B. De Hoogh, "Ethical Behaviour and Big Five Factors of Personality," *Journal of Business Ethics* 100 (2011): 249–366.

29 Brown, Trevino, and Harrison, "Ethical Leadership," 117–34.

30 S.H. Schwartz and W. Bilsky, "Toward a Universal Psychological Structure of Human Values," *Journal of Personality and Social Psychology* 58 (1987): 878–91.

31 S.H. Schwartz, "Beyond Individualism/Collectivism: New Dimensions of Values," in *Individualism and Collectivism: Theory Application and*

Methods, ed. U. Kim, H.C. Triandis, C. Kagitcibasi, S.C. Choi, and G. Yoon (Newbury Park, CA: Sage Publications, 1994).

32 See for example V.R. Krishnan, "Impact of Transformational Leadership on Followers' Influence Strategies," *The Leadership and Organization Development Journal* 25, no. 1 (2003): 58–71.

33 J.C. Sarros and J.C. Santora, "Leaders and Values: A Cross-Cultural Study," *Leadership and Organization Development Journal* 22, no. 5 (2001): 243–8.

34 M.E.P. Seligman, *Authentic Happiness* (New York: Free Press, 2002).

35 F. Luthans, K.W. Luthans, and B.C. Luthans, "Positive Psychological Capital: Beyond Human and Social Capital," *Business Horizons* 47, no. 1 (2004): 45–50.

36 A.D. Stajkovic, "Introducing Positive Psychology to Work Motivation" (Paper presented at Academy of Management, Seattle, WA, August 2003).

37 A. Bandura, "Self-Efficacy Mechanism in Human Agency," *American Psychologist* 37, no. 2 (1982): 122.

38 Luthans, Luthans, and Luthans, "Positive Psychological Capital," 45–50; F. Luthans et al., "Positive Psychological Capital: Measurement and Relationship with Performance and Satisfaction," *Personnel Psychology* 60 (2007): 541–72.

39 F. Luthans et al., "Positive Psychological Capital: Measurement and Relationship"; F. Luthans et al., "The Mediating Role of Psychological Capital in the Supportive Organizational Climate–Employee Performance Relationship," *Journal of Organizational Behaviour* 29 (2008): 219–38.

40 F. Luthans et al., "The Mediating Role"; F. Luthans et al., "Positive Psychological Capital: Measurement and Relationship," 45–50; F. Luthans et al., "The Psychological Capital of Chinese Workers: Exploring the Relationship with Performance," *Management and Organization Review* 1, no. 2 (2005): 249–71.

41 F. Luthans et al., "Positive Psychological Capital: Measurement and Relationship," 541–72.

42 F. Luthans et al., "The Mediating Role," 219–38.

43 Walumbwa et al., "Linking Ethical Leadership," 204–13.

44 G. Clapp-Smith, J. Vogelgesang, and J. Avey, "Authentic Leadership and Positive Psychological Capital: The Mediating Role of Trust at the Group Level of Analysis," *Organizational Studies* 15, no. 3 (2009): 227–40.

45 Walumbwa et al., "Linking Ethical Leadership," 204–13.

46 M.F. Peterson et al., "CEO Positive Psychological Traits, Transformational Leadership, and Firm Performance In High-Technology Start-Up And Established Firms," *Journal of Management* 35, no. 2 (2009): 348–68.

47 L. Kohlberg and R.H. Hersh, "Moral Development: A Review of the Theory," *Theory into Practice* 16, no. 2 (1977): 53–9.

48 Turner et al., "Transformational Leadership and Moral Reasoning," *Journal of Applied Psychology* 87, no. 2 (2002): 304–11.
49 Brown and Trevino, "Ethical Leadership," 595–616.
50 B. Victor and J.B. Cullen, "The Organizational Bases of Ethical Work Climate," *Administrative Science Quarterly* 33, no. 1 (1988): 102.
51 T. Barnett and C. Vaicys, "The Moderating Effect of Individuals' Perceptions of Ethical Work Climate on Ethical Judgments and Behavioural Intentions," *Journal of Business Ethics* 27 (2000): 304–11; Y. Vardi, "The Effects of Organizational and Ethical Climates on Misconduct at Work," *Journal of Business Ethics* 29 (2001): 325–37.
52 B. Schneider, "Organizational Climate: An Essay," *Personnel Psychology* 28 (1975): 447–79; B. Schneider, "The Psychological Life of Organizations," in *Handbook of Organizational Culture and Climate*, ed. N.M. Ashkanasay, C.P.M. Wilderon, and M.F. Peterson (London: Sage Publications, 2000), 21–36.
53 Schneider, "Organizational Climate," 447–79.
54 L.K. Bartels, E. Harrick, K. Martell, and D. Strickland, "The Relationship Between Ethical Climate and Ethical Problems within Human Resource Management," *Journal of Business Ethics* 17, no. 7 (1998): 799–804.
55 D.F. O'Keefe, "Assessing the Moderating Effects of Ethical Climate on the Relation Between Social Dominance Orientation/Right Wing Authoritarianism and Unethical Behaviour" (Guelph, ON: PhD dissertation, University of Guelph, 2006).
56 Victor and Cullen, "The Organizational Bases of Ethical Work Climate," 101–25.
57 Barnett and Vaicys, "The Moderating Effect of Individuals' Perceptions," 304–11.
58 Vardi, "The Effects of Organizational and Ethical Climates," 325–37.
59 J.A. Colquitt, J.M. Greenberg, and C.P. Zapata-Phelan, "History of Organizational Justice," in *Handbook of Organizational Justice*, ed. J. Greenberg and J. Colquitt (Mahwah, NJ: Erlbaum, 2005), 12–20.
60 Ibid., 12–20; E.A. Lind and T.R. Tyler, *The Social Psychology of Procedural Justice* (New York: Plenum Press, 1988).
61 Colquitt, Greenberg, and Zapata-Phelan, "History of Organizational Justice," 12–20.
62 R. Folger and M.A. Konovsky, "Effects of Procedural And Distributive Justice on Reactions to Pay Raise Decisions," *Academy of Management Journal* 32, no. 1 (1989): 115–30.
63 D.B. McFarlin and P.D. Sweeney, "Distributive and Procedural Justice as Predictors of Satisfaction with Personal and Organizational Outcomes," *Academy of Management Journal* 35, no. 3 (1992): 626–37.

64 D.P. Skarlicki and R. Folger, "Retaliation in the Workplace: The Roles of Distributive, Procedural, and Interactional Justice," *Journal of Applied Psychology* 82 (1997): 434–43.

65 J.A. Colquitt, D.E. Conlon, M.J. Wesson, C.O.L.H. Porter, and K.Y. Ng, "Justice at the Millennium: A Meta-Analytic Review of 25 Years of Organizational Justice Research," *Journal of Applied Psychology* 86, no. 3 (2001): 425–45.

66 J. Bennett, M.K. Duffy, C.A. Henle, and L.S. Lambert, "Procedural Injustice, Victim Precipitation, and Abusive Supervision," *Personnel Psychology* 59, no. 1 (2006): 101–23.

67 B.M. Wiesenfeld, J, Brockner, and V. Thibault, "Procedural Fairness, Managers' Self-Esteem, and Managerial Behaviours Following a Layoff," *Organizational Behaviour and Human Decision Processes* 83, no. 1 (2000): 1–32.

68 W. Mischel, "Toward a Cognitive Social Learning Reconceptualization of Personality," *Psychological Review* 80 (1973): 252–83.

69 Y. Shoda, W. Mischel, and J.C. Wright, "Intraindividual Stability in the Organization and Patterning of Behaviour: Incorporating Psychological Situations into the Idiographic Analysis of Personality," *Journal of Personality and Social Psychology* 67, no. 4 (1994): 674–87.

70 Mischel, "Toward a Cognitive Social Learning," 252–83.

71 W. Mischel and Y. Shoda, "A Cognitive-Affective System Theory of Personality: Reconceptualizing Situations, Dispositions, Dynamics, and Invariance in Personality Structure," *Psychological Review* 102, no. 2 (1995): 246–68.

72 L.K. Trevino, "Ethical Decision Making in Organizations: A Person-Situation Interactionist Model," *The Academy of Management Review* 11, no. 3 (1986): 601–17.

73 Barnett and Vaicys, "The Moderating Effect of Individuals' Perceptions," 351–62.

74 O'Keefe, *Assessing the Moderating Effects of Ethical Climate*.

75 B. Monin and D.T. Miller, "Moral Credentials and the Expression of Prejudice," *Journal of Personality and Social Psychology* 81 (2001): 33–43.

76 A.C. Merritt, D.A. Effron, and B. Monin, "Moral Self-Licensing: When Being Good Frees Us to Be Bad," *Social and Personality Psychology* 4, no. 5 (2010): 344–57.

77 Monin and Miller, "Moral Credentials," 33–43.

78 S. Sachdeva, R. Illev, and D. Medin, "Sinning Saints and Saintly Sinners: The Paradox of Moral Self-Regulation," *Psychological Science* 20 (2009): 523–8.

79 U. Khan and R. Dhar, "Licensing Effect in Consumer Choice," *Journal of Marketing Research* 43 (2006): 259–66.

80 J. Jordan, E. Mullen, and J.K. Murnighan, "Striving for the Moral Self: The Effects of Recalling Past Moral Actions and Future Moral Behaviour," *Personality and Social Psychology Bulletin* 37, no. 5 (2011): 701–13.

81 Merritt, Effron, and Monin, "Moral Self-Licensing," 344–57.

82 Neubert et al., "The Virtuous Influence of Ethical Leadership," 313–26; M. Schminke, M.L. Ambrose, and D.O. Neubaum, "The Effects of Leader Moral Development," 135–51; Stringer, *Leadership and Organizational Climate.*

PART THREE

Integrating Ethical Sensitivity and Ethical Risk-Taking in Operations

6

Ethical Sensitivity during Military Operations: Without Mindfulness There Is No Reasoning[1]

ALLISTER MACINTYRE, JOSEPH DOTY,
AND DAPHNE XU

INTRODUCTION

Research into ethics and integrity in governance has increased dramatically in recent years;[2] however, this amplification of effort should not be taken as an indication that ethical violations are on the rise. Ethical dilemmas[3] have existed since the dawn of humanity and will persist as long as humans continue to interact with other humans and as long as humans continue to be flawed. Monson and Bock define ethics as "a process that can take place either within an individual or between members of a group. This process encompasses more than decision-making involved with justifying what is moral or ethical. It involves how we perceive situations, how we value ethical actions over other competing needs, and how we show ethical courage in acting upon our beliefs and values in adversity."[4] Hence, our behaviours will inevitably have some sort of impact on others. Naturally, there will be occasions when an outcome could be viewed as unethical. The recent rise in interest in ethics is possibly due to an increase in awareness of ethical misbehaviours, the far-reaching consequences of ethical misconduct in modern society, and the appreciation that doing the right thing can be a tremendous challenge.

This chapter will discuss the existing literature on ethical sensitivity and concepts associated with it, followed by our proposed model of ethical sensitivity. Thereafter, we will provide a brief overview of how ethical sensitivity has been measured thus far, discuss the limitations of these approaches, and conclude with our proposed approach to measuring ethical sensitivity.

ETHICAL THINKING

We cannot assume that, when given freedom of choice and when conscious of their thinking and decisions, people will choose the most ethical course of action. Two historical psychological studies, Zimbardo's Stanford Prison Study[5] and Milgram's obedience study,[6] suggest that individuals can get so psychologically and/or emotionally caught up in whatever they are doing that ethical thinking does not seem to prevail, guide behaviour, or even occur. The unlawful behaviour of a few members of the US military at the notorious Abu Ghraib prison during the Iraq war appears to be a real-world example of the actions displayed in the Stanford Prison Study, and an example of a lack of ethical thinking and perhaps sensitivity.[7] It is also clear that many of the perpetrators of the Holocaust during the Second World War were not ethically sensitive nor thinking ethically. The story and trial of Adolf Eichmann,[8] a key participant in the death of many Jewish civilians during the Holocaust, is a stark example and reminder of how evilly some individuals can act by not consciously and intentionally thinking ethically, by compartmentalizing their thinking, or by having errors in their thinking. These examples also highlight how organizational, contextual, and external factors can and often will influence individual behaviours.[9]

The literature suggests that thinking morally or ethically[10] does not come naturally – but can be developed. An appropriate starting point for a discussion on ethical thinking is the popular Four Component Model (FCM)[11] developed by James Rest, which begins with an individual having moral/ethical awareness or being morally sensitive – meaning that they must *first be aware that an ethical issue even exists*. As discussed in chapter 4 of this book, moral/ethical sensitivity is a person's ability to recognize an ethical issue when it exists.[12] For example, if you were watching two young children in a park flying kites, an ethical issue would not exist, so you would not recognize one. However, if, while watching the kite-flyers, you were to observe some older teenagers come up and knock the children to the ground and steal their kites, then you should recognize that an

Figure 6.1 Four Component Model (FCM)

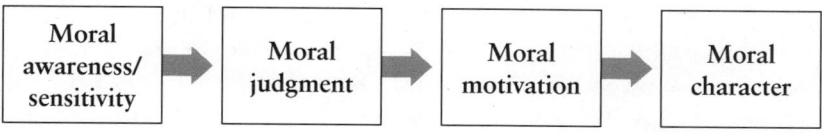

ethical issue exists. The FCM is illustrated in figure 6.1. Rest notes that moral awareness is a *domain-specific* ability, suggesting that individuals can compartmentalize their ethical thinking, thus implying that they may only think in ethical terms in specific contexts. So, theoretically, one can think (and behave) ethically in one's professional life but not in one's personal life – or vice versa. This line of thinking surfaces often in the political world, and reached a high note when then-president Clinton was sexually involved with a White House intern, Monica Lewinsky.

Reynolds introduces the construct of moral attentiveness and distinguishes moral awareness and/or moral sensitivity from moral attentiveness.[13] He defines moral attentiveness as "the extent to which an individual chronically perceives and considers morality and moral elements in his or her experiences"[14] and argues that "moral attentiveness is theoretically and conceptually distinct from moral awareness and moral sensitivity."[15] Reynolds notes that "moral attentiveness pertains to the process by which an individual actively screens and considers stimuli related to morality" and is "a more intentional reflective aspect by which the individual uses morality to reflect on and examine experience."[16] Here we suggest that moral attentiveness might have some 'early' aspects of moral judgment (Reynolds uses the words "reflect," "examine," and "consider"), as it appears to be a higher and more sophisticated cognitive level of moral awareness and moral sensitivity. For our purposes, we do not distinguish between the three terms – all three mean an individual's ability to recognize an ethical situation/dilemma when one exists.

ETHICS AND ETHICAL SENSITIVITY IN TERMS OF DOMAIN SPECIFICITY

As noted above, Rest suggests that moral awareness is a domain-specific ability. Clarifying what is meant by 'domain-specific' is important to discussions on ethics and ethical sensitivity, in order to ensure a common picture and shared mental models. Rest further clarifies his understanding of domain specificity by suggesting that moral sensitivity is "the awareness of how our actions affect other people. It involves being aware of different possible lines of action and how each line of action could affect the parties concerned. It involves imaginatively constructing possible scenarios, and knowing cause-consequence chains of events in the real world; it involves empathy and role-taking skills."[17] The infinite number of domains (contexts) in which one's "actions affect other people," and how each of these domains may or may not be interpreted, helps clarify why ethical sensitivity is a domain-specific ability.

Ethical sensitivity being domain-specific is taken from the perspective of the individual, not from an 'objective' view of the incident. Awareness and sensitivity result from an individual's cognition and/or affect – how they see or feel about something they experience. Of course, *if an incident is not perceived, there cannot be any ethical awareness*. Perception and sensitivity are distinct, with sensitivity conceptualized as a conscious (mindful/thinking) process. As noted by Jones, "the details of moral decision-making and behaviour processes become irrelevant if the person does not recognize that he or she is dealing with a moral issue. Future models of ethical decision making should include some consideration of the effect of the moral agent's failure to recognize the moral issue."[18] Our proposed model does just that.

Our position is that ethics, like gravity, is present whether humans think about it or not. As such, the 'rightness' or 'wrongness' of an event (ethical or unethical) or behaviour is socially and/or culturally determined by thinking, reasoning, and emotive human beings. As Shakespeare once wrote, "there is nothing either good or bad, but thinking makes it so."[19] This important point is best illustrated when we consider that such behaviours as 'honour killings' and female genital mutilation are acceptable and not considered wrong in some cultures.

Although much of the literature and research focuses on business ethics, military ethics, sports ethics, dental/medical ethics, or social ethics, ethics remains omnipresent. For example, there are public transportation ethics, shopping ethics, classroom ethics, hunting ethics, airline ethics, and coffee shop ethics – the list is endless. In any setting where humans are engaged with or interacting with other humans, or animals, or the environment, ethics is present. Consequently, we argue that perception and/or sensitivity to the ethics in a given situation becomes a mindful (conscious) endeavour. Empathy, discussed later, also plays a large role in this process. Furthermore, we argue that even though ethical violations are domain-specific, the ability to detect unethical behaviours (sensitivity) is not. For example, running full speed at someone and slamming him or her to the ground would be considered inappropriate (by most people) if it happened during someone's wedding ceremony. Yet, the identical behaviour is not only expected, it is desirable, when it happens on a North American football field. We contend that most people will be able to differentiate the uniqueness inherent in these two settings (domains) and display levels of sensitivity that are appropriate for the circumstances.

ETHICAL DECISION-MAKING RESEARCH

The FCM provides an appropriate launching pad from which to explore how people deal with and reason through ethical situations. Ho describes the FCM as "perhaps the most widely accepted model about ethical decision-making in psychology."[20] Furthermore, countless research studies have used the approach in an attempt to better understand ethical reasoning.[21] However, a review of the empirical literature into the study and use of Rest's model reveals a serious limitation: there is a paucity of research into the first stage of the model, sensitivity.[22] Most studies tend to focus on the second stage of the FCM, with little attention to the other three stages. It has been noted that in attending to the four processes of the FCM, "prior research has not sufficiently examined the individual capacities that explain the variance across individuals enabling someone to effectively execute the steps or actions related to these four processes."[23]

According to Jordan, "moral judgment is the most studied of the four components, but a focus only on Component 2 leaves a significant amount of moral behaviour unexplained. Moral judgment explains only about 10–15 per cent of the variance in moral-related behaviour."[24] Is it not conceivable that some of the unexplained variance can be attributed to a lack of ethical sensitivity, if the individual is not even aware that an ethical dilemma exists? Similarly, Sadler argues for the importance of ethical sensitivity and states that even though "literally hundreds of studies have examined moral judgement, relatively little work has been devoted to the explication of moral sensitivity."[25]

This shortage of research on ethical sensitivity is perplexing, yet presents a number of challenges for both academia and practitioners. After all, if there are observers present during a given situation with ethical components, and the observers do not perceive or recognize the ethical components of the situation, *then they will be incapable of engaging in ethical evaluation or judgment.* As argued by Sparks and Hunt, "recognizing an ethical issue in a decision-making situation is a necessary precursor to perceiving the conflict that constitutes an ethical problem, which in turn is the starting point for the cognitive processing involved in ethical decision-making."[26] However, in most ethical models and research, the perception of an ethical issue is almost taken as a given. The focus then is on addressing how the situation is handled, or not. But what if the observer is oblivious (mindless) to the fact that something unethical is taking place? Does this mean that an ethical dilemma does not exist? Or is it a failing on the part of the observer to recognize the ethical dimensions of the situation? As already mentioned, until we perceive that something unethical is taking place, ethical reasoning will not and cannot occur. As noted by Seiler and colleagues, "the moral decision-making process is activated only when a moral conflict (or problem) is perceived."[27] Yet it is evident that the bulk of research, by focusing on the second stage of the FCM, makes the assumption that perception and sensitivity have already taken place. This chapter specifically challenges that assumption.

PERCEPTION VERSUS SENSITIVITY

As a starting point in terms of understanding sensitivity, it is important to ask if it is sufficient for *only* perception to take place. Or is it possible that something more is required? For example, Wittmer argues that ethical perception and ethical sensitivity are not synonymous.[28] In Wittmer's opinion, with which we concur, we may perceive the ethical situation, but unless we assign appropriate importance to the issues, either cognitively or emotionally, then ethical sensitivity has not taken place. In other words, people need to attend to more than just the situational characteristics; they need the cognitive and affective awareness and capability to appreciate the *ethical dimensions* within the situation. Jones suggests that the intensity of the context/issues (based on any or all of the following: issue framing; magnitude of consequences; competitive context; temporal immediacy; proximity; probability of effect; concentration of effect) can increase one's moral awareness (one's ethical sensitivity).[29] It is also important for observers to be more than simply aware that a situation contains ethical elements; in many cases there must also be a desire to take appropriate action. Sparks and Hunt point out that "ethical sensitivity does not imply ethicality; being more ethically sensitive does not mean necessarily that a person is more ethical."[30] There are countless examples of situations where people stood idly by while atrocities were being committed in close proximity (sometimes due to the "bystander effect").[31] Hence, when faced with any situation that may be viewed as having an ethical dimension, we also need to understand how any observers, if they are present, fit into the dynamics that are taking place. This means that individual characteristics such as self-awareness, empathy, and emotional intelligence should play a critical role in determining whether people are sensitized to the presence of an ethical issue, and whether they may then experience a sense of responsibility to take action.

SELF-AWARENESS, EMPATHY, AND PERSPECTIVE-TAKING

Among other things, self-awareness should contribute to our appreciation of whether we are physically, emotionally, and psychologically capable of responding to situational demands. Self-awareness, sometimes referred to as self-consciousness,[32] has been conceptualized as a capability to sustain, or expand upon, an abundant and comprehensive concept of the self.[33] Morin defines it as representing "a state in which one actively identifies, processes, and stores information about the self."[34] In terms of ethical sensitivity, self-awareness is a critical part of the equation. For example, Peterson and Ritz report that "research has found that heightened self-awareness leads to more on-line processing of internal information and can make individuals less suggestible, more resistant to placebo effects, and is more likely to lead to correct causal attributions."[35] This suggests that those with a heightened sense of self-awareness will be more likely to accurately assess ethical situations. Thus, it is evident that we cannot truly understand the ethical decision-making process unless we first gain an appreciation of our own individual factors and characteristics – a knowledge of the self. This is why ethics researchers consistently highlight the importance of individual elements such as self-concept,[36] self-reflection,[37] self-responsibility,[38] and self-consciousness.[39] As noted by Robichaux, even though "affective responses such as emotion enable engagement, they are subject to personal motives and misunderstandings. Thus, increasing self-knowledge, critical reflection, and awareness of individual biases and assumptions also become important aspects of the development of ethical sensitivity."[40] Here, the importance of self-awareness and the ability to habitually meta-cognize (think about one's thinking), as it relates to being ethically sensitive, should not be understated.

When scholars have considered aspects of ethical sensitivity and reasoning, two highly related individual characteristics have emerged as being especially critical: empathy and perspective-taking.[41] Empathy is a largely affective response consisting of being able to appreciate how others are feeling, being able to react to these feelings, and thus gaining a sense of connection to others. It has been described as "the spark of human concern for others, the glue that makes social life possible. It may be fragile but it has, arguably, endured throughout evolutionary times and may continue as long as humans exist."[42] Perspective-taking, sometimes referred to as role-taking, is highly related to empathy because it reflects not only an ability to sense the feelings of others, but a capacity to interpret a situation from their point of view. Robichaux contends that both empathy and role-taking skills are highly related to ethical sensitivity because they enable people to constructively use their imaginations to envision scenarios, visualize possible outcomes, and anticipate long-term consequences as they affect other human beings.[43] Likewise, it has been argued that "sensitivity involves imaginatively constructing possible scenarios (often from limited cues and partial information), knowing cause-consequent chains of events in the real world, and having empathy and role-taking skills. Moral sensitivity is necessary to become aware that a moral issue is involved in a situation."[44] Here we note that the vast majority of ethical issues and dilemmas have an effect on other human beings (and to a lesser extent animals) – thus making the link back to empathy.

Although it may seem easy to appreciate the importance of self-awareness, especially as it relates to ethical sensitivity, we need to acknowledge that becoming self-aware or improving on one's self-awareness can be a challenge. In general, people are motivated to maintain a positive self-concept. This means that we may even, on occasion, engage in self-delusion by rationalizing, denying, or repressing uncomfortable perceptions of our own behaviours; people can cognitively mislead themselves, often resulting in a lack of ethical sensitivity or reasoning. The literature on self-deception[45] and self-serving bias[46] suggest individuals deceive themselves (lie to themselves) to maintain a positive self-identity and to feel good about themselves. Self-deception and self-serving biases are often a result of moral disengagement[47] where individuals rationalize or explain away unethical thinking or behaviours. Ogletree and Archer suggest that individuals can ease or shift the blame for unethical behaviour due to factors that cause an emotive reaction (abuse of alcohol, an abusive childhood) – a form of transfer of responsibility.[48] Kross and Grossmann note that individuals often psychologically distance themselves on issues they find very personal.[49] This form of self-deception can result in a lack of ethical sensitivity or in unethical behaviour. Epley and Caruso suggest that people have difficulty reasoning ethically on issues of personal importance.[50] It is easier to say someone else is doing something wrong than to say that about ourselves.

THINKING, MINDFULNESS, AND MINDLESSNESS

It seems intuitive that people in general would focus on what is important to them – work, winning games, information technology, money, relationships, social media, food, material goods, etc. Interestingly, how many people (besides those whose job is to do so) *really think* about ethics, or right and wrong, or good and bad? Research supports the commonly held belief that people think about what they choose to think about[51] or think about those things that support their goals and plans.[52] Furthermore, successful individuals who have years of experience in their field, often referred to as having expertise or tacit knowledge, do not always think ethically.[53] This line of research is informed by social cognition theory,[54] which suggests that people think about things that interest them or can help them to achieve their goals, and do not think about things that do not interest them or cannot help them achieve their goals. Most highly successful individuals have attained their level of success by being singularly focused on success in their particular field (arguably the success and subsequent tragedies that befell both Lance Armstrong and Joe Paterno are examples of this).

Jordan, when examining how (and if) business professionals thought ethically, specifically looked at three hypotheses to help categorize the respondent's thinking:

1 Individuals can only focus on so much (selective encoding).
2 Experts think about things in a way they are used to thinking about them (entrenchment).
3 Expertise and vast experience result in fallacies of thinking.[55]

Her results suggest that expert business practitioners do not think and practise outside of their domains of expertise, or only think (often erroneously or unethically) in ways that support their goals – again, they think about what is important to their work and what will make them successful. That could be summarized, in many cases, as personal benefits trumping ethical values.

The research on ethical thinking suggests that when individuals possess a high level of moral awareness, or are ethically primed, their thoughts, attitudes, and behaviours are often more ethically sensitive.[56] Such individuals think more carefully about, or are more sensitive to, the ethics (the rightness and wrongness) behind their decisions and actions. Internal psychological constructs such as moral potency, moral efficacy, moral agency, moral identity,[57] moral complexity, moral ownership, moral conation, and moral cognition[58] can have an effect on an individual's ethical thinking and perhaps his or her behaviour, *assuming* two things: 1) an individual possesses these psychological constructs at a high and usable level; and 2) the individual thinks about and is conscious of them (self-awareness). These assumptions cannot be taken for granted or simply dismissed, especially when taking into account the infinite number of individual differences in human beings. It can be argued that when individuals' professional or personal lives emphasize morals and ethical behaviour, they will think and act more often in those terms,[59] while those whose lives do not emphasize morals or ethics will not think or act in those terms. Again, people think about and are mindful of things that are important to them.

The conceptual model of moral maturation and moral conation proposed by Hannah and his colleagues[60] provides support to understanding individual differences as they attempt "to identify the specific individual capacities that help account for the level of variation across individuals in terms of how they process, formulate judgments about, and respond to moral challenges."[61] Note that the *starting point or assumption* of their conceptual model, as with Trevino's[62] and Rest's,[63] is that the individual has some knowledge, no matter how little, of the existence of a moral/ethical issue. But this may *not* be true. As noted above, our focus for this chapter is this obvious gap. While Hannah and his colleagues[64] must be given due credit for their attempt to provide greater clarity to the processes underlying the FCM, like many other theorists and scholars they only pay limited attention to the critical first stage – moral/ethical sensitivity. Their definition of moral sensitivity ("processes related to being aware of a moral problem, interpreting the situation, and identifying various options to address the problem"[65]) includes aspects of judgment and decision-making that *are* the latter stages of Rest's model.

There is also literature[66] which suggests that intuition and/or non-rational thinking can influence ethical decision-making. Haidt argues "against rationalist models and proposes an alternative: the social intuitionist model. Intuitionist approaches in moral psychology say that moral intuitions (including moral emotions) come first and directly cause moral judgment."[67] This line of research supports the idea of mindlessness, or of individuals acting without thinking – often deciding on a 'gut feeling.' Someone who says "I feel like that behaviour is wrong but I don't know why or can't explain why I think it is wrong" would be an example of this intuitive approach.

The intuitionist model approach is similar to the rational ethical decision-making models previously discussed because it begins with the *assumption* that the agent has a response (in this case emotive/affective as opposed to cognitive) to a moral/ethical event. Such assumptions are fraught with error. Clearly, a person can be in the presence (perception) of an unethical act and have no emotive response to it. And their lack of an emotive response does not negate the existence of the unethical act – it points to a lack of ethical sensitivity.

Individuals also may act without thinking during routine behaviours that are "performed automatically"[68] or mindlessly.[69] Simplistic examples include brushing one's teeth, pouring a cup of coffee, or putting on one's shoes. At some level, even potentially dangerous behaviours, such as driving a car or mowing the lawn, can be performed mindlessly – because they become routine in nature. Bargh reinforced Langer's work by noting that "if 'mindlessness' is restricted to referring just to the phenomenon that certain relevant information is overlooked or not used as rationally as it should have been, there is certainly plenty of evidence in support of it."[70] Bargh's conclusions also support more current research suggesting that "individuals focus on those stimuli that best fit current purposes or observational goals."[71] Braden discusses mindlessness by noting that "one of the ways we avoid taking responsibility for our actions when doing something we are not proud of or will be ashamed of later is to blank out awareness, in the moment of action, that it is we who are doing what we are doing."[72] Argyris and Schön found mindlessness to be commonplace where people espoused one thing and then did another.[73] It is important to note that mindlessness does not mean one's brain is not functioning – it means a task is being performed without the doer thinking about it. For example, individuals can drive their cars while thinking about the fights they had with their bosses earlier in the day or what they are going to have for dinner. Daydreaming is a form of mindlessness.

One cannot be ethically sensitive while being mindless. When faced with an ethically sensitive situation, observers and actors must not only perceive the critical elements of the situation, they must be sensitive to its moral and ethical characteristics. They must be empathetic; be capable of engaging in perspective-taking; be able to appreciate the potential consequences that are embedded in the set of circumstances; and be self-aware. If the actor is in a mindless state, regardless of the reasons for the mindlessness, these situational responses will never be activated, and there will be no hope for ethical judgment or appropriate action.

ETHICAL SENSITIVITY MINDFULNESS MODEL – A PROPOSED MODEL OF ETHICAL SENSITIVITY

Taking into consideration the above discussion, we propose the Ethical Sensitivity Mindfulness Model (ESMM) presented in Figure 6.1 as a comprehensive approach to understanding ethical sensitivity. This conceptual model takes into account the following considerations:

1 Distinguish between perception and sensitivity.
2 Ascribe importance to the aspects of Jones' concept of moral intensity with the strongest empirical support (see subsequent discussion of Jones' model).[74]
3 Highlight both the cognitive and affective components of ethical sensitivity.
4 Consider the effects of mindfulness and mindlessness on sensitivity.
5 Use the FCM as the basis for understanding ethical thinking and ethical decision-making.

The focus and unique aspect of our model is the "Degree of Mindfulness." At the lower end (bottom of the Mindfulness box), one cannot be ethically sensitive if they are in a mindless state (for example, daydreaming). The more mindful (aware of what they are thinking and feeling, and why) a person is, the greater the possibility of their being ethically sensitive.

The Cognitive/Affective Processes and Mindfulness boxes in our model are also informed by the Elaboration Likelihood Model of persuasion,[75] which suggests individuals have and use both central and peripheral routes in their thinking. These routes are influenced by the individual's ability to process information, their motivation to process the information, and the strength or clarity of the information. The ability to meta-cognize, challenge one's thinking, be conscious of one's thinking, and correct errors in one's thinking, all speak to the spectrum and variety available in the Mindfulness box (the human brain at work). Braden notes that, in terms of being mindful or thinking, human beings have the "free will and choice to turn consciousness bright or dimmer. We are free to:

- focus our mind, or not to bother, or to actively avoid focusing,
- think or not to bother, or to actively avoid thinking,
- strive for greater clarity with regard to some issues confronting us, or not to bother, or to actively seek darkness,
- examine unpleasant facts or to evade them."[76]

As noted above, the literature suggests that mindfulness is a conscious choice. As such, higher levels of self-awareness with a focus on "what am I thinking? and/or what am I feeling? and why?" may result in a higher level of ethical sensitivity.

Our ESMM should not be viewed as a sequential process, as also argued by Rest[77] and by Hannah et al.[78] about their proposed models. Our focus on ethical sensitivity highlights the notion that some level of ethical sensitivity is required in each component of the FCM.[79] Not only is ethical sensitivity necessary for the process to be initiated, it must persist for the final three processes to continue. Ethical sensitivity can be viewed as a light switch: if it is on, it is on, and the FCM process continues; and when it is turned off, the FCM process stops. This relationship is illustrated in our model. For example, if a person is walking across campus and observes two students beating up another student, hopefully ethical sensitivity is activated and the observer will rush to the aid of the victim. However, when the observer gets closer to the beating, the physical activity ceases and the three 'actors' start consulting their scripts for their upcoming play. At this point, the ethical sensitivity light switch should be turned off and the FCM become no longer relevant.

MEASURING ETHICAL SENSITIVITY

As explained earlier, the research efforts that purport to study ethical judgment and decision-making have largely ignored ethical sensitivity. There seems to be an almost magical assumption that this will naturally occur. This apparent attitude is evident in a recent review of the ethical decision-making literature that was able to identify 185 studies of ethical judgment, eighty-six investigations into ethical intent, and eighty-five explorations of ethical behaviour, but only twenty-eight ethical sensitivity studies.[80] This represents a mere 7.3 per cent of the identified studies. Yet, though limited, the little research into ethical sensitivity that does exist is not encouraging. For example, Sperry states: "the research literature on ethical sensitivity, also called moral sensitivity, is sobering. For instance, a review of several studies indicates that 25 and 33 per cent of trainees and experienced healthcare professionals in psychology, counseling, and social work failed to recognize ethical and moral issues in clinical settings ... In other words, up to one-third of these healthcare professionals were found to be ethically insensitive."[81] For healthcare professionals, this result should be unexpected (and perhaps surprising).

It can be argued that the scant research that has been conducted into ethical sensitivity appears to be fraught with inconsistencies, methodological issues, imprecise measurements, flawed operationalizations, limited generalizability, and context-specific approaches. In fact, when examined with a critical eye, many of the approaches discovered in our literature review do not measure ethical sensitivity in its truest sense. Unfortunately, many studies[82] use Rest's Defining Issues Test[83] as a measure of ethical sensitivity, even though "the methodology of DIT doesn't measure real ethical sensitivity"[84] and, as argued by Shawver and Sennetti,

> studies using the DIT often show mixed results and there are at least seven limitations of the DIT. It uses a set of (1) fixed and limited dilemmas, (2) which are not associated directly with business, and creates (3) a one-dimensional score not validly useful as (4) a valid pretest/post test (repeated) measurement from the same respondent; (5) it measures only at most the first two of

Figure 6.2 Ethical Sensitivity Mindfulness Model (ESMM)

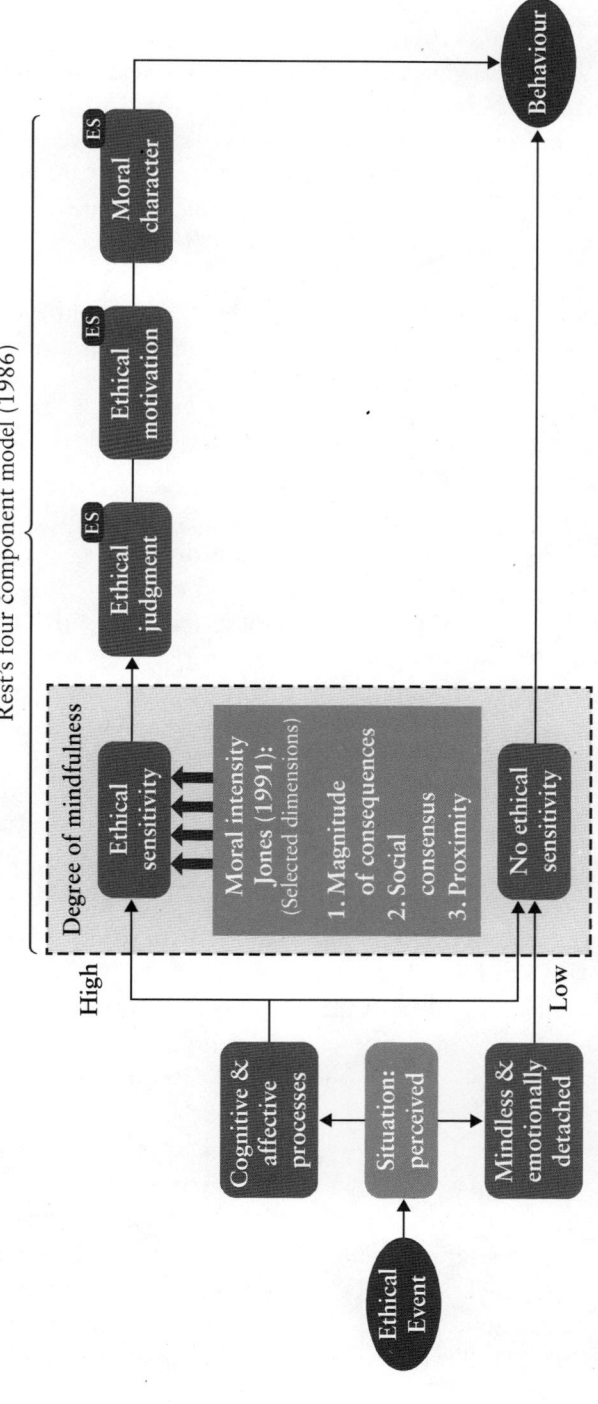

the required four activities (sensitivity, judgment, motivation, and character) that are needed to predict behaviour...; (6) it is known to be subject to gender, geographic, religious, and discipline-related biases or disadvantages ... Also, (7) because the DIT measures cognitive moral growth from children to adults and since it increases with age ... beginning college students under the age of 20 would not be expected to create much variation in their DIT scores.[85]

Each vignette on the DIT is an ethical dilemma and the respondent is asked to *define the issue* – hence the "Defining Issues Test." We are not arguing whether the DIT is a psychometrically sound test; we are challenging whether it is a sound test that measures ethical sensitivity – in its truest sense.

According to Richmond, research examining the first component of the FCM indicates that many individuals have difficulty identifying moral dilemmas and people exhibit differences in terms of their sensitivity to the needs and welfare of others.[86] Richmond also illustrated some of the common problems associated with using the early version of the DIT in ethics research. In particular, some of the scenarios needed rewording, mainly because they were dated, and the participation reliability checks were questionable. She conceded that Rest and his colleagues did revise the test in 1999, including clearer instructions and fewer dilemmas. Nevertheless, Sadler offers the compelling argument that "a consistent theme across all of the moral sensitivity research dictates that this construct cannot be measured by instruments that provide subjects with an explicit treatment of moral aspects and pre-existing options, as in the DIT."[87]

Triki also acknowledges that there is a scarcity of research in ethical sensitivity, and asserts that "previous operationalizations of ethical sensitivity suffer from several limitations: the absence of a control for social desirability bias, the lack of attention to moral intensity elements, the homogeneous structure of the instruments, the scarcity of dimensions and vignettes and a lack of generalizability."[88] In a recent comprehensive review of the measurement of ethical sensitivity, Jordan explains that the definitions of ethical sensitivity "fall into three categories: (a) a combination of recognition and affective response, (b) solely the recognition of moral issues, and (c) a combination of recognition and the ascription of importance to moral issues."[89] A careful review of the methodologies described by Jordan[90] for assessing ethical sensitivity is revealing on a number of levels.

First, there seems to be an underlying premise that ethical sensitivity should be assessed within the context of a specific domain (e.g. a healthcare or business professional setting). Consequently, we see instruments designed to tap into the ethical frameworks for target groups such as dentists, medical professionals, counsellors, social workers, accountants, and auditors. However, this approach appears to be grounded in the assumption that dentists, counsellors, and accountants should only be focused on violations of their professional codes of ethics, or should have a higher level of ethical sensitivity than other professionals. In other words, ethical sensitivity in general is largely ignored, which does not seem helpful because, as discussed previously, being ethically sensitive is *not* domain-specific but rather transcends domains. A domain-specific approach also means that respondents have been primed, in some respects, to attend to the ethical components of the situation. Any priming when testing for ethical sensitivity is problematic.

Second, of the fourteen instruments described, ten used a single vignette/scenario (two used two vignettes, one used three, and one used five videotaped scenes). If we accept the premise that ethics tend to be context-specific (an acceptable behaviour in one setting may be unacceptable in another), then it is difficult to accept that these instruments will be able to provide an accurate understanding of a participant's ethical sensitivity across domains and situations – again, the general nature of ethical sensitivity.

Third, for thirteen of the fourteen approaches, the vignettes contained unethical behaviours for the respondents to recognize and identify (the "Ethical Awareness in Accounting Auditors" instrument was an exception – it included one severe problem, one low-level problem, and one scenario without an ethical issue). This is tantamount to priming participants with respect to their task – "find the unethical elements in the scenario." In her review of the ethical sensitivity literature for accountants, Triki identified this research approach as particularly problematic. Triki states that "in order to measure ethical sensitivity, respondents need to distinguish between ethical and unethical issues. Interestingly, some of the research on ethical sensitivity (one out of nine) did not include an ethical statement in their instrument. The prevalence of unethical issues in the scenarios jeopardizes the balance of the instrument. Individuals were asked to identify to what extent they perceived the issue as unethical knowing that it was unethical."[91] In other words, not only are most of the scenarios unbalanced, the respondents clearly know that the vignette contains unethical issues and that the identification of these issues is their task. From a measurement and validity perspective, this is clearly problematic and confounding.

Fourth, many of the instruments appear to be measuring something other than ethical sensitivity. If we accept that ethical sensitivity is the first stage of the FCM, then asking respondents to recognize potential consequences of behaviours and identify potential courses of action is an approach that will shift the focus to the later stages of the FCM. Ethical sensitivity moves beyond perception to an awareness or recognition that a situation contains components of an ethical nature. It will entail a cognitive aspect (we need to think about the situation) and will undoubtedly contain an affective component (if unethical aspects are present, we might feel some level of discomfort), but judgments and considerations of courses of action will be subsequent to ethical sensitivity.

Finally, very little attention seems to be given to ethical intensity. Jones states that "ethical decision-making is issue contingent; that is, characteristics of the moral issue itself, collectively called *moral intensity*, are important determinants of ethical decision-making and behaviour."[92] As noted earlier, she describes the components of moral intensity as: magnitude of consequences (sum of harm/benefits); social consensus (the level of social agreement that an act is evil or good); probability of effect (the likelihood that an act will take place and cause the predicted harm/good); temporal immediacy (the time lapse from the present to the onset of consequences caused by the act in question); proximity (the feeling of social, cultural, psychological, or physical nearness the observer has for the recipients of the evil/good); and concentration of effect (an inverse function of the quantity of individuals impacted by a behaviour of a given magnitude).[93] Hence, being ethically sensitive includes being mindful (aware) and perhaps emotively affected by the ethical intensity of a given situation.

According to Carlson, Kacmar, and Wadsworth, "moral intensity influences every step in the decision-making process."[94] Similarly, Simga-Mugan and his colleagues argue that "an individual's ethical sensitivity and behaviour may be primarily affected by moral intensity."[95] Furthermore, Triki asserts that "moral intensity needs to be considered when establishing an ethical sensitivity measure."[96] However, the ethical decision research into intensity has not been consistent. The exceptions are strong support for magnitude of consequences and social consensus,[97] and moderate support for proximity.[98]

In sum, we posit that a global ethical sensitivity instrument should not be domain-specific; should provide a variety of contexts and situations; should include ethically neutral, moderate, and extreme situations; should not be transparent in nature; should remain focused on pure ethical sensitivity; and should incorporate elements of intensity.

A PROPOSED APPROACH TO MEASURING ETHICAL SENSITIVITY

The final objective of this chapter is to describe an approach to the measurement of ethical sensitivity that will effectively address the shortcomings in the literature. We have argued here that ethical sensitivity should be viewed as the stage of ethical decision-making that has the greatest importance. Where sensitivity is lacking, judgment, motivation, and action will *never* be part of the behavioural equation – by definition they cannot be. Ethical reasoning and decision-making would thus become a non-event. Our proposed ethical sensitivity instrument will be developed in the following manner:

1 It will contain a large number of very brief vignettes (examples follow), thus permitting a global assessment of ethical sensitivity in a variety of contexts. The items/vignettes will be short, easy to read, clear, direct, and include only one idea or thought. They will avoid items containing universals such as "all," "always," and "never." Furthermore, they will avoid double negatives and words that may not be understood, and will be general enough to cover many different topics.[99]
2 The vignettes will not be domain-specific. We should view ethical sensitivity as a personal characteristic[100] or skill[101] that will cross all domains. People's ethical sensitivity should not be restricted to a specific domain nor tied to a particular or professional code of ethics.
3 The vignettes will vary in intensity (magnitude of consequences) from benign, to moderate, to extreme. This will prevent participants from adopting a particular response set, and will encourage the recognition of both ethical and non-ethical components.
4 The vignettes will also provide manipulations to the proximity aspect of intensity by deliberately varying word choices such as family member, best friend, colleague, neighbour, and stranger.
5 By using a substantial variety of vignettes, situations, and intensity, we expect to be able to mask the intent of the questionnaire

(the questionnaire title will also be nondescript). If respondents recognize that many of the situations are benign or moderate, it is less likely that the ethical focus of the questionnaire will be salient. The benign items will also serve a double purpose as distractor items. Including distractor items in a survey is a psychometrically sound technique to disguise the construct being measured, mitigate social desirability,[102] and maintain respondent interest. This approach should not only reduce the likelihood of adopting a response pattern it should also help to reduce the possibility that social desirability will be an influence.

6 To the greatest extent possible, the items in the questionnaire will be gender-neutral. We will avoid the use of pronouns such as "he," "she," "his," and "her," and instead use names that could just as easily be for males or females. In this manner, the instrument will avoid generating affective responses triggered by gender stereotypes.

7 Similarly, the vignettes will be factual and descriptive, without emotional qualifiers or value-laden descriptive words, to mitigate and control for respondents' thinking and affective responses.

8 Respondents will not be asked to think in terms of appropriate courses of action. The focus will be purely on sensitivity, without forcing a consideration of the remaining steps in the FCM.

9 For each item/vignette, respondents will respond to two statements on a six-point Likert type scale (without a neutral midpoint).[103] The first statement will be "This would upset me," thus tapping into an affective type response. The second statement will be "I would not think negatively about this," thus providing some insight into the respondents' cognitive response. Bunk and Magley support this affective and cognitive approach: "Given that we define sensitivity as the strength of one's cognitive and affective responsiveness to interpersonal encounters, it is not simply being aware of interpersonal treatment that marks high sensitivity; one must be aware of and react strongly to these encounters."[104]

Example Items

a "While going for a walk one day you hear some noises coming from behind a large fence. You peek through a hole in the fence and notice a few people hitting dogs with sticks and clubs." (Ethical – Extreme) b "You are a soldier serving in combat. You discover that your 'battle buddy' and best friend has been torturing prisoners to obtain information that you are confident is saving the lives of soldiers in your unit." (Ethical – Extreme)

c "Your work colleague has an urgent and important report to submit the following day and decides to report sick for the day so as to complete and submit the report on time." (Ethical – Moderate).

d "You are a soldier on a peacekeeping mission in a foreign country. After 2 months in the country you have come to the realization that the only way to get host nation support is through bribes." (Ethical – Moderate).

e "You overhear two colleagues gossiping about the boss." (Distractor – Moderate)

f "You are walking home from work one sunny day and notice some kids playing football in a park." (Distractor – Benign)

CONCLUSION

As an instrument that has a pure focus on ethical sensitivity, this approach will offer tremendous potential benefits. First, once a sufficiently large database has been accumulated, it will be relatively easy to calculate statistical norms for the items and for the instrument. We anticipate that some people will be ethically sensitive (represented by the mean response level) while others will be what we term "Hypo-Sensitive" (more than one standard deviation below the mean) or "Hyper-Sensitive" (more than one standard deviation above the mean). This would make it a useful tool for understanding individuals, groups, and cultures, and it has the potential to be a tremendous feedback tool for developmental purposes. The calculated means would also provide some accurate insights into Jones' concept of social consensus[105] for each item and permit analyses from that perspective. Once again, with a sample large enough, a series of factor analyses could also be conducted to determine how the items themselves cluster. It would be relatively easy to determine if the vignettes could be categorized as "harm" (some harm will occur regardless of the action taken), "competing values" (satisfying one value puts us in conflict with a second value), or "uncertainty" (there are equally compelling arguments for more than one action).

NOTES

1 We would like to thank the Singapore Armed Forces (SAF) Centre for Leadership Development for their generous support for this research and manuscript.

2 D.C. Menzel, "Research on Ethics and Integrity in Governance: A Review and Assessment," *Public Integrity* 7, no. 2 (2005): 147–68.

3 An ethical dilemma is a situation where a person (or persons) can make a 'right' (ethical) or 'wrong' (unethical) decision.

4 V.E. Monson and T.S. Bock, "Educating for Ethical Action: MBA Student Perceptions of Peer Needs and Acceptance," *Journal of College and Character* 1, no. 5 (200): 1–18.

5 P. Zimbardo, *The Lucifer Effect: Understanding How Good People Turn Evil* (New York: Random House, 2007).

6 S. Milgram, *Obedience to Authority – An Experimental View* (London: Tavistock Publications, 1974).

7 S. Hersh, *Chain of Command – The Road from 9/11 to Abu Ghraib* (New York: Harper Collins, 2004).

8 H. Arendt, *Eichmann in Jerusalem – A Report on the Banality of Evil* (New York: Viking Press, 1963).

9 J. Schaubroeck et al., "Embedding Ethical Leadership within and across Organizational Levels," *Academy of Management* 55 (2012): 1055–78; L. Trevino, "Ethical Decision Making in Organizations: A Person-Situation Interactionist Model," *Academy of Management Review* 11, no. 3 (1986): 601–17.

10 For the purpose of this chapter the terms 'moral' and 'ethical' are used interchangeably.

11 J.R. Rest, *Moral Development: Advances in Research and Theory* (Westport, CT: Praeger, 1986).

12 J.R. Sparks and S.D. Hunt, "Marketing Researcher Ethical Sensitivity: Conceptualization, Measurement and Exploratory Investigation," *The Journal of Marketing* 62, no. 2 (1998): 92–109.

13 S. Reynolds, "Moral Attentiveness: Who Pays Attention to the Moral Aspects of Life?" *Journal of Applied Psychology* 91, no. 5 (2008): 1027–41.

14 Ibid., 1028.

15 Ibid.

16 Ibid.

17 J.R. Rest, "Background Theory and Research," *Moral Development in the Professions: Psychology and Applied Ethics*, ed. James Rest and Darcia Narvaez (Hillsdale, NJ: Lawrence Erlbaum Associates, 1994), 23.

18 T.M. Jones, "Ethical Decision Making by Individuals in Organizations: An Issue Contingent Model," *Academy of Management Review* 16, no. 2 (1991): 366–95.

19 W. Shakespeare, *Hamlet*, Act 2 Scene 2.

20 Y.H. Ho, "A Review of Research on Ethical Decision-Making of Purchasing Professionals," *Information Management and Business Review* 4, no. 22 (2012): 72–8.

21 M.J. Bebeau, "The Defining Issues Test and the Four Component Model: Contributions to Professional Education," *Journal of Moral Education* 31, no. 3 (2002): 271–95, doi:10.1080/0305724022000008115; R.A. Bernardi and K.L. LeComte, "Impressions of Questionable Marketing Practices in Indonesia: The Influence of Gender and Social Desirability Response Bias," *Journal of Business Ethics and Organization Studies* 13, no. 1 (2008): 42–50; J.R. Rest, D. Narvaez, S.J. Thoma, and M.J. Bebeau, "A Neo-Kohlbergian Approach to Morality Research," *Journal of Moral Education* 29, no. 4 (2000): 381–95, doi:10.1080/030572400200015001; C. Robichaux, "Developing Ethical Skills: From Sensitivity to Action," *Critical Care Nurse* 32, no. 2 (2012): 65–72; S. Sirin, M. Brabeck, A. Satiani, and L. Rogers-Serin, "Validation of a Measure of Ethical Sensitivity and Examination of the Effects of Previous Multicultural and Ethics Courses on Ethical Sensitivity," *Ethics and Behaviour* 13, no. 3 (2003): 221–35; S.J. Thoma, D. Narvaez, J. Rest, and P. Derryberry, "Does Moral Judgment Development Reduce to Political Attitudes or Verbal Ability? Evidence Using the Defining Issues Test," *Educational Psychology Review* 11, no. 4 (1999): 325–41.

22 D.M. Choi and J.L. Perry, "Developing a Tool to Measure Ethical Sensitivity in Public Administration and Its Application," *International Review of Public Administration* 14, no. 3 (2010): 1–12; T.D. Sadler, "Moral Sensitivity and Its Contribution to the Resolution of Socio-Scientific Issues," *Journal of Moral Education* 33, no. 3 (2004): 339–58; L. Sperry, "Ethical Sensitivity in Christian Healthcare Practice," *The Journal of Christian Healing* 26, no. 2 (2010): 29–34.

23 S. Hannah, B. Avolio, and D. May, "Moral Maturation and Moral Conation: A Capacity Approach to Explaining Moral Thought and Action," *Academy of Management Review* 36, no. 4 (2011): 663–85.

24 J. Jordan, "Taking the First Step toward a Moral Action: A Review of Moral Sensitivity Measurement across Domains," *The Journal of Genetic Psychology* 168, no. 3 (2007): 323–59.

25 Sadler, "Moral Sensitivity," 341.

26 Sparks and Hunt, "Marketing Researcher Ethical Sensitivity," 93.

27 S. Seiler, A. Fisher, and Y. Ooi, "An Interactional Dual-Process Model of Moral Decision Making to Guide Military Training," *Military Psychology* 22 (2010): 490–509.

28 D.M. Choi and J.L. Perry, "Developing a Tool to Measure Ethical Sensitivity," 1–12.

29 Jones, "Ethical Decision Making."

30 Sparks and Hunt, "Marketing Researcher Ethical Sensitivity," 95.

31 J.M. Darley and M. Latane, "Bystander Intervention in Emergencies: Diffusion of Responsibility," *Journal of Personality and Social Psychology* 8 (1968): 377–83; B. Latane and J.M. Darley, "Group Inhibition of Bystander Intervention in Emergencies," *Journal of Personality and Social Psychology* 10, no. 3 (1968): 215–21; B. Latane and S. Nida, "Ten Years of Research on Group Size and Helping," *Psychological Bulletin* 89, no. 2 (1981): 308–24.

32 Y. Ishihara, "Later Nishida on Self-Awareness: Have I Lost Myself Yet?" *Asian Philosophy* 21, no. 2 (2011): 193–211.

33 J. Wain and J. Muldoon, "Wanting to Be 'Known': Redefining Self-Awareness through an Understanding of Self-Narration Processes in Educational Transitions," *British Educational Research Journal* 35, no. 2 (2009): 289–303.

34 A. Morin, "Self-Recognition, Theory-of-Mind, and Self-Awareness: What Side Are You On?" *Laterality* 16, no. 3 (2011): 367–83.

35 S. Peterson and T. Ritz, "The Role of Fearful Beliefs in the Relationship between Situational Self-Awareness and Report of Breathing-Related Sensations," *British Journal of Health Psychology* 16 (2011): 359–72.

36 Y.S. Kim, J.W. Park, Y.J. Son, and S.S. Han, "Nurse Managers' Moral Self-Concept and Ethical Sensitivity," *Journal of Korean Academy of Nursing* 32, no. 7 (2002): 1072–8; D. Narvaez and D.K. Lapsley, "Moral Identity, Moral Functioning, and the Development of Moral Character," in *The Psychology of Learning and Motivation*, ed. D.M. Bartels, C.W. Bauman, L.J. Skitka, and D.L. Medin (Burlington, VT: Academic Press, 2009), 237–74.

37 E.G. Constable, T.B. Kreider, T.F. Smith, and Z.R. Taylor, *The Confidentiality of a Confession: A Counseling Intern's Ethical Dilemma* (2011): 1–11, http://www.counseling.org/resources/library/vistas/2011-v-online/article_37.pdf (accessed 28 May 2015).

38 Narvaez and Lapsley, "Moral Identity."

39 Kim et al., "Nurse Managers."

40 Robichaux, "Ethical Reasoning," 66.

41 M.J. Bebeau, J.R. Rest, and D. Narvaez, "Beyond the Promise: A Perspective on Research in Moral Education," *Educational Researcher* 28, no. 4 (1999): 18–26; J. Jordan, "Taking the First Step"; Sadler, "Moral

Sensitivity"; Sparks and Hunt, "Marketing Researcher Ethical Sensitivity"; K. Tirri, P. Nokelainen, and K. Holm, "Ethical Sensitivity of Finnish Lutheran 7th–9th Graders," in *Getting Involved: Global Citizenship Development and Sources of Moral Values*, ed. F.K. Oser and W. Veuglers (Rotterdam, Netherlands: Sense Publishers, 2008), 327–41.

42 M.L. Hoffman, *Empathy and Moral Development: Implications for Caring and Justice* (New York: Cambridge University Press, 2000), 3.

43 Robichaux, "Developing Ethical Skills."

44 Bebeau et al., "Beyond the Promise," 22.

45 A. Tenbrunsel, K. Diekmann, K. Wade-Benzone, and M. Baserman, "The Ethical Mirage: A Temporal Explanation as to Why We Aren't as Ethical as We Think We Are," *Research in Organizational Behaviour* 30 (2010): 153–73; A. Tenbrunsel and D. Messick, "Ethical Fading: The Role of Self-Deception in Unethical Behaviour," *Social Justice Research* 17 (2004): 223–36.

46 K. Campbell and C. Sedikides, "Self-Threat Magnifies the Self-Serving Bias: A Meta-Analytic Integration," *Review of General Psychology* 3 (1999): 23–43; F. Heider, *The Psychology of Interpersonal Relations* (Hillsdale, NJ: Erlbaum, 1958).

47 A. Bandura, *Social Foundations of Thought Action: A Social Cognition Theory* (Englewood Cliffs, NH: Prentice Hall, 1986); A. Bandura, *Self-Efficacy: The Exercise of Control* (New York: Freeman, 1997).

48 S. Ogletree and R. Archer, "Interpersonal Judgments: Moral Responsibility and Blame," *Ethics and Behaviour* 21, no. 1 (2011): 35–48.

49 E. Kross and I. Grossmann, "Boosting Wisdom: Distance from Self Enhances Wise Reasoning, Attitudes and Behaviour," *Journal of Experimental Psychology, General*, doi: 10.1037/a0024158.

50 N. Epley and E. Caruso, "Perspective Taking: Mis-Stepping into Other's Shoes," in *Handbook of Imagination and Mental Simulation*, ed. K.D. Markman, W.P. Klein, and J.A. Suhr (Hove, UK: Psychology Press, 2008), 297–311.

51 D. Broadbent, *Perception and Communication* (Oxford, UK: Pergamon Press, 1958); D. Rumelhart and A. Ortony, "The Representation of Knowledge in Memory," in *Schooling and the Acquisition of Knowledge*, ed. R.C. Anderson, R.J. Shapiro, and W.E. Montague (Hillsdale, NJ: Erlbaum, 1977), 99–136; S. Taylor and J. Crocker, "Schematic Bases of Social Information Processing," in *Social Cognition – The Ontario Symposium* 1, ed. E.T. Higgins, C.P. Herman, and M.P. Zanna (Hillsdale, NJ: Erlbaum, 1981), 89–134.

52 S. Fiske and L. Dyer, *Cognitive Analysis of Involvement in Persuasion* (Washington, DC: paper presented to the meeting of the American

Psychological Association, 1982); D. Gioia, "Pinto Fires and Personal Ethics: A Script Analysis of Missed Opportunities," *Journal of Business Ethics* 11 (1982): 379–89; R. Hastie, "Schematic Principles in Human Memory," in *Social Cognition – The Ontario Symposium 1*, ed. E.T. Higgins, C.P. Herman, and M.P. Zanna (Hillsdale, NJ: Erlbaum, 1981), 39–88; C. Lord, L. Ross, and M. Lepper, "Biased Assimilation and Attitude Polarization: The Effects of Prior Theories of Subsequently Considered Evidence," *Journal of Personality and Social Psychology* 37 (1979): 2098–2109; R. Wyer, T. Stull, S. Gordon, and J. Hartwick, "Effects of Processing Objectives on the Recall of Prose Material," *Journal of Personality and Social Psychology* 43, no. 4 (1982): 674–88.

53 D. DeSteno and P. Valdesolo, *Out of Character – Surprising Truths about the Liar, Cheat, Sinner (and Saint) Lurking in All of Us* (New York: Crown Publishing Group, 2011); P. Gioia, D. Ludwig, and C. Longenecker, "The Bathsheba Syndrome: The Ethical Failures of Successful Leaders," *Journal of Business Ethics* 12 (1993): 265–73; J. Wiley, "Expertise as Mental Set: The Effects of Domain Knowledge on Creative Problem Solving," *Memory and Cognition* 26 (1998): 716–30.

54 A. Bandura, "Social Foundations," in *Social Cognition*, ed. S. Fiske and S. Taylor (New York: Random House, 1991); G. Moskowitz, *Social Cognition: Understanding Self and Others* (New York: Guilford, 2005); R.Wyer and D. Carlston, *Social Cognition, Inference and Attribution* (Hillsdale, NJ: Erlbaum, 1979).

55 J. Jordan, "Business Experiences and Moral Awareness: When Less May Be More" (New Haven, CT: Yale University, unpublished doctoral dissertation, 2005).

56 K. Butterfield, L. Trevino, and G. Weaver, "Moral Awareness in Business Organizations: Influences of Issue-Related and Social Context Factors," *Human Relations* 53, no. 7 (2000): 981–1018; L. Godwin, "Examining the Impact of Moral Imagination on Organizational Decision Making" (Cleveland, OH: Case Western University, unpublished doctoral dissertation, 2008); Jordan, *Business Experiences* and "Taking the First Step."

57 S. Hannah and B. Avolio, "Moral Potency: Building the Capacity for Character-Based Leadership," *Consulting Psychology Journal: Practice and Research* 62, no. 4 (2010): 291–310.

58 S. Hannah, B. Avolio, and D. May, "Moral Maturation and Moral Conation: A Capacity Approach to Explaining Moral Thought and Action," *Academy of Management Review* 36, no. 4 (2011): 663–85.

59 Naturally, there will be exceptions to this stance. The child abuse scandals that have plagued the Roman Catholic Church come to mind as a counter-example.

60 Hannah et al., "Moral Maturation."
61 Ibid., 664.
62 Trevino, "Ethical Decision Making."
63 Rest, "Moral Development."
64 Hannah et al., "Moral Maturation."
65 Ibid., 666.
66 Desteno and Valdesolo, *Out of Character*; J. Haidt, "The Emotional Dog and Its Rational Tail: A Social Intuitionist Approach to Moral Judgment," *Psychology Review* 108, no. 4 (2001): 814–34; J. Haidt, *The Righteous Mind: Why Good People Are Divided by Politics and Religion* (New York: Random House, 2012); M. Rogerson, M. Gottlieb, M. Handelsman, et al., "Nonrational Processes in Ethical Decision Making," *American Psychologist* 66, no. 7 (2011): 614–62; Seiler et al., "An Interactional Dual-Process Model."
67 Haidt, "The Emotional Dog," 814.
68 E. Langer, A. Blank, and B. Chanowitz, "The Mindlessness of Ostensibly Thoughtful Action: The Role of 'Placebic' Information in Interpersonal Interaction," *Journal of Personality and Social Psychology* 36 (1978): 635–42.
69 E. Langer, *Mindfulness* (Reading, MA: Addison-Wesley, 1989).
70 J.A. Bargh, "Automatic and Conscious Process of Social Information," in *Handbook of Social Cognition 3*, ed. R.S. Wyer and T.K. Stull (Hillsdale, NJ: Erlbaum, 1984), 1–44.
71 Ibid., 36.
72 N. Braden, *The Art of Living Consciously – The Power of Awareness to Transform Everyday Life* (New York: Simon-Schuster, 1997), 77.
73 C. Argyris and D. Schön, *Organizational Learning II: Theory, Method, and Practice* (Reading, MA: Addison Wesley, 1996).
74 Jones, "Ethical Decision Making."
75 R. Petty and J. Cacioppo, "Issue Involvement Can Increase or Decrease Persuasion by Enhancing Message Relevant Cognitive Responses," *Journal of Personality and Social Psychology* 37 (1979): 1915–37.
76 Braden, *The Art of Living Consciously*, 46.
77 Rest, "Moral Development."
78 Hannah et al., "Moral Maturation."
79 Ibid.
80 A. Triki, "Accountants' Ethical Sensitivity" (St Catharines, ON: Unpublished master's dissertation, Brock University, 2011).
81 Sperry, "Ethical Sensitivity," 29–30.
82 For example: R.A. Bernardi and K.L. LeCompt, "Impressions," in K.A. Richmond, "Ethical Reasoning, Machiavellian Behaviour, and Gender: The

Impact on Accounting Students' Ethical Decision Making" (Blacksburg, VA: Unpublished PhD dissertation, Virginia Polytechnic Institute and State University, 2001).

83 J. Rest, *Development in Judging Moral Issues* (Minneapolis: University of Minnesota Press, 1979).

84 Choi and Perry, "Developing a Tool," 4.

85 T.J. Shawver and J.T. Sennetti, "Measuring Ethical Sensitivity and Evaluation," *Journal of Business Ethics* 88 (2009): 663–78, doi: 10.1007/s10551-008-9973-z.

86 Richmond, "Ethical Reasoning."

87 Sadler, "Moral Sensitivity," 342.

88 Triki, *Accountants' Ethical Sensitivity*, 2–3.

89 Jordan, "Taking the First Step," 326.

90 Ibid.

91 Triki, *Accountants' Ethical Sensitivity*, 5.

92 Jones, "Ethical Decision Making," 371.

93 Ibid.

94 D.S. Carlson, K.M. Kacmar, and L.L. Wadsworth, "The Impact of Moral Intensity Dimensions on Ethical Decision-Making: Assessing the Relevance of Orientation," *Journal of Managerial Issues* 21 (2009): 534–51.

95 C. Simga-Mugan, B.A. Daly, D. Onkal, and L. Kavut, "Ethical Sensitivity of Professionals and Future Professionals: A Context Based Examination," *MARC Working Paper Series, Working Paper No. 2007-01*, Management and Administration Research Center, METU (2007): 1–32.

96 Triki, *Accountants' Ethical Sensitivity*, 4.

97 Carlson et al., "The Impact of Moral Intensity Dimensions."

98 Simga-Mugan et al., "Ethical Sensitivity."

99 R. DeVillis, *Scale Development: Theory and Application, 2nd ed.* (London: Sage, 2004).

100 D. Klein, "Why Learners Choose Plagiarism: A Review of Literature," *Interdisciplinary Journal of E-Learning and Learning Objects* 7, no. 1 (2011): 97–110; Sparks and Hunt, "Marketing Researcher Ethical Sensitivity"; Sperry, "Ethical Sensitivity."

101 Constable et al., "The Confidentiality of a Confession"; S. Monteverde, "The Importance of Time in Ethical Decision Making," *Nursing Ethics* 16, no. 5 (2009): 613–24, doi: 10.1177/0969733009106653; D. Narvaez, "Integrative Ethical Education," in *Handbook of Moral Development*, ed. M. Killen and J. Smetana (Mahwah, NJ: Erlbaum, 2006), 703–33.

102 S. Crowne and D. Marlowe, *The Approval Motive* (New York: John Wiley & Sons, 1964).

103 R. Garland, "The Mid-Point on a Rating Scale: Is It Desirable?" *Marketing Bulletin* 2 (1991): 66–70; J.T. Kulas and A.A. Stachowski, "Middle Category Endorsement in Odd Numbered Likert Response Scales: Associated Item Characteristics, Cognitive Demands and Preferred Meanings," *Journal of Research in Personality* 43, no. 3 (2009): 489–93; P. Sturgis, C. Roberts, and P. Smith, "Middle Alternatives Revisited: How the Neither/Nor Response Acts as a Way of Saying 'I Don't Know?'" *Sociological Methods and Research* 43, no. 1 (2012): 15–38.

104 J.A. Bunk and V.J. Magley, "Sensitivity to Interpersonal Treatment in the Workplace: Scale Development and Initial Validation," *Journal of Occupational and Organizational Psychology* 84 (2011): 395–402.

105 Jones, "Ethical Decision Making."

7

The Continuing Evolution of Post-Cold War Operational Ethics in the Canadian Armed Forces[1]

HOWARD G. COOMBS

[T]he true aim of war is peace and not victory.[2]
　　　Major-General J.F.C. Fuller, *The Conduct of War, 1789–1961* (1961)

INTRODUCTION

The environment of conflict presents many challenges. Primary among these trials is dealing with negative influences that are difficult to detect and discern, then resolving them in a fashion conducive to the establishment of a lasting and durable peace. One could opine that such an outcome, particularly in a post-Westphalian world, is more easily said than achieved.[3] Western militaries, and in this case the Canadian Armed Forces, routinely operate in complex and complicated settings that create many ethical predicaments. These challenges, in combination with a professional ethos that puts successful accomplishment of assignments as one's *raison d'être*, create ethical risk. On top of that, space for ethical discourse is not created by the manner in which orders and instructions are made. However, with the use of frameworks for ethical decision-making, training, and education, as well as minor changes to the Canadian Forces Operational Planning Process, this oversight can be rectified in a fashion that will allow for military accomplishment and at the same time ensure that the ethical risks are examined.

The security environment is fraught with complexity. The fragmentation of the Soviet Union and Warsaw Pact during the early 1990s was matched by a concomitant rise in the level of intrastate conflict. Through participation in United Nations missions, Canada was drawn into conflicts in the former Yugoslavia, Rwanda, Haiti, and East Timor, among others. Involvement in UN efforts demonstrated Canadian commitment to maintaining saliency as a middle power within Western states while furthering her bilateral interests within NATO and NORAD. In sum, this increased international security commitment permitted Canada to be a loyal member of the Western alliance and "an international arbiter with sufficient freedom to act decisively in the cause of peace."[4]

Unfortunately, these missions exposed a force that was unprepared for the realities of a fragmenting post–Cold War world. This outcome was combined with declining defence budgets in a country eager to reap the peace dividend that was to result from the elimination of the bipolar world. Events such as those that occurred during Canadian deployments to Somalia in 1993 and Bacovici (in the former Republic of Yugoslavia) during 1993–94 created a great deal of public and private introspection regarding the nature of the profession of arms in Canada.[5] There were public boards of inquiry in addition to a number of reports. These in turn prompted governmental supervision, through the Minister of National Defence, to deal with the most pertinent recommendations arising from those cases, particularly those from the Somalia Inquiry. Following on from that were projects such as the *Report to the Prime Minister on the Leadership and Management of the Canadian Forces* (1997), *A Strategy for 2020* (1999), and *Officership 2020* (2001), which rejuvenated efforts to 're-professionalize' the Canadian military.[6] At the same time, these post–Cold War deployments 'blooded' the Canadian military for the first time since the Korean War and prepared a cadre of leaders who were better able to deal with the challenges to come.

It was during this period of reform that the attacks of 9/11 took place. Canada soon became involved in the global activities that were part of the Western reaction to these attacks, and continues to be involved today. This security engagement took shape in a myriad of forms, at home and abroad, as despite the far-reaching reforms of the 1990s, further events only heightened the need for ethical awareness, discourse, and institutionalized process.

THE PAST AS PROLOGUE: THE KILLINGS
IN SOMALIA

Although these were discussed in the second chapter of this book, I would like to explain in further details the incidents that occurred in Somalia at the end of the last century to better serve the argument I am discussing here. In late 1992, over 900 members of the elite Canadian Airborne Regiment were sent to war-torn Somalia as part of a United Nations peacekeeping effort. Their mission was to stabilize the security situation and facilitate the distribution of humanitarian aid to a starving population, who, in the absence of functioning government, were being terrorized by armed gangs. These lawless groups had also interfered with food deliveries to the regions experiencing famine.

The Canadians were deployed to the town of Belet Huen, which contained about 80,000 people and was located outside the areas of greatest need. The local people welcomed the armed peacekeepers and the gangs avoided confrontation. However, in the months that followed, trouble ensued. On 4 March 1993, after many days of providing security in more than fifty-degree-Celsius heat followed by nights of watching over their own compounds to deter locals who had been breaking in and stealing supplies, Canadian soldiers shot two Somalis, one fatally. It was later disclosed that the man who had been killed had been alive when shot "execution-style in the head." Within twelve days there was another incident, in which another local Somali, sixteen-year-old Shidane Arone, was tortured and murdered while in Canadian custody.

In the ensuing investigation the two main culprits were arrested, but as a result of the introspection and inquiries that followed, it was realized that there were endemic problems in the Canadian Airborne Regiment which, in turn, were indicative of larger issues within the Canadian Forces.

In the months immediately following the disclosure of the death of Arone, there were other documented instances of failures of leadership and discipline amongst the Canadian military in Somalia. When photos of the torture of Shidane Arone emerged, in addition to videotape of hazing ceremonies, the government disbanded the Canadian Airborne Regiment in March 1995 and called a commission of inquiry with wide-ranging powers to investigate the whole matter.[7]

The events in Somalia created a very public discourse regarding the nature of the profession of arms in Canada and its professional ethics. One could opine that, until the systemic reforms since the late 1990s, this discussion was lacking in Canada, and the events surrounding the disbandment of the Canadian Airborne Regiment indicated a deficiency in that regard. The military is a unique institution. It is part of society, yet by the nature of its role, it is distinct. The greater Canadian society demands that its military be proficient in the art of war and, at the same time, expects it to conform to societal norms. Given the nature of this dichotomy, members of the military will be faced with many instances that require ethical decision-making skills and the resultant ethical behaviour. The deontological or proportionalist systems on which the military relied before the 1990s did not meet the requirements of complex ethical decision-making. One can suggest that, at times, the necessity of making an ethical decision may transcend all other professional requirements.[8] In order to prepare the service member for such situations, it is necessary to encourage a climate where ethical decision-making and behaviour are taught, supported, and reinforced.[9] There must be a systematic progressive methodology to train members of the Canadian Armed Forces in how to consider relevant facts in order to arrive at an appropriate decision, and act accordingly, when faced with ethical dilemmas. This not only includes appropriate decision-making models and their inclusion in the military education system, but also the follow-through or reinforcement of ethical behaviour. Accordingly, while much advancement has occurred within the Canadian military since the reforms arising from governmental direction during the post-Somalia era, it is necessary to remain professionally vigilant to ensure that ethical awareness does not diminish in professional importance. This need is still relevant, as noted in a recent Foreign Policy article detailing ethical failures in the United States military, which only reinforces this idea.[10]

THE ETHICAL EVOLUTION OF THE CANADIAN ARMED FORCES

I agree with all the authors of this book that if the problem of ethical decision-making is certainly not unique to the last few decades, its challenges have been exacerbated by the changing nature of the military within society along with the transparency of its activities. I would suggest that the military is no longer the warrior caste of years gone by, ignored and unappreciated except in times of war, as alluded to by

Rudyard Kipling's poem "Tommy Atkins" – "It's Tommy this and Tommy that and kick him out the brute; but it's thank-you very much Mr. Atkins when the guns begin to shoot."[11] The secular military life-style espoused this century, by General Sir John Hackett, as a "contract of unlimited liability"[12] has become increasingly civilianized, with less separation between military members and the larger society. American military researcher Richard Gabriel noted in the 1970s that this progression was in part evidenced by the replacement of the ethos of the military community with that of the entrepreneur.[13] Following from this evolution in the values evidenced in the profession of arms, as well as the challenges shown during the operations of the 1990s, it remains essential that members of the military society internalize the societal norms and deal with problems in a manner appropriate to the military profession. Consequently, it becomes necessary to train them in rational methods to make principled decisions that reflect the values of both society and the military. Following from that is the ability to have these debates during all types of activities, not simply individual decision-making. This conclusion must take into account the norms advocated through the social contract with society and the ethical norms of the profession of arms.[14]

Some arguments that have been made against the course of the study of ethics are that this subject is simply a matter of preference; that such concern is not compatible with professional competence; or, most commonly, that the whole field of study is a waste of time. A *Canadian Army Journal* article by researcher Peter Bradley explores these issues and refutes them.

Ethical decision-making is an important part of the soldier's role. Ethical decisions are integral to military operations. Getting such decisions wrong can have far-reaching consequences, and the military's professional status requires that all its members, from the highest to the lowest ranks, know how to make ethical choices.[15]

Undoubtedly, to some, this may be self-evident, "much ado about nothing," as these issues were identified in the 1990s and resolved. However, one can suggest that this belief is fallacious. It has been demonstrated time and time again in the last decade during various operations that soldiers overseas face many challenges during their missions and that the ethical challenges may be some of the most difficult to deal with as well as to overcome. The recent case of Canadian officer Captain Robert Semrau, broadcast around the world, can serve as an example.

GABRIEL'S PARADIGM FOR ETHICAL CHANGE

Richard Gabriel and Paul Savage, in their seminal work on the Vietnam War *Crisis in Command: Mismanagement in the Army*, presented eight criteria necessary to produce substantive change in a military environment: overt elite support; elite conversion; indoctrination; peer support; perceptions of communal interest; functional linking of behaviour to career survival; external support; and time to create change.[16] The Defence Ethics Programme aims at meeting many of the aforementioned eight criteria, particularly regarding elites, indoctrination, communal interest, and external support, via its initial targeting of the senior leadership of the Canadian Armed Forces.

As indicated in the early Defence Ethics Programme Terms of Reference, all senior leaders had the responsibility to ensure that their subordinates possessed the required knowledge, skills, and attitudes to accomplish their functions in an ethical manner. More specifically, when it was instituted, each Environmental Chief of Staff and Group Principal had the responsibility to ensure that the Defence Ethics Programme was implemented within their areas of responsibility "in a manner consistent with their organizational cultures." They ensured, therefore, that their planning included the necessary resources to carry out that responsibility. Today, these ideas continue as direction in current iterations of the Defence Ethics Programme and related initiatives.[17]

Efficacious as it may have seemed to permit the service commanders and group principals to act as foci in implementing the tenets of this programme, these early top-down approaches have been continually reinforced and developed. There has been growing central direction of the ethical strategy vis-à-vis military training, education, and doctrine in order to improve upon the consistency of implementation. All formal training and education contain elements of ethical decision-making and ethical training in a manner commensurate with the level of experience of the attendees. Leadership doctrine is values-based. Even though all this has happened, ethical decision-making and ethics must continue to be taught during career milestones from entry-level to senior professional military education.[18]

Nevertheless, what is to some degree lacking in these directed programmes is a holistic implementation of Gabriel and Savage's criteria of the linking of ethical behaviour to career survival. It is the only manner in which we can remove from the CAF those who do not demonstrate acceptable ethical behaviours, in order to "encourage the others" to abide by institutional norms and values. It is an extremely necessary step.

One can take several approaches to link career success with appropriate ethical decisions and behaviours. Obviously, organizations can be ruthless in the punishment of those who do not adhere to the accepted values while simultaneously rewarding those who demonstrate acceptable ethical behaviours. As simplistic as it may sound, public castigation with administrative or disciplinary action of offenders, contrasted with praise, commendations, and career advancement for those who demonstrate ethical behaviour, will undoubtedly have a powerful effect on the military population in creating a positive ethical climate. The CAF must continue to strive for an atmosphere in which ethical behaviour is viewed as in the best interests of the Canadian military society as it performs its required tasks, roles, and missions. Consequently, a connection between ethical behaviour and career survival is a strong message.

Throughout this process, leaders at all levels reinforce acceptable military norms by being irreproachable examples. Essentially, they set the ethical climate within their units. When confronted with ethical dilemmas, they make difficult decisions and ensure the appropriate actions are enacted. All members of the military community must understand that outstanding performance is a result of a high standard of leadership and adherence to institutional values and behaviours.[19]

The only aspect of Gabriel's model that could not be directly addressed by these policies is the issue of peer support for ethical behaviour. Despite that, peer support will increase with the measures taken to further develop an ethical environment. Members of the military community will provide support to their comrades to "do the right thing" when making ethical choices.[20]

CREATING DISCOURSE: AN ETHICAL DECISION-MAKING AND PLANNING PROCESS

Even with the changes that have been implemented since the 1990s, the current security environment requires vigilance to ensure that ethical discourse occurs both during the extreme demands and exigencies of combat as well as during domestic operations and the mundane realities of garrison or static environments. As discussed in chapter 3 of this book, members of the CAF must be capable of making complex ethical decisions in conditions that can be time-constrained and extremely hazardous, where failure, or even success, may have severe consequences. Models provide a method of quickly ensuring that all aspects of an ethical dilemma have been examined. One such suggested holistic model, which takes in account facets of different ethical philosophies – deontology, consequentialism, proportionalism, virtue ethics, and situationism – has been proposed by Captain Karine Chapleau, during the 1998 Conference on Ethics in Canadian Defence, in "Giving a Voice to Ethics: A Personal Approach."[21]

CHAPLEAU'S MODEL FOR ETHICAL DECISION-MAKING

Chapleau proposes a five-step ethical decision-making model that provides a basis for ethical discourse on ethical dilemmas, including during operations and operational planning:

1 *Identify the ethical question*
   Is a moral issue involved and what is the dilemma?

2 *Identify all possible solutions*
   List *all* possible solutions in a manner analogous to brainstorming.

3 *Analyze the risks and advantages of each possible solution*
   Examine all advantages and disadvantages in a dispassionate manner. Some factors to consider:
   a The mission;
   b All persons involved;
   c The decision-maker; and
   d Relative strengths of the advantages and disadvantages when compared to the other options.

4 *Make the decision and accept the responsibility of that decision*
   Once the decision has been formulated, one must scrutinize it carefully. When confronted by the same set of circumstances, would the majority of reasonable people come to the same conclusion? If so, then the decision should bear public scrutiny. Enact the decision and bear full responsibility for any results of that action.

  5 Evaluate the efficiency of the decision
        In some ways, this may be the most important step for
        ethicists: evaluate the decision. Did it achieve the desired
        results? What was positive and negative? What should
        be altered if it were to be done again? In other words,
        conduct a mini after-action review of the ethical decision
        and its consequences with a view to improving perfor-
        mance when confronted with future ethical dilemmas.

Decision-making models such as this assist in creating the space for
ethical discourse, either internal or overt, when planning or carrying
out military activities. They support implementing the ideas imbued
within the profession of arms and the corresponding military ethos.

  The military ethos embodies the spirit that binds the military profession together. It is a living spirit that finds its full expression
through the conduct of members of the profession of arms. It clarifies how members view their responsibilities, apply their expertise,
and express their unique military identity. It establishes an ethical
framework for the professional conduct of all activities and military
operations.[22]

THE CANADIAN FORCES OPERATIONAL PLANNING PROCESS

One could argue that, given all the change that has happened within
the realm of ethical education and doctrine in the Canadian Armed
Forces, all measures have been taken to ensure recognition of ethical
dilemmas, permit a pause for ethical review, make appropriate decisions, and undertake measured actions in order to achieve the appropriate outcomes. That might be true if not for the Canadian Forces
Operational Planning Process.[23]

  Central to any understanding of a professional military is an awareness of the role of the staff officer in devising solutions to military
problems. Staffs have existed since ancient times, and assist senior
commanders in carrying out national direction. In its most rudimen-
tary form, the staff can consist of personal assistants to a commander;
however, in modern times, staffs have become large and highly spe-
cialized organizations. The staffs form the intellectual core of any
military organization. Staffs have continually evolved since the
Napoleonic Wars, a time when nations mobilized in order to meet the

threat imposed on Europe by the armies of post-Revolutionary France. Since that period, the scope and complexity of conflict has expanded immensely. Staffs have developed in order to deal with all aspects of military activities from operations to administration. In essence, staff officers prepare armed forces for what they have to do. The mathematician Gerald J. Whitrow wrote, "The primary function of mental activity is to face the future and anticipate the event which is to happen."[24] In this way, staff officers look ahead, attempt to foresee what is to come, and organize their services for the roles that they will be assigned by their government. In this fashion, they remove the burden of minutiae from military commanders in order to allow those leaders to guide and manage their forces.[25] One of the earliest modern iterations of the British Army staff manual from 1912 exhorted staff officers to act in concert with the wishes of their commander and

> be unsparing in their endeavours to help the troops by every possible means in carrying out their difficult task; foreseeing and providing for obstacles and dangers that may arise; making clear what is required without ambiguity or possibility of misunderstanding; and ever careful to attend to the comfort of those under their General's command before attending to their own.[26]

This directive also made sure that staff officers understood that they had no *de jure* power outside what was vested in them by the person in charge; theirs was an intellectual role:

> Staff officers, as such, have no authority over the troops or services and departments, and though they are responsible for the issue of orders, it is essential that they should remember that every order given by them is given by the authority and on the responsibility of the authorized commander.[27]

The concept of acting on behalf of a commander is key to any staff-conducted process such as the CFOPP that results in plans and corresponding orders, directives, and instructions. It expresses a commander's vision and guidance in the accomplishment of military pursuits. Accordingly, it is designed to produce viable options for a commander to consider and then to refine the best option that can be chosen in the form of direction. Regrettably, although legal considerations have become imbued within the CFOPP, at no point in this process is space deliberately created for systemic ethical discourse. This omission could be rectified with little modification to the existing process.

The CFOPP comprises five major parts. First, "Initiation" is the receipt of direction that commences the planning cycle. During Initiation, the planning staff is activated, and staff and commander's guidelines about the planning process are issued, as well as timelines and deliverables to be achieved. A warning order to subordinate formations or units is also an output of this step. Second, "Orientation" consists of gathering and analyzing information and intelligence pertinent to the problem at hand. It results in a mission statement with any conditions explicitly stated and with detailed commander's planning guidance. Other products might include an information brief, a situation analysis brief, and an amended warning order. Third, "Course of Action Development" consists of the testing of various options, or hypotheses, to determine an appropriate set of actions. During this phase, the courses of action are tested via wargaming. The results are then used to assist with determining supporting plans, such as logistics, or supporting related processes, such as targeting. Possible branches or sequels resulting in other future COAs are also identified. By the end of this step, a COA that identifies the commander's preferred option will be developed into a plan, or Concept of Operations (CONOPS), to be used to achieve the mission. Fourth, "Plan Development" results in the creation and issuance of the detailed direction required to implement the plan. These orders give subordinate and supporting units the requisite information to plan and execute operations. Last, "Plan Review" is the review, continual reassessment, and, where necessary, readjustment of the plan to ensure its viability. These periodic reviews are contingent on a myriad of factors, such as the situation, the type of operation, and the environment. Everything in the CFOPP, like other planning systems, is a process that is non-judgmental and allows many people to work in a coordinated fashion to generate a product that can set in motion momentous affairs.[28]

Accordingly, Chapleau's model of ethical decision-making provides a basis for command and staff introspection and discussion at a number of points in the process. The idea of ethical risk can be examined and expressed through the commander's initial and detailed planning guidance. The articulation of the mission statement has great ethical impact because military forces are "mission focused." The mission statement itself, or the constraints (that which must be done) and restraints (that which cannot be done) therein, can shape ethical activity. This applies to the staff producing the direction, as well as those receiving it, for all analysis and activity starts and ends with the mission statement. Military culture is explicit in its prioritization of "mission, men, self" during operations.

Also, during the Course of Action phase, war-gaming and the targeting process offer opportunities to identify areas of ethical risk and adjust options pertaining to potential COAs, as does the Plan Development phase. War-gaming and targeting are ongoing activities that support all aspects of planning and operations. In a similar fashion that legal aspects of these procedures are constantly examined, the same can be done for ensuring the ethical conduct of operations. Furthermore, Plan Review also provides a chance to test the plan against the ethical guidance that has resulted from the discussion and decision at various stages of the CFOPP to see whether changed circumstances have created the need to amend that ethical direction.

It can be said that one of the greatest differences between the military and other entities is that militaries have planning cultures – a great deal of effort is spent educating commanders and staffs in how to achieve Whitrow's vision of anticipating the future. Staff officers provide a critical role in the orderly conduct of military activities. They not only create directives in response to superior direction, but more importantly, they provide rigour to the orders, instructions, and plans that are prepared prior to and during operations through use of the CFOPP. Ideas flow from commanders and are given substance and form by their staffs, who then disseminate these concepts in the form of orders and instructions. Given the central role of the CFOPP in these activities and the impact that ethical choices have on the way one conducts operations, it is surprising that the need for ethical discourse and methodology to address that necessity within the CFOPP has not been previously highlighted. This process, used during war and peace to frame operations, is pervasive and too important to ignore in the continuing evolution of operational ethics, especially given that how we fight and win is sometimes more important than victory per se.

CONCLUSION

Although ethical training, education, and the inclusion of ethical consideration in doctrine has developed the capacity for ethical decision-making by members of the Canadian Armed Forces, it is a subject that must be given continuous, unambiguous, and focused direction. The events of the 1990s and beyond in Western militaries have demonstrated that behaviour that does not stand the test of outside scrutiny results in reprobation from the Canadian population at large. Our military ethics are a reflection of those of the country that our military serves; this must always be considered during military activities.

In order to ensure the highest possible standards of ethical conduct, the Canadian military leadership must develop in members of the CAF the capacity to make ethical decisions quickly and efficiently in the context of operations at home and abroad. This could be done by educating them in models of ethical decision-making, such as that suggested by Chapleau, among others. Chapleau provides a simple and holistic construct, a paradigm that can easily be remembered and retrieved when needed. Following from that, ideas of value-based leadership and ethical decision-making frameworks must continue throughout professional education and training. By the same token, neither do the dilemmas get easier with the passage of time nor with the gaining of seniority and rank – quite the contrary.

It is strongly suggested that ethical behaviour be strongly linked to career survival with a system of positive and negative reinforcement. Throughout this process, leaders must mentor their subordinates in ethical behaviour. They will have the responsibility to guide ethical conduct and create ethical discourse. This exigency extends to the seemingly mundane planning process – the CFOPP. In some respect, this last point may raise a critical issue. Process itself is neither good nor evil, and its results will depend on the inputs that are used. It is the subtext to the process or discussion that provides context and shapes the final product.

Although the Canadian Armed Forces is distinct from Canadian society by the nature of its profession, its members are an integral component of Canadian society and should always act in a manner that is acceptable to Canada and reflects her values. All military activities, including those derived from the CFOPP, need to be transparent and subject to scrutiny, with the ethical risk inherent in these operations identified wherever possible and appropriately dealt with. Simple modifications to the all-encompassing planning processes used to determine those actions will assist greatly with the goal of achieving a more perfect peace, even in the crucible of violence. In the words of Richard Gabriel, "There can be no question of an unethical military serving an ethical society. One will surely corrupt the other."[29]

NOTES

1 This chapter is based on Howard G. Coombs, "Ethical Dilemmas in Operational Planning" (presentation given at the *Military Ethics Conference*, Royal Military College of Canada, Kingston, ON, 19–20 September 2013). Also, I would like to thank my daughter, Lindsay Coombs, for her editorial review of this chapter.

2 J.F.C. Fuller, *The Conduct of War, 1789–1961* (New Brunswick, NJ: Rutgers University Press, 1961; reprinted Cambridge, MA: Da Capo Press, 1992), 76.

3 The Westphalian model arises from the Treaty of Westphalia in 1648, which ended the Thirty Years War. This agreement created an international system based on the recognition of the State and its prerogatives. In a post-Westphalian world, the power that was formerly exercised by recognizable nation-states is now exerted by non-governmental organizations, multinational corporations, regional organizations, terrorist groups, organized crime, and armed irregulars. Accordingly, threats are less identifiable, increasingly transnational, and ever more powerful.

4 N. Hillmer, "Peacemakers, Blessed and Otherwise," *Canadian Defence Quarterly* 19, no. 1 (Summer 1989): 57.

5 For more detail into these events see Donna Winslow, "Misplaced Loyalties: The Role of Military Culture in the Breakdown of Discipline in Two Peace Operations," *Journal of Military and Strategic Studies* 6, no. 3 (Winter 2004): 345–67; see also Barry Came, Luke Fisher, and Mark Cardwell, "Military Investigates Misconduct," *Maclean's* (29 July 1996).

6 Canada, Department of National Defence, *Canadian Officership in the 21st Century (Officership 2020): Strategic Guidance for the Canadian Forces Officer Corps and the Officer Professional Development System* (February 2001), i.

7 CBC *Newsworld*, "Flashback: The Killings in Somalia," http://www.newsworld.cbc.ca/flashback/1996/somalia2.html (accessed 12 April 2001).

8 Captain Howard G. Coombs, "A Formal Ethical Code For The Canadian
   Forces: Is It Required" (Petawawa, ON: Unpublished Service Paper, The
   Canadian Airborne Regiment, 1991), 1.

9 K.D. Johnson, "Ethical Issues of Military Leadership," in *The Parameters
   of Military Ethics*, ed. Lloyd J. Mathews and Dale E. Brown (London:
   Brassey's Defence Publishers Ltd, 1989), 77.

10 See G. Lubold, "The Military Has Cataloged Its Ethical Failures, and
   They're Kind of Awesome," *Foreign Policy* (30 January 2014), http://com-
   plex.foreignpolicy.com/posts/2014/01/30/
   the_military_has_catalogued_its_ethical_failures_and_theyre_kind_of_
   awesome.

11 Lieutenant-General G.G. Simmonds, "Commentary and Observations,"
   in *The Canadian Military: A Profile* (Toronto: The Copp Clark Publishing
   Company, 1972), 289.

12 Sir John Winthrop Hackett, "Today and Tommorrow," in *War, Morality
   and The Military Profession, 2nd ed.*, ed. Melham W. Wakin (Boulder, CO:
   Westview Press, 1989), 99.

13 R.A. Gabriel and Paul L. Savage, *Crisis in Command: Mismanagement in
   the Army* (New York: Hill and Wang, 1978), 145.

14 Gerald Baxter and Charles Rarick, "The Manager as Kierkegaard's
   'Knight of Faith': Linking Ethical Thought and Action," *Journal of
   Business Ethics* 8, no. 5 (May 1989): 400–1.

15 D. Callahan, "How Shall We Incorporate Ethics Instruction at All Levels?"
   in *Ethics and National Defense: The Timeless Issues*, ed. James C. Gaston
   and Janis Brien Hietala (Washington, DC: National Defense Press, 1993),
   136–7; see also J. Peter Bradley, "Just Following Orders Is Not Sufficient:
   How to Make Ethical Decisions," *Canadian Army Journal* 14, no. 2
   (Summer 2012): 47.

16 Gabriel and Savage, *Crisis in Command*, 152–3.

17 Canada, Department of National Defence, "Defence Ethics Program:
   Standards For Defence Ethics Training," http://www.dnd.ca/crs/ethics/
   documents/Trgst_e.doc (accessed 12 April 2001); Dr Richard Walker,
   personal communication, 9 December 2013.

18 Coombs, "A Formal Ethical Code," 7.

19 A.E. Hartle, "A Military Ethic in an Age of Terror," in *The Parameters of
   Military Ethics*, ed. Lloyd J. Matthews and D.E. Brown (London: Brassey's
   Defence Publishers Ltd, 1989), 135.

20 Gabriel and Savage, *Crisis in Command*, 154.

21 Captain Karine Chapleau, "Giving a Voice to Ethics: A Personal
   Approach" (paper presented at the Conference on Ethics in Canadian

Defence, Ottawa, February 1998), http://www.dnd.ca/crs/ethics/documen-tary/conf/1998/chapleau_e.htm (accessed 6 August 2014).

22 Government of Canada, "Ethics Terms," in *Canada, National Defence and the Canadian Armed Forces*, http://www.forces.gc.ca/en/training-ethics/ethics-terms.page#ethics (accessed 30 April 2014).

23 See Canada, Department of National Defence, B-GJ-005-500/FP-000 *Canadian Forces Joint Publication 5.0 (CFJP 5.0) Change*, 2 (April 2008).

24 D. Kahn, "Note: The Prehistory of the General Staff," *The Journal of Military History* 71, no. 2 (April 2007): 500.

25 Ibid., 500–1; and for a history of military staffs see Brigadier-General (Retired) James D. Hittle, United States Marine Corps, *The Military Staff: Its History and Development, 3rd ed.* (Harrisburg: The Stackpole Company, 1961).

26 United Kingdom War Office, *Staff Manual War* Provisional *1912* (London: His Majesty's Stationery Office, 1912), 7.

27 Ibid.

28 Canada, Department of National Defence, B-GJ-005-500/FP-000 *Canadian Forces Joint Publication 5.0 (CFJP 5.0) Change* 2 (April 2008); M. Bélanger, A. Guitouni, and N. Pagea, "C2 and Agility: Decision Support Tools for the Operational Planning Process" (paper presented at the 14th International Command and Control Research and Technology Symposium, Fairfax, VA, 19–21 June 2012), 3; and for an example of CFOPP application at the strategic level see H.G. Coombs and General Rick Hiller, "Planning for Success: The Challenge of Applying Operational Art in Post Conflict Afghanistan," *Canadian Military Journal* 6, no. 3 (Autumn 2005): 5–14.

29 R.A. Gabriel, *To Serve with Honor: Treatise on Military Ethics and the Way of the Soldier* (Westport, CT: Greenwood Press, 1982): 228–9.

PART FOUR

Cultural Clashes and Decision-Making

8

Sex and the Soldier: The Effect of Competing Ethical Value Systems on the Health and Well-Being of Canadian Military Personnel and Veterans

ALLAN ENGLISH

INTRODUCTION

Factors other than disease and physical injury that nonetheless affect the health and well-being of Canadian military personnel and veterans are often overlooked in academic studies. Furthermore, studies that examine how competing ethical value systems can have an impact on their health are rare indeed. However, this ethical conflict has caused unnecessary suffering among Canadian military personnel and veterans, preventable losses that have reduced the effectiveness of the Canadian military, and additional costs to Canadian society, which provides support for injured veterans who cannot lead fully productive lives due to service injuries.[1]

One reason why these problems continue to recur is a failure to learn the lessons found in history, and a lack of interdisciplinary study of issues related to military healthcare.[2] This book has provided an opportunity to examine what might seem to be unrelated issues that can affect the health and well-being of Canadian military personnel and veterans. This chapter focusses more specifically on the issue of competing ethical value systems leading to preventable losses and unnecessary suffering by examining three case studies spanning one hundred years of Canadian military history. These case studies have been chosen because they include aspects of controversial sexual behaviour involving Canadian service personnel, thereby provoking highly visible responses and official reactions that enable us to more easily recognize conflicts among ethical value systems and deal with their adverse effects. It concludes with some suggestions on how to mitigate these adverse effects, in order to reduce the number of situations that may potentially cause harm to Canadian military personnel and veterans.

A main cause of preventable losses in the Canadian military, today and in the past, is the failure to deal with them systematically, treating all causes of loss as part of an interconnected structure. The personnel sustainment cycle model (Figure 8.1) is one way of seeing this issue from an organizational systems perspective, encompassing the creation (selection and training), employment, conservation, and recycling (re-employment) of military forces. In order to successfully optimize personnel sustainment, military organizations must address all parts of the sustainment cycle concurrently. Instead, militaries tend to deal with these issues separately, in "stovepipes," and rarely use an integrated system to effectively manage all aspects of personnel sustainment.[3] One important reason for this behaviour is conflicts among and within professions due to competing ethical value systems. Before looking at the case studies in detail, I will briefly discuss a few basic concepts that I will use in the analysis that follows.

BASIC CONCEPTS

The Profession of Arms

The first concept is the nature of a profession, particularly the unique characteristics of the profession of arms. The Canadian profession of arms manual, *Duty with Honour*, gives this definition of a profession, which reflects the traditional model of a profession often used by Western, English-speaking armed forces:

A profession is an exclusive group of people who possess and apply a systematically acquired body of knowledge derived from extensive research, education, training and experience. Members of a profession have a special responsibility to fulfill their function competently and objectively for the benefit of society. Professionals are governed by a code of ethics that establishes standards of conduct while defining and regulating their work. This code of ethics

Figure 8.1 Personnel sustainment cycle model

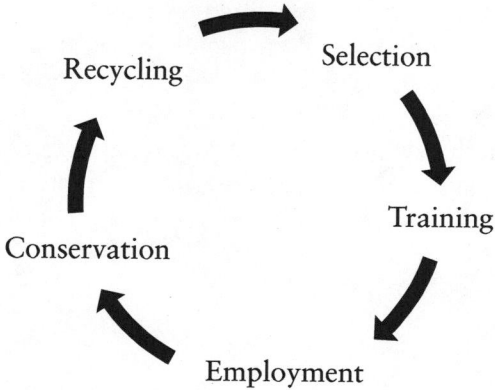

Recycling   Selection

Training

Conservation

Employment

is enforced by the members themselves and contains values that are widely accepted as legitimate by society at large.[4]

It goes on to make a critical distinction between traditional "associational professions" (e.g., medicine, law, clergy), where members often practise their profession "independently, dealing directly with their clients," and the military as a "collective profession," where all must work as a team to accomplish a mission.[5]

Dual Professionals

Duty with Honour recognizes that the military profession in Canada, as a "collective profession," includes experts in fields other than the profession of arms, such as doctors, lawyers, and clerics, who are members of other professions. It refers to them as "dual professionals," and it stresses that, while they wear a uniform, they also retain the responsibilities of their non-military profession. It acknowledges that having dual professional responsibilities can be challenging, especially when competing ethical value systems cause "a conflict between operational imperatives and other professional considerations." Nonetheless, as military professionals, they must "understand and conform to operational objectives and direction unless these are clearly unlawful."[6]

Military Medicine

A concrete example of the concept of dual professionals is the case of military medical officers. As dual professionals who are members of a collective profession, physicians in uniform must practise "military medicine," which is only very distantly related to "medicine in the military," to accomplish the objectives of the profession of arms.[7] Unlike medicine in the civilian sector, which generally puts the well-being of the patient first, military medicine holds a different first principle. Practitioners of "military medicine" have an obligation to conserve human resources for military purposes; this implies a return of military personnel to duty as soon as possible, even if this means likely death or injury for the individual.[8]

Values

Two other concepts that are also useful in understanding professions, because they help us to understand why differences in value systems exist within groups and organizations, are "espoused values" and "values-in-use." Espoused values are what people say they will do. They are "conscious, articulated values that are primarily normative statements which reflect attitudes, hopes, or beliefs about how people would like things to be as opposed to how they really are," and are often a group's or an organization's publicly stated values disseminated for the purposes of legitimization and image-building. Values-in-use, on the other hand, are what people actually do, despite what they might say they will do. They can be seen as the real guidelines for behaviour in a group or organization, and they influence the actions of all members. Values-in-use have varying degrees of congruence with espoused values, depending on the group or organizational culture.[9]

We will now examine the first case study involving competing ethical value systems and the health and well-being of Canadian military personnel and veterans: the case of reducing the incidence of sexually transmitted infections among Canadian service personnel, with examples ranging from the First World War to today.

CASE STUDIES

STIs and Canadian Service Personnel

STIs, or venereal disease (VD) as it was called in both world wars, were the cause of significant losses to the Canadian Expeditionary Force during the First World War. The 66,083 cases of VD outnumbered the 45,460 cases of influenza during the "Spanish flu"

pandemic, and constituted an "epidemic" that affected the equiva-
lent of almost the entire strength of the four divisions that comprised
the Canadian Corps in the field.[10] Although the rates of infection in
the Second World War were about half of what they were in the
First, they were very high in some areas and still caused tens of thou-
sands of unnecessary Canadian losses.[11]

VALUES

And yet, some of the senior physicians and religious leaders who
influenced healthcare policy at the time were prepared to forgo preventative measures because they believed that these measures would
promote "moral laxity," and their policies were responsible for
extremely high infection rates in units where they were followed. For
example, in 1917 Sir Francis Champneys, a physician and a leading
member of the British National Council for Combating Venereal
Disease, expressed the espoused values of many in positions of authority at the time when he said that it was "[f]ar better that venereal
diseases should be imperfectly combated than that, in an attempt to
prevent them, men should be enticed into mortal sin."[12] Similarly, in
the Second World War, one influential Canadian clergyman attacked
preventative measures for limiting the spread of vD, declaring that
"there ought to be an intensive Christian approach ... we should
insist on Christian idealism among the medical officers instead ... [of
the way that i]n some units prophylactics are distributed."[13]

PRACTICE

In the end, most Canadian medical officers at the time adopted values-
in-use that reflected what they called a "practical view" in dealing
with STIs, and they often ignored policies based on religious beliefs,
as well as existing laws which prohibited even providing information
about contraception, let alone distributing contraceptives themselves.
With the support of senior officers, they established programmes of
education and prevention which helped to control the incidence of
STIs. Some Canadian medical officers' "practical approach" to medicine went so far as to run a "local brothel" to reduce the incidence of
vD among Canadian soldiers and sex trade workers.[14]

Following in the footsteps of their predecessors, Canadian healthcare professionals in Afghanistan made condoms freely available to
all personnel, even though sexual activity was officially prohibited
among those deployed in the theatre of operations. The espoused

values were expressed in regulations that forbade displays of affection and sexual relations, even for married couples, while in theatre.[15] Nevertheless, the values-in-use that guided CAF Health Services were expressed by a spokesperson who said: "Our (role) isn't to be judgmental. It's to keep people safe." Therefore, condoms were made freely available. Interestingly, from an historical perspective, a defence spokesperson justified this practice using the precedent set by Canadian military doctors in the First World War.[16]

The examples above reflect an ongoing conflict in debates over what types of healthcare practices are acceptable in a given society. In today's language, the conflict is often portrayed as one between evidence-based medicine on the one hand, which can be characterized as medical practice based on the best available research and clinical evidence and as a way to accelerate useful knowledge from research into clinical healthcare practice, and faith-based medicine on the other hand, which can be represented by these statements: "fornication and adultery in the Christian system are mortal sins ... which ... destroy the soul"[17] and "we should insist on Christian idealism among the medical officers ... instead of peddling unsavoury attitude[s] among the forces."[18]

With this first case, I have tried to show that, despite the best efforts of some Canadian officers, the ability to deal with STIs systematically was disrupted by differences in ethical value systems among and within professions with influence on healthcare policies, resulting in less than optimal treatment for Canadians in uniform, which led to unnecessary personnel losses and suffering.

Treatment of "Homosexuals" in the Canadian Military 1939–45

The most complete study of these issues is found in Paul Jackson's book *One of the Boys: Homosexuality in the Military during World War II*, which examines same-gender sexual relations, principally among men, during the war. It studies the Canadian experience in detail, explaining the social, legal, medical, and administrative aspects of a phenomenon that was more widespread than generally known, and rarely discussed in public. Jackson's study concludes that there was no consistent way of dealing with homosexual relations in the Canadian military due to competing interests among and within those in the professions who dealt with these issues, principally the professions of medicine and law and, of course, the profession of arms.[19] Each will now be discussed in turn. This chapter uses the terms employed at the time, because they had a specific meaning which is not reflected in today's vocabulary.

MEDICAL

Espoused values among medical officers were complicated by differing views of homosexuality – from a "psychopathic personality" incapable of adapting, to just a stage of sexual development. One source of these differing values was a generational difference of opinion among doctors about what constituted "abnormal" sexual behaviour in a medical context. On the one hand, older physicians were often influenced by the assumption, common in many societies in the past, that in a male same-sex encounter, such as anal intercourse, the "active" partner (i.e., the one who was penetrating the "passive" partner) was in a normal male sexual role. Therefore, only the passive partner, who was acting in an "effeminate" manner, could be diagnosed as a "homosexualist," a medical term used at the time. On the other hand, a number of younger physicians were influenced by a new model of sexual development that depicted same-sex relations as a temporary, but normal, stage of development that some young men passed through, and, therefore, would not diagnose as a "homosexualist" any young soldier they thought to be passing through a phase on the road to a "normal" heterosexual lifestyle.

As a result of these differing values-in-use views on what constituted "normal" behaviour, the treatment of men referred to physicians because of their same-gender sexual activities was inconsistent. Furthermore, other issues, such as the social class of a soldier, affected physicians' judgment in determining a patient's diagnosis or disposition. The outcome was that, in most cases, the label "homosexual" was rarely applied to healthy, apparently well-adapted young men.[20]

LEGAL

Military lawyers had a different set of challenges in trying to articulate espoused values and in establishing a consistent approach to "homosexuality" from a legal perspective. One of the problems they faced was the considerable discretion allowed in defining "abnormal" behaviour in the laws related to sexual behaviour, which frequently used words such as "sodomy" as a shorthand for all sexual acts that were seen as "abnormal."[21]

This problem is still reflected in some of today's legal codes, such as the US Uniform Code of Military Justice. The Code defines sodomy in the following terms: "Any person subject to this chapter who engages in unnatural carnal copulation with another person of the same or opposite sex or with an animal is guilty of sodomy." This definition is further clarified as follows: "It is unnatural carnal copulation for a person to take into that person's mouth or anus the sexual organ of another person."[22] The problematic nature of this type of legal definition is reflected in the fact that, based on studies of sexual behaviour in the American population today, it is likely that a significant number of American military personnel have committed an offence under the Uniform Code of Military Justice.[23]

Similar ambiguity in rules and regulations in the Canadian Army during the Second World War, combined with differences in interpretation, led to the situation where sexual offences were rarely dealt with under laws relating to sodomy, but instead under the section of the Army Act that was used to prosecute all sorts of "disgraceful" behaviour, including fraud and theft.

A second problem for lawyers was the practical limits of a military justice system that had to deal with legal issues of all sorts for a wartime cohort of over one million uniformed Canadians – cases had to be prioritized and those related to "good order and discipline" received precedence. The net result was that values-in-use limited prosecutions, so as not to be a drain on resources, to only a relatively few cases to act as a deterrent by publicly shaming selected servicemen. Lawyers and commanding officers soon realized that courts-martial for same-gender sexual activity, especially when they involved popular and combat-effective soldiers, could be more damaging to unit morale and discipline than taking no legal action.[24]

MILITARY

Most COs' espoused values conformed to the social norms of the era, namely that same-sex relations were illegal and immoral. However, whatever personal beliefs a CO might have held, the majority saw their primary ethical duty as producing the most operationally effective unit possible, even if it meant overlooking some illegal activities. In this calculation, there were two main factors for them to consider when dealing with illegal activities of any kind: 1) does an illegal activity affect the good order, discipline, and operational effectiveness of a unit? 2) How much disruption to the unit would formal legal proceedings cause? The end result was the toleration of a certain amount of discreet male same-sex relations.[25]

The competition among all of the ethical value systems described above combined to produce broad "values-in-use" for dealing with homosexuality in the Canadian military, which Paul Jackson portrayed as unwritten, but widely followed, "Routine Orders," two key parts of which summarized the actual behaviour at the time:

> When officers become aware of homosexuals under their command, they are to ignore the situation as long as it does not interfere with the smooth functioning of the unit ... Popular soldiers, who are well established in their units, will be allowed much latitude in their romantic attachments with their comrades ... However, sensitive soldiers, unsure of themselves and embarrassed by their homosexual desires[,] should be harassed and intimidated.[26]

Predictably, this situation was rife with uncertainty, because of the wide discretion afforded the many persons making decisions in dealing with cases of soldiers involved in same-sex relations. Without a systemic and widely accepted approach to this issue, there was conflict and confusion in dealing with it, leading to preventable losses to the military and unnecessary suffering for certain members.[27]

Sexual Abuse of Boys Witnessed by CAF Members in Afghanistan

There were numerous reports of sexual abuse of boys by Afghan National Army and Afghan National Police personnel made by Canadian soldiers to the chain of command, chaplains, military police, and parliamentarians in the early 2000s. This issue was brought to widespread public notice in 2008 by a media report that detailed how "in late 2006 a Canadian soldier had heard an Afghan soldier raping a young boy at one of the outposts near Kandahar. The soldier later saw the injuries the boy sustained, including seeing his lower intestines falling out of his body, a sign of trauma from anal rape."[28]

VALUES
The espoused values of Canadian society and the CAF, at the time, were clearly articulated by Minister of National Defence Peter MacKay, who "said in the Commons that he had told senior military

leaders that soldiers should report any allegation of unlawful activity they see."[29] And the CAF profession of arms manual made it quite clear why these espoused values should be reflected in values-in-use: "The legitimacy of the profession of arms in Canada essentially depends on members fulfilling their professional responsibilities in accord with Canadian values, Canadian and international laws, and the Canadian military ethos."[30]

However, the espoused values were not congruent with the values-in-use that governed the behaviour of many involved with this issue. This statement by the United Nations Special Representative for Children and Armed Conflict is typical of those made by many others, including our coalition partners, and represents the prevailing values-in-use related to the sexual abuse of young boys in Afghanistan at the time: "What I found was nobody talks about it; everyone says 'Well, you know, it's been there for 1,000 years so why do we want to raise this now?'"[31] Furthermore, many CAF members, like our coalition partners, saw a practical reason for the existence of values-in-use that clashed with our espoused values: "There was a belief that we have to keep those relationships with the Afghan army. You go attacking their cultural ways and the next day, when you're both fighting the Taliban, you're going to get a bullet in the back of the head."[32]

The CAF profession of arms manual recognizes that these types of value conflicts may occur and it says that competing societal "imperatives" (i.e., the requirement in Canadian law and values to report the abuse) and functional "imperatives" (i.e., the behaviour required to successfully accomplish the mission – in this case not reporting the sexual abuse) may cause "tensions" that must be resolved. It tells us that these tensions can be reconciled by a "healthy military ethos" which should be nurtured by the senior leadership of the CAF.[33] In theory, this might be true; however, more than a "healthy military ethos" is required to deal with situations similar to the ones highlighted by this case study, when requiring Canadian soldiers to attempt to apply a Canadian ethos in a foreign theatre of operations might jeopardize the mission and their lives.

Nevertheless, this is a challenge that must be dealt with by senior leaders, who are charged with "exercising stewardship of the profession," and, no matter what actions they take, they will be watched closely by members of the CAF. Ideally, their actions should conform to the standards set out in Canadian leadership and profession of arms doctrine, namely that they "set an example that inspires and encourages all members to reflect these standards in their day-to-day conduct ... [and] contribute to professionalism through their influence on education, training and self-development ... They demand excellence in performance and generally shape the environment."[34] They do these things because "[w]hat leaders pay attention to ... and control sends strong signals to others about what is important to them ... What they ignore or overlook sends equally strong signals about what is culturally unimportant."[35]

ACTIONS OF SENIOR CAF LEADERS

In summary, incidents of sexual assault of boys by Afghan forces were reported by members of the CAF to the chain of command as early as 2005. After three years of internal investigations and debate about what to do, a Board of Inquiry (BOI) was convened in late 2008 – almost five years later, it has still not reported. In total, eight years have passed without any answers to the soldiers' complaints and questions, since the Department of National Defence has declined to comment further on the incidents, on the grounds that the events are still under investigation.[36]

The incidents of sexual assault of boys by Afghan forces illustrate a significant problem with the CAF's method of dealing with this type of issue that has developed over the past decade, as BOIS now tend to take years rather than months to report their findings and make recommendations. Recall, for example, that the Croatia BOI, which dealt with a much more complex set of issues, reported six months after receiving its mandate in August 1999, and many of its recommendations were implemented quickly, thereby reducing losses to the CAF and suffering among service personnel.[37] In the case of the Afghanistan sex assault BOI, instructions from the commander of the Canadian Army in 2008 seemed to indicate that similar results to the ones produced by the Croatia BOI were expected: "The board is to 'identify the actions taken by individual CAF members and the chain of command in response to that incident' ... Recommendations will be made on how to address future incidents of that nature."[38]

Leaders have a duty of care to ensure a prompt investigation of problems so that they may be rectified as soon as possible, on the assumption that it is better to implement the fifty percent solution quickly rather than produce the ninety percent solution too late for anything to be done. BOIs are one tool leaders can use to fulfill their responsibilities for the health and welfare of personnel under their command. If nothing is done, unresolved problems can fester, damaging the credibility of leaders, causing preventable losses to the system, and allowing unnecessary suffering to occur among personnel. For example, not addressing the issues raised by the troops caused uncertainty in how CAF personnel should act when they witnessed incidents of sexual abuse in Afghanistan. In one case, a senior military police officer told his superiors, "Of greatest concern to the M[ilitary]P[olice] members was the belief that if they were [to] intervene in any instances of this nature that they would not be supported by the C[hain] o[f] C[ommand]."[39] In another case, CAF personnel were apparently told not to abide by the espoused values articulated by the MND, as a padre "complain[ed] that Canadian soldiers were ordered by their commanding officers in Afghanistan to ignore such incidents of sexual assault ... Other military chaplains have said they too heard similar complaints from Canadian troops."[40]

ANOTHER SOMALIA SCANDAL IN OUR FUTURE?

The Somalia Commission of Inquiry, thoroughly discussed in the previous chapter, investigated the misconduct of some Canadian troops in Somalia in 1993. One of the Commission's principal findings was that failures in Somalia were due to shortcomings in Canada's Professional Military Education (PME) system.[41] A key recommendation of the Somalia Commission was that education, not just training, was necessary to prepare CAF leaders adequately for complex operations in areas of the world that were culturally different from Canada. And yet, major reforms to the CAF's PME based on this recommendation are now being dismantled due to budget cuts, while some education related to ethics and the military profession is being reduced or eliminated altogether.[42] One of the most insidious influences on how these cuts are being made is described by the expression "teeth versus tail ratio" (i.e., the proportion of combat versus support functions) when used as a biological metaphor for the CAF. It is used, for example, to justify cuts to PME based on the logic that it is always preferable to make cuts to the "tail" of the CAF instead of its "teeth."[43] However, the flawed logic in this false dichotomy is obvious when we consider that no higher-order animal is composed of only teeth and a tail. We know that any such animal is a complex biological system that includes a brain, nervous system, lungs, muscles, skeleton, and so on. Consequently, when considering what cuts to make to the CAF, one might pose the question, "Is it better for the animal to lose a tooth or two or a significant part of its brain?"

The disappearance of important aspects of the CAF's PME, especially those related to the effective as well as ethical practice of the profession of arms, should cause us grave concern lest future generations of CAF leaders find themselves as poorly prepared to deal with these issues as their predecessors were in the 1990s – a "Decade of Darkness" for the CAF.[44]

CONCLUSION

This study focused on how competing ethical value systems, especially among and within certain professions, has caused preventable losses and unnecessary suffering among Canadian military personnel and veterans. In analyzing three case studies, we have seen that a major cause of these losses and suffering was the failure to deal with all of the issues systematically and in a timely manner.

However, while leaders have a responsibility to resolve problems as expeditiously as possible, because unresolved problems can worsen leading to preventable losses, solutions are not always obvious or easy to implement. Ethical conflicts will always exist and there is no "perfect" way to address them; there will always be tradeoffs. As some commentators have noted, "what is ethical is not always legal and what is legal is not always ethical."[45] Therefore, leaders must sometimes make difficult choices in deciding what action to take.

The CAF's profession of arms manual provides invaluable advice for leaders who must evaluate problematic courses of action. In the following quote from it, I have highlighted some parts that I think summarize well the lessons from our history about effective and ethical military leadership:

[Leaders in the CAF] demonstrate that loyalty can and must be applied both upwards to superiors and civil authority and downwards to subordinates. Such *loyalty can only be sustained*, particularly when the tension between achieving the mission and ensuring the well-being of subordinates is high, *through exhibiting unassailable integrity.* All must know that a leader's decisions reflect an honest and truthful assessment of the situation. Professionals account for these decisions and stand by them. Finally, *leaders act courageously*, both physically, but more *especially, morally*. In sum, *doing what is right* on the basis of available information *encapsulates all of these values.*[46]

In other words, leaders who do the right thing gain the trust and loyalty of their subordinates, a key ingredient in mission success, and we have seen some examples of this type of behaviour in the three cases studies discussed here. On the other hand, leaders who use rules, regulations, and technicalities to avoid doing the right thing have often failed and have even been the targets of mutinies or combat refusals, and in extreme cases have been attacked by their own troops.[47] However, leaders in the CAF will only be able to know how to act professionally if they receive the proper PME in those aspects of their profession related to leadership and ethical conduct. This is a fact, especially in times of budget cuts, which should be foremost in the minds of those senior leaders in the CAF who are charged with being the stewards of the profession of arms in Canada.

In examining three case studies spanning one hundred years of Canadian military history we have seen that the health and well-being of Canadian military personnel and veterans has been adversely affected because of a failure to deal with preventable losses systematically due to conflicts among and within professions due to competing ethical value systems. Despite the diversity of the causes of adverse effects on the health and well-being of Canadian military personnel and veterans – whether from varying treatments of STIs in the First World War or different ways of dealing with "homosexuals" in the Second World War or the inability of the chain of command to effectively meet the needs of CAF members traumatized by witnessing the sexual abuse of boys by Afghan National Army and Afghan National Police personnel – the most effective method for mitigating these adverse effects is the same. This method is for senior leaders in DND to assume responsibility for co-ordinated, systematic, and ethical action in all cases.

NOTES

1 A. English, "Not Written in Stone: Social Covenants and Resourcing Military and Veterans Health Care in Canada," in *Shaping the Future:*

Military and Veteran Health Research, ed. Alice B. Aiken and Stéphanie
A.H. Bélanger (Kingston, ON: Canadian Defence Academy Press, 2011),
230–8.

2 The Surgeon General of the Canadian Armed Forces addresses some of
these issues from a force health protection perspective in Jean Robert
Bernier, "Threats to Operational Force Health Protection," in *The
Operational Art – Canadian Perspectives: Health Service Support*, ed.
Allan English and James C. Taylor (Kingston, ON: Canadian Defence
Academy Press, 2006), 41.

3 A. English and J.C. Taylor, "Introduction," in *The Operational Art*, ed.
English and Taylor, vii–x; and Allan English, "From Combat Stress to
Operational Stress: The CF's Mental Health Lessons from the 'Decade
of Darkness,'" *Canadian Military Journal* 12 (Autumn 2012): 9–17.

4 Canada, Department of National Defence (DND), *Duty with Honour: The
Profession of Arms in Canada* (Kingston, ON: CF Leadership Institute,
2003), 6.

5 Canada, DND, *Duty with Honour*, 9.

6 Ibid., 1, 51–2.

7 R.F. Bellamy and Craig H. Llewellyn, "Preventable Casualties: Rommel's
Flaw, Slim's Edge," *Army* 40 (May 1990): 52–6.

8 The issue of "military medicine" in a Canadian context was discussed by
a panel on "The Mission and Medical Ethics: Is There a Conflict?" in
Proceedings in the Conference on Ethics in Canadian Defence (Ottawa:
Public Works and Government Services Canada, 1999), http://www.forces.
gc.ca/assets/FORCES_Internet/docs/en/about-reports-pubs-ethics/
conf1999-eng.pdf (accessed 24 November 2013). See also Desmond
Morton, "Military Medicine and State Medicine: Historical Notes on the
Canadian Army Medical Corps in the First World War 1914–1919," in
Canadian Health Care and the State, ed. David C. Naylor (Montreal and
Kingston, ON: McGill-Queen's University Press, 1992), 55; and Arthur
M. Smith, "The Influence of Medicine on Strategy," *Naval War College
Review* 41 (Spring 1988): 28.

9 A. English, *Understanding Military Culture: A Canadian Perspective*
(Montreal and Kingston, ON: McGill-Queen's University Press, 2004), 21,
23, 28, 69, 110, 124, 155.

10 Morton, "Military Medicine and State Medicine," 58.

11 W.R. Feasby, ed., *Official History of the Canadian Medical Services,
1939–1945, Vol. 2: Clinical Subjects* (Ottawa: Queen's Printer, 1953),
442–4, 446–7; and Christopher Webb, "Protecting our Privates: V.D. and
the Canadian Military in WWI and WWII," Margaret Angus Research

Fellowship Manuscript (Kingston, ON: Museum of Health Care at Kingston, 2005).

12 E.H. Beardsley, "Allied Against Sin: American and British Responses to Venereal Disease in World War I," *Medical History* 20 (April 1976): 191.

13 Rev. G.N. Luton, cited in "History as We Saw It," *Kingston Whig Standard* (2 June 2010).

14 The details of the Canadian approach to dealing with STIs in the First World War are described in Jay Cassel, *The Secret Plague* (Toronto: University of Toronto Press, 1987), 122–44. Second World War approaches are in Feasby, ed., *Official History of the Canadian Medical Services, 1939–1945, Vol. 2*, 109–22. The example of running a brothel is from Mitch Kline et al., "Obituary, Hubert (Hughie) J. Kline," *Globe and Mail* (3 April 2012).

15 E. Anderssen, "No Sex, Please. We're Soldiers," *Globe and Mail* (30 May 2010), http://www.theglobeandmail.com/news/national/no-sex-please-were-soldiers/article1390372/#dashboard/follows/.

16 A. Panetta, "Canadian Soldiers Issued a Large Amount of Military Condoms," *Canadian Press* (11 June 2006), http://forum.argent.canoe.ca/dcboard.php?az=printer_friendly&forum=121&topic_id=93708.

17 Beardsley, "Allied Against Sin," 191.

18 Luton cited in "History as We Saw It," 26.

19 P. Jackson, *One of the Boys: Homosexuality in the Military during World War II* (Montreal and Kingston, ON: McGill-Queen's University Press), 265–9.

20 Ibid., 3–7, 13, 110–46.

21 Ibid., 110–46.

22 United States, *Manual for Courts-Martial United States* (2012 edition), IV-84, http://www.apd.army.mil/pdffiles/mcm.pdf (accessed 17 November 2013).

23 See for example the results of this large-scale study published in 2010: Indiana University, Center for Sexual Health Promotion, "National Survey of Sexual Health and Behaviour (NSSHB)," http://www.nationalsexstudy.indiana.edu/ (accessed 17 November 2013).

24 Jackson, *One of the Boys*, 78–109, 268.

25 Ibid., 221–61, 266–7.

26 Ibid., 76–7.

27 Ibid., 28, 265–8.

28 CanWest MediaWorks Publications Inc., "Rape of Boys in Afghanistan Sparks Inquiry," *Ottawa Citizen* (4 October 2008), http://www.canada.com/ottawacitizen/news/story.html?id=8b51ebd6-164d-4537-bffb-277c88f8c4d0.

29 Ibid.

30 Canada, DND, *Duty with Honour*, 6.

31 CanWest, "Rape of Boys in Afghanistan Sparks Inquiry."

32 Lieutenant-Colonel Stephane Grenier cited in R. Westhead, "Canadian Military Still Investigating Afghanistan Sex Assault Claim," *Toronto Star* (4 July 2013), http://www.thestar.com/news/world/2013/07/04/canadian_military_still_investigating_afghanistan_sex_assault_claim.html.

33 Canada, DND, *Duty with Honour*, 45–50.

34 Ibid., 57.

35 Canada, DND, *Leadership in the Canadian Forces: Conceptual Foundations* (Kingston, ON: Canadian Defence Academy, 2005), 116, 118.

36 Westhead, "Canadian Military Still Investigating."

37 For a detailed account of the Board's activities, see G.E. (Joe) Sharpe, *Croatia Board of Inquiry: Leadership (and Other) Lessons Learned* (Kingston, ON: Canadian Forces Leadership Institute, 2002).

38 D. Pugliese, "Sex Abuse and Silence Exposed," *Ottawa Citizen* (21 September 2009), http://www.ottawacitizen.com/news/abuse+silence+exposed/2010032/story.html.

39 Ibid.

40 CanWest, "Rape of Boys in Afghanistan Sparks Inquiry."

41 D. Bercuson, *Significant Incident: Canada's Army, the Airborne, and the Murder in Somalia* (Toronto: McClelland and Stewart, 1996), describes this process in detail. See also Randy Wakelam, "Senior Professional Military Education for the 21st Century," *Canadian Defence Quarterly* (Autumn 1997): 14–18; and D.J. Bercuson, "Defence Education for 2000 … and Beyond," in *Educating Canada's Military* (report of a workshop held at the Royal Military College of Canada, Kingston, ON, 7–8 December 1998).

42 J.L. Granatstein, "A Soldier's Best Weapon Is a Well-Trained Mind," *Globe and Mail* (3 May 2012), http://www.theglobeandmail.com/globe-debate/a-soldiers-best-weapon-is-a-well-trained-mnd/article4104387/#dashboard/follows/.

43 M. Fitzpatrick, "DND Report Lays out Plan to Save $1B," *CBC News* (19 August 2011), http://www.cbc.ca/news/politics/dnd-report-lays-out-plan-to-save-1b-1.992916.

44 For a description of the term "Decade of Darkness" see English, "From Combat Stress to Operational Stress."

45 See for example C. MacDonald, "What's Legal Isn't Always Ethical," *Canadian Business* (22 December 2011), http://www.canadianbusiness.com/blogs-and-comment/whats-legal-isnt-always-ethical/.

46 Canada, DND, *Duty with Honour*, 57–8.
47 The Canadian Defence Academy's three-volume series on actions against
    authority documents these types of behaviour. See for example Howard G.
    Coombs, ed., *The Insubordinate and the Noncompliant: Case Studies of
    Canadian Mutiny and Disobedience: 1920 to Present* (Toronto and Kingston,
    ON: Dundurn Group and Canadian Defence Academy Press, 2007).

9

Mitigating the Ethical Risk of Sexual Misconduct in Organizations

DEANNA L. MESSERVEY AND KAREN D. DAVIS

INTRODUCTION

The Canadian Armed Forces instituted its first sexual harassment policy in 1988. Throughout the 1990s, however, harassment and assault in the CAF made national news in Canada. In 1992, a *Montreal Gazette* headline read, "Complaints of Harassment Heard from Every Base across Canada."[1] A 1993 *Globe and Mail* front-page headline read "Sex and the Military: Battling Harassment."[2] A front-page headline in the *Toronto Sunday Star* in May 1994 announced, "Gulf War Hero Officer Guilty of Harassment." The officer in question had faced accusations of sexual assault against a female officer while he had served as the senior CAF officer in the Persian Gulf in 1991.[3] In 1992, the Chief of the Defence Staff (CDS) issued a CAF-wide message making it clear that harassment would not be tolerated in the CAF:

Sexual harassment in particular is an insidious behaviour that victimizes people and attacks their dignity and self-respect. It erodes mutual trust and confidence, adversely affects morale and unit cohesion, and can reduce operational effectiveness. Armed Forces council endorse quote zero tolerance unquote of sexual harassment. This means that sexual harassment will not be tolerated in the CAF, that our goal is zero incidents of sexual harassment, and that if incidents occur, they will be resolved quickly, effectively, and fairly.[4]

Yet public outrage persisted. In May and June 1998, the popular Canadian weekly newsmagazine *Maclean's* published two consecutive front-cover issues that featured charges of rape and harassment in the CAF.[5] The stories described numerous cases of sexual harassment, assault, and rape against military women, spanning the 1980s and 1990s.

In 1998, the Minister of National Defence and the CDS took a public stand. In an edition of the widely distributed internal CF newspaper *The Maple Leaf*, the MND emphasized his commitment to Canadians and the Canadian Forces to make the CAF a safe place for women as well as men.[6] The CDS expressed both his professional and personal disappointment:

> What upsets me most in light of these articles is that many women – and some men – have been harassed or assaulted, and have emerged from this unfortunate experience traumatized and too frightened to talk about it with their superiors, at all levels, and to report that they had been hurt, that they had been harmed, that their lives had been ruined, that their careers had been ruined.[7]

His disappointment was evident, as were his expectations that such behaviour had to be addressed by the chain of command. Clearly, there were members of the Canadian military who had failed to live up to the stated values of the organization and had failed to do the right thing.

This chapter examines the relationship between individual motivation, situational factors, organizational context, ethical decision-making, and sexual misconduct in a military context. We begin by arguing that sexual harassment and sexual assault behaviours are moral issues that create particularly difficult dilemmas for leaders in the organization. We then present an overview of the individual motivations, situational factors, and organizational contexts that contribute to inappropriate sexual behaviour, followed by evidence suggesting that situational factors and organizational context influence ethical decision-making, including that which results in inappropriate sexual conduct. As such, we propose that ethical decision-making models can both inform and be informed by the decisions and processes that surround these behaviours within a military context. We close the chapter with recommendations for further research, concluding that such knowledge has the potential to strengthen policy and leadership strategy in ways that will help organizations, including the military, mitigate sexually inappropriate behaviours.

APPROACHING SEXUAL HARASSMENT AS A MORAL AND ETHICAL PROBLEM

According to T.M. Jones, moral issues are defined as the freely performed actions of persons that "may harm or benefit others,"[8] and unethical decisions are decisions that are "either illegal or morally unacceptable to the larger community."[9] Sexual harassment and sexual assault have been shown to cause psychological and physical harm, including negative impacts on job satisfaction and work productivity,[10] attitudes toward the organization, and the victim's relationships with his or her family.[11] The severity and the source of harassment have also been linked to employee decisions to leave an organization.[12] Several studies of military veterans have also found an association between sexual harassment and mental health outcomes.[13] Research has consistently found that military women are more likely than military men to report sexual harassment[14] and sexual trauma.[15] However, some research also suggests that incidents of a sexual nature may be a stronger predictor of mental stress among men than women.[16] Regardless of the role of gender, a significant number of studies have concluded that sexual harassment and sexual assault harm the individuals who experience them and have a negative impact on organizations.

Moreover, sexual assault is a crime in Canada and other Western nations with which Canada is allied, including Australia, New Zealand, the United Kingdom, and the United States. In the Canadian context, sexual assault constitutes an offence under the *Criminal Code of Canada* and the *Code of Service Discipline*,[17] and it is dealt with at a military court-martial overseen by a military judge. Sexual harassment is not a *Criminal Code* offence in Canada;[18] nonetheless, it is morally unacceptable in the larger community[19] and victims of sexual harassment have been provided with legal recourse under provincial human rights tribunals.

Since the Canadian military instituted harassment policy, reported rates of harassment have declined. In an anonymous 1992 survey of CAF members, 26.2 percent of female respondents indicated that they had experienced sexual harassment in the previous twelve months. In similar surveys administered in 1998 and 2012, the reported rate of sexual harassment among female respondents had dropped to 14 percent[20] and 7.6 percent respectively.[21] However, even as rates of harassment drop, there is a persistent expectation within the broader community that organizations, and in particular the military, will substantially reduce, if not completely eliminate, incidents of harassment. In spite of a substantial reduction in the rate of anonymously reported rates of sexual harassment in recent years, by May 2014, the Canadian media was once again claiming that sexual violence was plaguing Canadian soldiers.[22]

Clearly, both sexual harassment and sexual assault cause harm and are morally unacceptable, thus meeting Jones' definition of a moral issue and underscoring the responsibility of the military to implement policies and strategies to prevent sexual violence, ensure appropriate recourse for individuals, and minimize harm. And although there are important distinctions between behaviours that are considered to be sexual harassment and those that are considered to be sexual assault, for the purpose of this analysis, we do not make a distinction between them. Harassment, including sexual harassment, is typically addressed through processes such as alternative dispute resolution, administrative investigations, or a military summary trial before a commanding officer. Regardless, the implicated behaviours and their outcomes are not mutually exclusive. It is not unusual in a military context, for example, for a sexual assault charge to result in a finding of the lesser transgression of sexual harassment. Notwithstanding the potential for further research in this area, we suggest that the theories and models used to understand ethical decision-making in organizations can be applied to sexual harassment and sexual assault, and inform organizational policy and strategy to create conditions that discourage such behaviours.

ETHICAL DECISION-MAKING

Psychologists' understanding of ethical decision-making has long been dominated by Lawrence Kohlberg's theory of moral development.[23] Kohlberg was interested in "the transformations that occur in a person's form or structure of thought," or, in other words, how an individual's moral thinking develops over time.[24] Kohlberg studied moral development by presenting people with hypothetical moral dilemmas, and then analyzing how they reasoned about the dilemmas.

He found that moral reasoning could be characterized by six sequential and hierarchical moral stages that range from pre-conventional moral reasoning, where the rightness of an action is dependent on the direct consequences of the act, to post-conventional moral reasoning, where moral reasoning is based on abstract reasoning and universal principles. Most adults reason at the conventional level, in which people determine the morality of an action based on society's rules and expectations. James Rest's four-component model builds on Kohlberg's theory,[25] which underscores the role of rational thought and deliberative thinking. According to Rest, people recognize and become aware of a moral issue (Component 1), make an ethical judgment (Component 2), are motivated to act (Component 3), and then may carry out the act (Component 4).

But recent research has called into question Kohlberg and his followers' account of the role of rational thinking. Although deliberative thinking may be the dominant type of decision-making when thinking about hypothetical moral dilemmas, it is not the dominant type of decision-making used in real-world situations.[26] A large body of research now suggests that people engage in automatic processing that is below their level of awareness.[27] Deliberative thinking is generally slow and effortful, involves awareness, and requires controlled attention, which is linked to a working memory resource.[28] In contrast, automatic processing is generally fast and effortless, occurs below the level of awareness, and does not require controlled attention.[29] Automatic processing is a core aspect of several influential ethical decision-making models, including Haidt's social intuition model,[30] Reynolds' neurocognitive model of ethical decision-making,[31] and Sonenshein's sense making-intuition model.[32]

Haidt uses the metaphor of a rider on an elephant to illustrate how the mind is divided by conscious reasoning and automatic processing. The rider represents deliberative reasoning, which requires controlled attention, while the elephant represents mental processes that take place beyond our awareness (e.g., emotion, intuition). The elephant is portrayed as bigger than the rider because, in Haidt's model, "the rider's job is to serve the elephant."[33] One way the rider serves the elephant is by developing post hoc justifications for the elephant's actions and by finding reasons to justify what the elephant wishes to do next. According to Haidt's social intuition model,[34] therefore, moral judgments are made rapidly, and often without conscious awareness of engaging in a search or that one has weighed evidence and come to a conclusion. Once an intuitive and rapid moral judgment has been made, people *then* engage in moral reasoning. Haidt argues that "reason is the servant of the intuitions,"[35] whereby people seek reasons to justify their moral intuitions.

One implication of Haidt's model is that the primary purpose of post hoc moral reasoning is to influence others. It is plausible, for example, that post hoc reasoning was used to justify the moral intuitions of an American lieutenant-general in a high-profile case involving Lieutenant-Colonel James Wilkerson of the United States Air Force. On 2 November 2012, Wilkerson was found guilty of aggravated sexual assault by a jury. He was sentenced to serve a year in prison and dismissed from the US military.[36] Lieutenant-General Craig Franklin, the General Court-Martial Convening Authority in Wilkerson's case, overturned Wilkerson's guilty verdict, even though he did not attend the trial. Franklin's actions sparked outrage among members of Congress and in the American public. In response Franklin wrote a letter to the Pentagon, dated 12 March 2013,[37] to explain his decision. The following justification was included in that letter:

> Lt Col Wilkerson was a selectee for promotion to full colonel, a wing inspector general, a career officer, and described as a doting father and husband. However, according to the version of events presented by the prosecution, Lt Col Wilkerson, in the middle of the night, decided to leave his wife sleeping in bed, walk downstairs past the room of his only son, and also near another room with two other sleeping guest-children, and then he decided to commit the egregious crime of sexually assaulting a sleeping woman who he and his wife had only met earlier that night. Based on all the letters submitted in clemency, in strong support of him, by people who know him, such behavior appeared highly incongruent. Accordingly, this also contributed, in some small degree, to my reasonable doubt.

According to a member of the House Armed Services Committee, "Franklin clearly substituted his own independent judgment for that of the convened fact-finding panel ... He took some information that was outside the proceeding and not deemed credible and used his own judgment of what to accept."[38] Although it is impossible to know exactly how Franklin reached his judgment, it is possible that his decision to overturn the guilty verdict was shaped by his emotions and intuitive judgments.

Several studies have demonstrated that situational factors also influence ethical decision-making.[39] Situational factors are external influences that shape people's behaviour,[40] and they can interact with individual differences (e.g., moral development) to influence ethical decision-making.[41] For example, being reminded of one's ethical standards before completing a task where there is an opportunity to cheat, being ordered by a person in a position of authority to harm somebody else, and seeing a peer being sanctioned for harassing someone else are all examples of situational factors that can influence ethical behaviour. Organizational culture and one's immediate work environment are also situational factors.[42] When situational factors are especially powerful, individual factors are less likely to influence ethical decision-making.[43] Situational factors can lead people to experience emotions and visceral factors (e.g., thinking that is influenced by the "heat of the moment"). Loewenstein uses the term *visceral factors* for negative emotions (e.g., fear, anger), feeling states (e.g., pain), and drive states (e.g., hunger, sexual arousal) that can influence behaviour.[44] Negative emotions are the "complex pattern of changes, including physiological arousal, feelings, cognitive processes, and behavioural reactions, made in response to a situation perceived to be personally significant"[45] that impact how people respond to situations. Drive states are internal bodily states that affect behaviour. Anger, for example, is a visceral factor that can increase people's preference for aggressive behaviour.[46] Researchers have found that US soldiers who reported experiencing high levels of anger were more likely than those who reported low levels of anger to mistreat noncombatants and damage civilian property unnecessarily.[47] Of course, anger is not the only visceral factor that can influence ethical behaviour.

Research on sexually inappropriate behaviour conducted on a sample of male university students suggests that sexual arousal is a visceral factor that can influence a person's willingness to engage in date-rape-like behaviours. Ariely and Loewenstein examined the impact of sexual arousal on moral judgment under conditions of low and high sexual arousal.[48] As part of the study, they asked the students to indicate their willingness to engage in morally questionable behaviours, such as whether they would urge their date to increase her drinking so she would be more likely to have sex with them, whether they would persist in trying to obtain sex after their date said "no," and whether they would give a woman a drug to increase the possibility of her having sex with them. Male students who were highly sexually aroused were significantly more likely than male students who had lower sexual arousal levels to indicate that they would engage in date-rape-like behaviours. These findings are consistent with another study that examined sexual arousal and willingness to engage in morally questionable behaviour. Men in the study who viewed pornography were more likely than men who did not to indicate that they would coax a date into removing her clothes, even though she had indicated that she was not interested in having sex.[49] These findings suggest that sexual arousal is a visceral factor whereby people get caught up in "the heat of the moment," which can influence subsequent ethical judgments and behaviour.

Sexual arousal may also affect men's perception of a woman's willingness to engage in sexual activity. In one study, researchers found that self-reported level of sexual arousal was related to a misperception of a partner's willingness to engage in sexual activity.[50] In this study, reported high levels of sexual arousal among male participants correlated with participants' perceptions of sexual interest by a woman presented to them in a hypothetical situation. Moreover, an overperception of sexual interest was related to coercive behaviour; that is, the more the men in the laboratory study overperceived sexual interest, the more they indicated they would try to get a woman intoxicated. Other researchers have also identified the link between a misperception of sexual interest and coercive behaviours,[51] especially among men who hold sex-role stereotypes.[52] Extrapolating from these research findings, it is logical to suggest that increasing people's awareness of how perceptions can be flawed when they are sexually aroused is a potential strategy to reduce sexually inappropriate behaviour. Clearly, more research is needed to examine whether such strategies would reduce this type of behaviour in real-world situations.

Sexual arousal as a visceral factor is not only salient in laboratory settings, but also appears to be important for ethical conduct in real-world settings.[53] Rampant sexual violence by members of the rebel forces and members of the Congo Armed Forces has been well documented.[54] When M.E. Baaz and M. Stern asked members of the Congo Armed Forces in the Democratic Republic of the Congo why sexually violent acts against women occurred, they found that soldiers distinguished between two types of rape: (a) rapes that are the result of lust and the desire for sexual gratification, and (b) rapes that are driven by "a wish to humiliate the dignity of people."[55] The first type of rape, called lust rape, is consistent with the notion that sexual arousal is a visceral factor that has the potential to influence ethical behaviour. The second type of rape, called evil rape, derives from "a sense of moral disengagement that accompanies the climate of warring and violence in which they [members of the Congo Armed Forces] have been living; previously unthinkable behavior becomes conceivable and even dedramatized through the process of dehumanizing."[56] Albert Bandura examined moral disengagement and how it affected ethical behaviour. He theorized that people feel good about themselves when they act in accordance with their internalized moral standards and feel badly when they do not. However, Bandura identified several psychological processes that people use to deactivate or disengage their moral standards so they can act unethically without feeling badly for doing so. For example, people morally disengaged by using euphemistic labelling (e.g., calling women by derogatory labels instead of by their rank and name), advantageous comparison (e.g., "I only call her names; other guys grab her"), attributing blame to the victim (e.g., "What does she think will happen if she dresses that way?"), minimizing the consequences of one's behaviour (e.g., "She is just trying to get out of work, she is not that hurt"), and dehumanizing victims of moral transgressions (e.g., "She is a witch").[57]

Understanding the different factors underlying sexual assault (and other unethical behaviour) is critical for eliminating the behaviour. If sexually inappropriate behaviour is motivated by the desire to humiliate others (i.e., evil rape), then an understanding of the psychological processes perpetrators use to morally disengage (e.g., euphemistic labelling, advantageous comparison) may be crucial for developing effective interventions. For example, future research could examine whether leaders who discipline personnel harshly for using derogatory labels to describe women actually influence attitudes and behaviour regarding sexually inappropriate behaviour when compared with leaders who do not. Likewise, more research is needed to understand the effectiveness of training interventions that focus on "humanizing" women.

Alternatively, if sexually inappropriate behaviour is caused by being caught up in the heat of the moment (i.e., lust rape), then efforts to enhance self-control may be an important way to reduce the behaviour. This approach is consistent with research conducted by C.M. Barnes and colleagues,[58] who found that lack of sleep (a visceral factor) increases the likelihood that people will engage in unethical behaviour. More importantly, they argue that depletion of willpower (i.e., self-control resources) is the reason lack of sleep increases the likelihood that people will engage in unethical behaviour.

Self-control – the effort exerted when people try to alter the manner in which they think or behave – is a limited resource.[59] Any time a person's words or actions require self-regulation, they are depleting their self-control resources.[60] When people are presented with two tasks that require self-control, for example, the ability to exert self-control on the second task is impaired.[61] Self-control involves controlled attention,[62] like other examples of deliberative thinking. When self-control strength is depleted, people are less likely to recognize moral issues and to act ethically.[63] Self-control has been found to be related to sexual restraint.[64] For example, M.T. Gailliot and R.F. Baumeister found that people who had just completed a task that required a great deal of controlled attention were more likely than those who had not depleted their self-control resources to report that they would engage in sexual infidelity.[65]

Fortunately, there are ways that people can improve and restore their self-control. Because "a single act of self-control" can cause glucose levels to drop, which can impede an individual's ability to exert self-control on a subsequent task, consuming high-glucose beverages (e.g., Kool-Aid) can replenish people's ability to exert self-control.[66] Rest and relaxation can also restore an individual's self-control resource.[67] In addition, the act of changing a habitual behaviour, such as using one's non-dominant hand for routine activities or avoiding the use of slang in one's speech, requires exerting self-control, which has been found to increase willpower in general.[68] For example, Megan Oaten and Ken Cheng developed an exercise program that required self-control training and found that fitness levels improved. They also found that self-control training led to a variety of positive outcomes, including less alcohol and caffeine consumption, less smoking, less impulse spending, and a lower frequency of lost tempers.[69] They found similar results in an academic study intervention program that involved self-control training.[70]

Organizations that seek to promote ethical behaviours, including preventing sexually inappropriate behaviour, need to understand the motivation behind such behaviours. If morally questionable behaviour is driven by visceral factors that lead to heat-of-the-moment thinking, then strategies need to focus on self-control techniques. If inappropriate sexual behaviour is driven by a desire to humiliate others, then efforts to address the ways people morally disengage may be effective. Once the factors and causes are identified, organizations can pursue preventative measures.

To understand situational impacts on decision-making within organizational cultures, it is important to understand the role of leadership. In an organization such as the military, in which there is a clear structure of reporting and control and accountability over explicit tasks and responsibilities, leadership plays a key role in creating and shaping both climate and culture. According to Daniel Denison:

> Climate refers to a situation and its link to thoughts, feelings, and behaviours of organizational members. Thus it is temporal, subjective, and often subject to direct manipulation by people with power and influence. Culture, in contrast, refers to an evolved context (within which a situation may be embedded). Thus it is rooted in history, collectively held and sufficiently complex to resist many attempts at direct manipulation.[71]

The climate of a work environment is those factors or characteristics that can be directly influenced in the short term; the culture is the more permanent context that has evolved over time, as the organization has adapted to its external environment.

Drawing from the leadership and organization research of Edgar Schein, Canadian Armed Forces doctrine states, "Culture and leadership are two sides of the same coin in that leaders first create cultures when they create groups and organizations."[72] J.M. Schaubroeck and colleagues showed how leaders in the US Army "embed shared understandings through their influence on the ethical culture of units at various levels, which in turn influence followers' ethical cognitions and behaviour."[73] Given this symbiotic relationship between leadership and organizational culture, leaders in the military not only have a particular responsibility to respond appropriately to sexual harassment or sexual assault in their units, but can also be instrumental in setting the conditions for appropriate behaviours. When such events do occur in an organization that places significant emphasis on team cohesion and operational success, leaders may face ethical decision-making challenges as they strive to ensure that their responses do not allow alleged transgressions to damage the reputation and primary operational goals of the unit.

Despite the strong influence of organizational cultures and the leadership within those cultures on decision-making and associated behaviours, harassment has frequently been addressed within organizations as the isolated behaviours of a few individuals or a personal issue between aggressors and victims. However, Catharine Mackinnon's groundbreaking 1979 analysis in *Sexual Harassment of Working Women: A Case of Sex Discrimination*[74] moved sexual harassment from a personal and isolated experience within organizations into the public, legal, economic, social, and political realms. Mackinnon's analysis was instrumental in establishing a relationship between sexual inequality and the social conditions set by employer-employee relations. In spite of developments in subsequent decades to frame harassment within the context of leadership and organizational climate and culture, within some cultures there is continued risk that such transgressions will be attributed solely to individuals, explained as isolated incidents, or handled in a manner that ensures that outsiders do not become aware of the behaviours. According to military sociologists Joseph Soeters, Donna Winslow, and Alise Weibull, subcultural patterns related to a range of behaviours, including sex and violence, can develop with rules and codes that are not considered acceptable within the larger organization or society.[75] Furthermore, they claim that unit members might be forbidden by influential peers or leadership to discuss these behaviours. As a result, the behaviours are informally sanctioned until a critical insider or informed outsiders, such as the news media, expose the inappropriate behaviour.

Some organizations have implemented bystander intervention programs to increase the likelihood that sexually inappropriate behaviours will be acknowledged and addressed.[76] Bystander intervention programs are based on Bibb Latané and John Darley's early bystander research, which identified barriers that prevented helping behaviour and sought ways to overcome bystander inaction in emergency situations.[77] Drawing on lessons learned from Latané and Darley's research, bystander intervention programs have been further developed with a focus on preventing sexual aggression by addressing barriers to inaction and encouraging bystanders to intervene. For example, intervention programs teach bystanders to take action when others may be at risk, such as walking a friend home who has had too much to drink.[78] Furthermore, a recent meta-analysis of bystander intervention programs provides support for their effectiveness in increasing bystander helping behaviours.[79] Of particular note to military organizations, one bystander intervention program targeted toward an American military sample found that soldiers exposed to the program were more likely to demonstrate a sense of responsibility and awareness regarding their role in preventing sexual assault than soldiers who were not exposed to the program.[80] While approaches vary, in this particular case a poster campaign was a key part of the program strategy, and in other cases on-line training has served as an important yet cost-effective element of bystander intervention programs.[81] This research demonstrates that bystander intervention programs may help promote an organizational culture that challenges sexual misconduct.[82]

Given the difficulty of dealing with sexual misconduct and the associated risk that it presents to individuals, to organizations, and to operational effectiveness, our discussion thus far suggests that there are specific strategies that may mitigate these behaviours. However, these strategies must be considered within the broader cultural context within which they will be applied. Specific strategies directed at the tendencies of a relatively small number of potential transgressors will have minimal impact if the climate and culture of the organization is not effectively positioned to address the behaviours in an appropriate way when they do occur; that is, effective values-based processes are an important part of prevention. In the following section, we discuss Kaptein's model of ethics auditing, which places particular emphasis on the organizational context.

IDENTIFYING THE RISK OF UNETHICAL AND SEXUALLY INAPPROPRIATE BEHAVIOUR

Kaptein conducted an "ethics audit" in 1998,[83] in which he used qualitative research methods to ascertain which "moral aspects can be revealed in order to improve the moral functioning of the organization."[84] Based on this research, Kaptein identified numerous virtues or factors that increase the likelihood that people will engage in ethical behaviour in organizational settings:[85]

> *Clarity:* the degree to which organizations communicate expected moral standards that are well-defined, comprehensive, and concrete.
> *Role modelling:* the extent to which the moral behaviour of senior leaders in an organization is seen as being consistent with organizational expectations.
> *Achievability* (or *feasibility*): the degree to which an organization creates the conditions (e.g., sufficient time, authority) that enable employees to act ethically.

Supportability: the extent to which employees identify with organizational expectations and the extent to which organizations create a supportive work environment.

Transparency (or *visibility*): the extent to which the conduct of employees can be observed by others and acted upon by those in a position to do so.

Discussability: the degree to which employees feel they can raise and talk about issues.

Sanctionability: the extent to which organizations tolerate or punish unethical behaviour.

Kaptein's research on corporate ethical virtues can be used to shed light on the factors that influence inappropriate sexual behaviour in other organizations and to gauge whether an organization is promoting sexually appropriate behaviour. Each of Kaptein's virtues, as they apply to the context of inappropriate sexual behaviours, is discussed below:

Clarity: Are the rules clear regarding what is appropriate and inappropriate behaviour regarding others in the organization, regardless of differences such as gender and rank/status?

Role modelling: Do senior leaders model exemplary behaviour toward women?

Achievability: Do informal norms send mixed messages that endorse sexually inappropriate behaviour?

Supportability: Do personnel take the formal rules regarding sexual conduct seriously? Do they treat each other with respect?

Transparency: Are victims or observers of sexually inappropriate conduct encouraged to come forward?

Discussability: Are there ample opportunities to discuss sexually appropriate conduct? Are reports of misconduct taken seriously?

Sanctionability: Are people who commit sexually inappropriate acts held accountable for their behaviour, or are they rewarded (e.g., with higher social status) in spite of their inappropriate behaviour?

RECOMMENDATIONS AND DIRECTIONS FOR FUTURE RESEARCH

For change to occur, leaders need to understand the tug-of-war between rational thought (the rider) and intuitive decision-making (the elephant), and the powerful role of situational factors in decision-making.[86] Moral judgments and behaviour are often not guided by deliberative thinking in many real-world situations,[87] which means that attempts to deal with sexual harassment and assault using methods rooted in deliberative approaches will likely fail. As we saw in the sexual arousal study conducted by Ariely and Loewenstein, sexual arousal has a dramatic impact on self-reported willingness to engage in unethical behaviour (e.g., giving a woman a drug without her knowledge to increase one's likelihood of having sex). According to the authors:

> the failure to appreciate sexual arousal by those who are not themselves aroused can also help explain the enactment of misguided and ineffective policies such as "just say no" ... At a practical level, our results suggest that efforts to promote safe, ethical sex should concentrate on preparing people to deal with the "heat of the moment" or to avoid it when it is likely to lead to self-destructive behavior.[88]

By understanding how decision-making is influenced by situational factors, such as sexual arousal; individual factors, such as depleted self-control resources; and informal cultural practices, leaders and policy-makers can develop more effective training programs and policies to promote ethical conduct and sexually appropriate behaviour and discourage inappropriate behaviours. Below are some recommendations to help organizations foster ethical behaviour.

Effective Training

We argue that realistic training that incorporates real-world situational and contextual factors is imperative for helping personnel overcome situations where they would be at risk of acting unethically. This approach is consistent with other research that suggests that ethics training be carried out in a way that is consistent with the "train as you intend to fight" approach.[89] Future research could examine whether personnel who are taught to follow specific behavioural steps when caught up in the heat of the moment and confronted with the temptation to act unethically will behave more ethically than those who have not learned such strategies. Likewise, future research could investigate whether self-control training (i.e., enhancing controlled attention) is an effective way to prevent sexually inappropriate behaviour. Furthermore, as suggested earlier, bystander intervention training has the potential to change behaviours; however, more research is needed to identify bystander intervention training strategies that will be most effective in a military setting.

Role Models

It is possible that some areas of an organization may have higher rates of inappropriate sexual behaviour than others. For example, the 2012 documentary *The Invisible War*[90] suggests that some military units have higher rates of sexually inappropriate behaviour than others. Rather than focusing largely on problematic areas in an organization, organizations may benefit from an examination of the reverse question, "Are there areas in the organization where behaviour can be emulated?"[91] By identifying areas in an organization that provide models for dealing with sexual harassment and assault, important lessons and strategies may be learned that can benefit the entire organization.

Self-Control

The capacity to exert self-control is limited. Leaders might therefore consider minimizing other demands when dealing with especially challenging situations that require a great deal of willpower. Likewise, it may be worth training people to use their willpower to stay away from situations where temptations to act inappropriately may be high.[92] More research is needed to understand how self-control research can be applied in the military context.

Conducting an Audit of Ethical Behaviour

It is possible to assess ethical risk within one's organization. Although Kaptein developed a measure of ethical culture that did not directly address sexually inappropriate behaviour, the virtues he identified can be used to better understand the moral functioning of an organization.[93] Other factors have also been shown to predict unethical behaviour.[94] Organizations could consider administering a survey that measures factors that predict ethical and unethical behaviour, such as the Defence Ethics Survey used by the Department of National Defence.[95]

In sum, this discussion suggests not only that the prevention of inappropriate sexual behaviours requires good policy and effective leadership in response to such behaviour when it does occur, but that there are strategies which can be applied to mitigate the occurrence of sexual misconduct. Notwithstanding the important role of training and leadership, further research is required to better understand the relationship between individual motivation, situational factors, leadership, and cultural practices within organizations, including the military, in preventing inappropriate sexual behaviours.

NOTES

1 Sarah Scott, "Complaints Taught Women Lesson about Military Life," and "Harassment Heard from Every Base Across Canada," *Montreal Gazette* (28 November 1992).

2 Anne Fuller, "Sex and the Military: Battling Harassment," and "Female Soldiers Entering Battlefield of Sexual Harassment," *The Globe and Mail* (7 August 1993).

3 Darcy Henton, "Gulf War Hero Officer Guilty of Harassment," *The Sunday Star* (15 May 1994).

4 Department of National Defence, National Defence Headquarters, Chief of the Defence Staff, "CF Harassment Policy," CANFORGEN 64/92 271920Z (November 1992).

5 Jane O'Hara, "Rape in the Military," *Maclean's* (25 May 1998), and "More Rape in the Military," *Maclean's* (1 June 1998).

6 Minister of National Defence, "Minister's Message," Special Report to *The Maple Leaf* 1, no. 6 (1998).

7 Chief of the Defence Staff, "Exclusive Interview with the CDS," Special Report to *The Maple Leaf* 1, no. 6 (1998): 12.

8 T.M. Jones, "Ethical Decision Making by Individuals in Organizations. An Issue-Contingent Model," *Academy of Management Review* 16, no. 2 (1991): 366–95. See also Tom L. Beauchamp, Norman E. Bowie, and G. Arnold Denis, *Ethical Theory and Business* (Upper Saddle River, NJ: Pearson/Prentice Hall, 2009); and Robert Audi, ed., *The Cambridge Dictionary of Philosophy* (New York: Cambridge University Press, 1999).

9 Jones, "Ethical Decision Making by Individuals in Organizations," 366–95.

10 L.F. Fitzgerald, F. Drasgow, C.L. Hulin, M.J. Gelfand, and V.J. Magley, "The Antecedents and Consequences of Sexual Harassment in Organizations: A Test of an Integrated Model," *Journal of Applied Psychology* 82, no. 4 (1997): 578–89, quoted in William D. Murry, Nagaraj Sivasubramaniam,

and Paul H. Jacques, "Supervisory Support, Social Exchange Relationships, and Sexual Harassment Consequences: A Test of Competing Models," *The Leadership Quarterly* 12 (2001): 1–29.

11   J.B. Pryor, "The Psychological Impact of Women in the U.S. Military," *Basic and Applied Social Psychology* 17, no. 4 (1995): 581–603, quoted in Murray, Sivasubramaniam, and Jacques, "Supervisory Support," 1–29.

12   J.E. Gruber and M.D. Smith, "Women's Responses to Sexual Harassment: A Multivariate Analysis," *Basic and Applied Social Psychology* 17, no. 4 (1995): 543–62, quoted in Murray, Sivasubramaniam, and Jacques, "Supervisory Support," 1–29.

13   E.A. Bell, M.A. Roth, and G. Weed, "Wartime Stressors and Health Outcomes: Women in the Persian Gulf War," *Journal of Psychosocial Nursing* 36 (1998): 19–25, quoted in Dawne S. Vogt, Anica P. Pless, Lynda A. King, and Daniel W. King, "Deployment Stressors, Gender, and Mental Health Outcomes Among Gulf War I Veterans," *Journal of Traumatic Stress* 18, no. 2 (2005): 115–27; J. Wolfe, E.J. Sharkansky, J.P. Read, R. Dawson, J.A. Martin, and P.C. Ouimette, "Sexual Harassment and Assault as Predictors of PTSD Symptomatology Among U.S. Female Persian Gulf War Military Personnel," *Journal of Interpersonal Violence* 13 (1998): 40–7, quoted in Vogt et al., "Deployment Stressors," 115–27.

14   N.J. Holden and K.D. Davis, "Harassment in the Military: Cross-National Comparisons," in *Challenge and Change in the Military: Gender and Diversity Issues*, ed. Franklin C. Pinch, A. MacIntyre, P. Browne, and A. Okros (Kingston, ON: Canadian Defence Academy Press, 2004), 97–121.

15   L. Katz, L. Bloor, G. Cojucar, and T. Draper, "Women Who Served in Iraq Seeking Mental Health Services: Relationships Between Military Sexual Trauma, Symptoms, and Readjustment," *Psychological Services* 4, no. 4 (2007): 239–49; L.S. Katz, G. Cojucar, C.T. Davenport, C. Pedram, and C. Lindl, "Post-Deployment Readjustment Inventory: Reliability, Validity and Gender Differences," *Military Psychology* 22 (2010): 41–56.

16   Vogt et al., "Deployment Stressors," 115–27.

17   Department of National Defence, *Sexual Misconduct and Sexual Disorders*, Defence Administrative Order and Directive 5019-5 (last modified 5 November 2012), http://www.forces.gc.ca/en/about-policies-standards-defence-admin-orders-directives-5000/5019-5.

18   While sexual harassment is not in itself a criminal offence in Canada, it can be considered a criminal offence if it meets the conditions identified within the broader concept of criminal harassment, under Section 264 of the *Criminal Code of Canada*. Department of Justice, *Criminal Code of Canada*, current to 27 April 2015, retrieved from http://laws-lois.justice.gc.ca.

19 A.M. O'Leary-Kelly and L. Bowes-Sperry, "Sexual Harassment as Unethical Behaviour: The Role of Moral Intensity," *Human Resources Management Review* 11 (2001): 73–92.

20 Holden and Davis, "Harassment in the Military."

21 Julie Coulthard, *The 2012 Canadian Forces Workplace Harassment Survey*, National Defence, Director General Military Personnel Research and Analysis and Chief of Military Personnel, Technical Memorandum (2013): 18.

22 Noémi Mercier and Alec Castonguay, "Crimes sexuels: le cancer qui ronge l'armée canadienne," *L'Actualité* (24 April 2014); and Noémi Mercier and Alec Castonguay, "Our Military's Disgrace," *Maclean's* (5 May 2014).

23 L. Kohlberg and R. Hersh, "Moral Development: A Review of Theory," *Theory into Practice* 16, no. 2 (1977): 53–9.

24 Ibid.

25 J.R. Rest, *Moral Development: Advances in Research and Theory* (New York: Praeger, 1986).

26 S. Sonenshein, "The Role of Construction, Intuition, and Justification in Responding to Ethical Issues at Work: The Sensemaking-Intuition Model," *Academy of Management Review* 32, no. 4 (2007): 1022–40.

27 J.A. Bargh, M. Chen, and L. Burrows, "Automaticity of Social Behaviour: Direct Effects of Trait Construct and Stereotype Activation on Action," *Journal of Personality and Social Psychology* 71, no. 2 (1996): 230–44; Ap Dijksterhuis and Ad van Knippenberg, "The Relation Between Perception and Behavior, or How to Win a Game of Trivial Pursuit," *Journal of Personality and Social Psychology* 74 (1998): 865–77; Matthew D. Lieberman, "Social Cognitive Neuroscience: A Review of Core Processes," *Annual Review of Psychology* 58 (2007): 259–89, doi: 10.1146/annurev.psych.58.110405.085654; Evans and Stanovich, "Dual-Process Theories of Higher Cognition," 225.

28 J.St.B.T. Evans, "Dual-Processing Accounts of Reasoning, Judgment, and Social Cognition," *Annual Review of Psychology* 59 (2008): 255–78; J.St.B.T. Evans and K.E. Stanovich, "Dual-Process Theories of Higher Cognition: Advancing the Debate," *Perspectives on Psychological Science* 8 (2013): 223–41.

29 Evans, "Dual-Processing Accounts," 255–78.

30 J. Haidt, "The Emotional Dog and Its Rational Tail: A Social Intuitionist Approach to Moral Judgment," *Psychological Review* 108, no. 4 (2001): 814–34.

31 S.J. Reynolds, "A Neurocognitive Model of the Ethical Decision-Making Process: Implications for Study and Practice," *Journal of Applied Psychology* 91, no. 4 (2006): 737–48.

32 Sonenshein, "The Role of Construction," 1022–40.
33 J. Haidt, *The Righteous Mind: Why Good People Are Divided by Politics and Religion* (Toronto: Vintage, 2012).
34 Haidt, "The Emotional Dog and Its Rational Tail," 814–34, and *The Righteous Mind.*
35 Haidt, *The Righteous Mind*, 54.
36 Craig Whitlock, "Air Force General Defends Overturning Sex Assault Verdict," *Washington Post* (10 April 2013), http://www.washingtonpost. com/world/national-security/air-force-general-defends-overturning-sexual-assault-conviction/2013/04/10/42f8162c-a215-11e2-ac00-8ef7caef5e00_ story.html
37 Ibid.
38 Ibid.
39 T. Eyal, N. Liberman, and Y. Trope, "Judging Near and Distant Virtue and Vice," *Journal of Experimental Social Psychology* 44 (2008): 1204–9; S. Milgram, "Some Conditions of Obedience and Disobedience to Authority," *Human Relations* 18 (1965): 57–76; P. Valdesolo and D.A. DeSteno, "Moral Hypocrisy: Social Groups and the Flexibility of Virtue," *Psychological Science* 18 (2007): 689–90.
40 R.J. Gerrig and Philip G. Zimbardo, *Psychology and Life, 16th ed.* (Boston: Allyn and Bacon, 2001).
41 L.K. Trevino, "Ethical Decision Making in Organizations: A Person-Situation Interactionist Model," *Academy of Management Review* 11, no. 3 (1986): 601–17.
42 Jones, "Ethical Decision Making," 366–95.
43 Ibid.
44 G. Loewenstein, D. Nagin, and R. Paternoster, "The Effect of Sexual Arousal on Expectations of Sexual Forcefulness," *Journal of Research in Crime and Delinquency* 34 (1997): 443–73.
45 Gerrig and Zimbardo, *Psychology and Life.*
46 Loewenstein, Nagin, and Paternoster, "The Effect of Sexual Arousal on Expectations," 443–73.
47 C.A. Castro and D. McGurk, "Battlefield Ethics," *Traumatology* 13 (2007): 24–31.
48 D. Ariely and G. Loewenstein, "The Heat of the Moment: The Effect of Sexual Arousal on Sexual Decision Making," *Journal of Behavioural Decision Making* 19 (2006): 87–98.
49 Loewenstein, Nagin, and Paternoster, "The Effect of Sexual Arousal on Expectations," 443–73.

50 J.A. Bouffard and H.A. Miller, "The Role of Sexual Arousal and Overperception of Sexual Intent Within the Decision to Engage in Sexual Coercion," *Journal of Interpersonal Violence* (2014): 1–20.

51 A. Abbey, "Sex Differences in Attributions for Friendly Behaviour: Do Males Misperceive Females' Friendliness?" *Journal of Personality and Social Psychology* 43, no. 5 (1982): 830–8.

52 C. Farris, T.A. Treat, R.J. Viken, and R.M. McFall, "Perceptual Mechanisms that Characterize Gender Differences in Decoding Women's Sexual Intent," *Psychological Science* 19 (2008): 348–54.

53 M.E. Baaz and M. Stern, "Why Do Soldiers Rape? Masculinity, Violence, and Sexuality in the Armed Forces in the Congo (DRC)," *International Studies Quarterly* 53, no. 2 (2009): 495–518.

54 E. Schroeder, "A Window of Opportunity in the Democratic Republic of the Congo: Incorporating a Gender Perspective in the Disarmament, Demobilization and Reintegration Process," *Peace, Conflict & Development* 6, no. 6 (2005): 1–45.

55 Baaz and Stern, "Why Do Soldiers Rape?" 510.

56 Ibid.

57 A. Bandura, "Moral Disengagement in the Perpetration of Inhumanities," *Personality and Social Psychology Review* 3 (1999): 193–209.

58 C.M. Barnes, J. Schaubroeck, M. Huth, and S. Ghumman, "Lack of Sleep and Unethical Conduct," *Organizational Behaviour and Human Decision Processes* 115 (2011): 169–80.

59 M. Muraven and R.F. Baumeister, "Self-Regulation and Depletion of Limited Resources: Does Self-Control Resemble a Muscle?" *Psychological Bulletin* 126, no. 2 (2000): 247–59.

60 Chip Heath and Dan Heath, *Switch: How to Change Things When Change Is Hard* (Toronto: Random House, 2010).

61 R.F. Baumeister, E. Bratslavsky, M. Muraven, and D.M. Tice, "Ego Depletion: Is the Active Self a Limited Resource?" *Personality Processes and Individual Differences* 74, no. 5 (1998): 1252–65.

62 Muraven and Baumeister, "Self-Regulation and Depletion of Limited Resources," 247–59.

63 F. Gino, M.E. Schweitzer, N.L. Mead, and D. Ariely, "Unable to Resist Temptation: How Self-Control Depletion Promotes Unethical Behaviour," *Organizational Behaviour and Human Decision Processes* 115 (2011): 191–203.

64 M. Friese and W. Hofmann, "Just a Little Bit Longer: Viewing Time of Erotic Material From a Self-Control Perspective," *Applied Cognitive*

Psychology 26 (2012): 489–96; M.T. Gailliot and R.F. Baumeister, "The Physiology of Willpower: Linking Blood Glucose to Self-Control," *Personality and Social Psychology Review* 11, no. 4 (2007): 303–27.

65 Gailliot and Baumeister, "The Physiology of Willpower," 303–27.

66 Ibid.

67 J.M. Tyler and K.C. Burns, "After Depletion: The Replenishment of the Self's Regulatory Resources," *Self and Identity* 70, no. 3 (2008): 305–21.

68 E. Finkel, C. DeWall, E. Slotter, M. Oaten, and V. Foshee, "Self-Regulatory Failure and Intimate Partner Violence Perpetration," *Journal of Personality and Social Psychology* 97 (2009): 483–99; M.T. Gailliot, E.A. Plant, D.A. Butz, and R.F. Baumeister, "Increasing Self-Regulatory Strength Can Reduce the Depleting Effect of Suppressing Stereotypes," *Personality and Social Psychology Bulletin* 33 (2007): 281–94.

69 M. Oaten and K. Cheng, "Longitudinal Gains in Self-Regulation from Regular Physical Exercise," *British Journal of Health Psychology* 11, no. 4 (2006): 717–33, doi:10.1348/135910706X96481; and Oaten and Cheng, "Improvements in Self-Control from Financial Monitoring," *Journal of Economic Psychology* 28, no. 4 (2007), 487–501, doi:10.1016/j.joep. 2006.11.003.

70 M. Oaten and K. Cheng, "Improved Self-Control: The Benefits of a Regular Program of Academic Study," *Basic and Applied Social Psychology* 28, no. 1 (2006): 1–16, doi:10.1207/s15324834basp2801_1.

71 D.R. Denison, "What Is the Difference Between Organizational Culture and Organizational Climate? A Native's Point of View on a Decade of Paradigm Wars," *The Academy of Management Review* 21 (1996): 619–54.

72 E.H. Schein, *Organizational Culture and Leadership* (San Francisco, CA: Jossey-Bass, 1998), quoted in Canadian Armed Forces Leadership Institute, *Leadership in the Canadian Forces: Conceptual Foundations* (Kingston, ON: Canadian Defence Academy, 2003).

73 J.M. Schaubroeck, S.T. Hannah, B.J. Avolio, S.W. Kozlowski, R.G. Lord, L.K. Trevino, N. Dimotakis, and A.C. Peng, "Embedding Ethical Leadership within and across Organization Levels," *Academy of Management* 55, no. 5 (2012): 1053–78.

74 C.A. Mackinnon, *Sexual Harassment of Working Women: A Case of Sex Discrimination* (New Haven, CT, and London: Yale University Press, 1979).

75 J.L. Soeters, Donna J. Winslow, and Alise Weibull, "Military Culture," in *Handbook of the Sociology of the Military*, ed. Giuseppe Caforio (New York: Kewar Academic/Plenum, 2003).

76 C.A. Gidycz, L.M. Orchowski, and A.D. Berkowitz, "Preventing Sexual
    Aggression Among College Men: An Evaluation of a Social Norms and
    Bystander Intervention Program," *Violence Against Women* 17, no. 6
    (2011): 720–42; V.L. Banyard, M.M. Moynihan, and E.G. Plante, "Sexual
    Violence Prevention through Bystander Education: An Experimental
    Evaluation," *Journal of Community Psychology* 35, no. 4 (2007): 463–81;
    S.J. Potter and J.G. Stapleton, "Translating Sexual Assault Prevention from
    a College Campus to a United States Military Installation: Piloting the
    Know-Your-Power Bystander Social Marketing Campaign," *Journal of
    Interpersonal Violence* 27, no. 8 (2012): 1593–1621.

77 B. Latané and J. Darley, "Bystander 'Apathy,'" *American Scientist* 57
    (1969): 244–68.

78 A. Kleinsasser, E.N. Jouriles, R. McDonald, and D. Rosenfield, "An Online
    Bystander Intervention Program for the Prevention of Sexual Violence,"
    Psychology of Violence (2014), doi:http://dx.doi.org/10.1037/a0037393
    (accessed 13 August 2014).

79 J. Katz and J. Moore, "Bystander Education Training for Campus Sexual
    Assault Prevention: An Initial Meta-Analysis," *Violence and Victims* 28,
    no. 6 (2013): 1054–65.

80 S.J. Potter and J.G. Stapleton, "Translating Sexual Assault Prevention from
    a College Campus to a United States Military Installation," *Journal of
    Interpersonal Violence* 27, no. 8 (2012): 1614.

81 Kleinsasser et al., "An Online Bystander Intervention Program."

82 S. McMahon and V.L. Banyard, "When Can I Help? A Conceptual
    Framework for the Prevention of Sexual Violence Through Bystander
    Intervention," *Trauma Violence Abuse* 13 (2012): 3–14.

83 M. Kaptein, *Ethics Management: Auditing and Developing the Ethical
    Content of Organizations* (Dordrecht, Netherlands: Kluwer, 1998).

84 Ibid.

85 M. Kaptein, "Developing and Testing a Measure for the Ethical Culture of
    Organizations: The Corporate Ethical Virtues Model," *Journal of
    Organizational Behaviour* 29, no. 7 (2008): 923–47.

86 C. Heath and D. Heath, *Switch*.

87 M.D. Rogerson, M.C. Gottlieb, M.M. Handelsman, S. Kapp, and J.
    Younggren, "Nonrational Processes in Ethical Decision Making,"
    American Psychologist 66, no. 7 (2011): 614–23.

88 D. Ariely and G. Loewenstein, "The Heat of the Moment: The Effect of
    Sexual Arousal on Sexual Decision Making," *Journal of Behavioural
    Decision Making* 19 (2006): 96.

89 D.L. Messervey, *What Drives Moral Attitudes and Behaviour?* Director
    General Military Personnel Research and Analysis Technical Report TR
    2013-003 (Ottawa: Defence Research and Development Canada, 2013);
    D. Messervey and Jennifer M. Peach, "Battlefield Ethics: What Influences
    Ethical Behaviour on Operations?" in *The Human Dimension of
    Operations: A Personnel Research Perspective* (Kingston, ON: Canadian
    Defence Academy Press, forthcoming).

90 Kirby Dick, dir., *The Invisible War*, produced by Amy Ziering (Chain
    Camera Pictures, 2012).

91 C. Heath and D. Heath, *Switch*.

92 R.F. Baumeister and John Tierney, *Willpower: Rediscovering the Greatest
    Human Strength* (New York: Penguin, 2012).

93 Kaptein, "Developing and Testing a Measure," 923–47.

94 D.L. Messervey, "Using Decision-Making Research to Mitigate Ethical
    Risk," Canadian Armed Forces Mental Health and Defence Ethics
    Working Group (April 2014); D.L. Messervey and K. Lavergne, *The
    Re-Development of the 2014/2015 Defence Ethics Survey*, Defence
    Research and Development Canada Scientific Report (Ottawa: Defence
    Research and Development Canada, forthcoming).

95 The 2014 iteration of the Defence Ethics Survey, developed by Dr Deanna
    Messervey at Director General Military Personnel Research and Analysis
    in collaboration with the Defence Ethics Programme, will be administered
    in the fall of 2014. The survey focuses on ethical risk and ethical climate.
    Inquiries should be directed to Deanna.Messervey@forces.gc.ca.

Contributors

STÉPHANIE A.H. BÉLANGER, PhD, is the associate scientific director of the Canadian Institute for Military and Veteran Health Research, and she has co-edited many collections, including *Beyond the Line: Military and Veteran Health Research* (Montreal & Kingston, ON: McGill-Queen's University Press, 2013). She is an associate professor in the French department of the Royal Military College of Canada, where her research focuses on war testimony, soldier identity, and moral injuries. She also specializes in just war theories, the topic of her monograph *Guerre, sacrifices et persécutions* (Paris: L'Harmattan, 2010). She has served as an officer in the Naval Reserve since 2004.

PETER BRADLEY, PhD, is an associate professor emeritus at the Royal Military College of Canada in the Department of Military Psychology and Leadership, and specializes in combat stress reactions, moral decision-making, and moral injury. He retired from the Canadian Armed Forces as a lieutenant-colonel.

VICTOR M. CATANO, PhD, is an industrial/organizational psychologist and a professor of psychology at Saint Mary's University, Halifax, Nova Scotia. He has also served as a special lecturer at the Technical University of Nova Scotia, as an adjunct professor at Dalhousie University, and as a visiting research fellow at the Canadian Forces Personnel Applied Research Unit in Toronto. Dr Catano has served as president of the Association of Psychologists of Nova Scotia, a member of the Nova Scotia Board of Examiners in Psychology (the body responsible for regulating the profession within Nova Scotia), and president of the Canadian Society of Industrial/Organizational Psychology. Dr

Catano also chaired the Canadian Council of Human Resources Associations' (CCHRA) Independent Board of Examiners, the agency that was responsible for developing and running the examinations and assessments that lead to the Certified Human Resources Professional (CHRP) designation. In recognition of his contributions to the science and practice of psychology in Canada, Dr Catano was elected a fellow by the Canadian Psychological Association, and an honorary member by Canadian Forces Personnel Selection Officers Association. He was recently awarded the Canadian Psychological Association's Award for Distinguished Contributions to Education and Training and the Canadian Society for Industrial and Organizational Psychology's Award for Distinguished Contributions to Industrial and Organizational Psychology. His consulting clients include the Canadian Forces, the RCMP, the Nova Scotia Nurses Union, Capital District Health Authority, and Cape Breton District Health Authority. He has published over two hundred journal and technical articles and is the first author of *Recruitment and Selection in Canada*, which is used throughout colleges and universities and government offices.

DANIELLE CHARBONNEAU, PhD, is an associate professor at the Royal Military College of Canada in the Department of Military Psychology and Leadership, completed her doctoral studies in clinical psychology, and specializes in leadership and motivation.

HOWARD G. COOMBS, PhD, is a graduate of the Canadian Forces Staff School, Canadian Land Force Command and Staff College, United States Army Command and General Staff College, and the US Army School of Advanced Military Studies, which awarded him his master's degree in military planning. Coombs received his PhD in military history from Queen's University in Kingston, Ontario, and is currently an assistant professor of the Royal Military College of Canada. He is also a member of the Canadian Army Reserve assigned on a part-time basis to the staff of 4th Canadian Division Headquarters, Toronto. Coombs deployed with Joint Task Force Afghanistan from September 2010 to July 2011 as a civilian advisor to the Task Force Commander.

KAREN D. DAVIS, PhD, is a defence scientist with the Director General Military Personnel Research and Analysis, Defence Research and Development Canada. She has published widely on topics related to gender, culture, and leadership in the Canadian military, and has provided presentations and expert testimony to numerous organizations including the Canadian Human Rights Commission, the Canadian Senate Committee on Constitutional and Legal Affairs, the Canadian House of Commons Standing Committee on the Status of Women, the US Defense Advisory Committee on Women in the Services, and the Australian Defence Force. Her current research interests include the intersections of military leadership and culture as they impact military identity, commitment, and performance.

Colonel RICHARD DICKSON, CD, MA, is director of the Canadian Army Land Warfare Centre. His academic qualifications include a bachelor of Mechanical Engineering, a master's of Mechanical Engineering and a master's of Military Arts and Science. He is also a graduate of the Canadian Land Force Command and Staff Course, the US Army Command and General Staff Course, and the US Army School of Advanced Military Studies (SAMS). Over the years, Colonel Dickson's operational assignments have included the UN Mine Awareness and Clearance Training Program in Pakistan (1989), CO Works and Design Company in Bosnia (1996–97), Deputy Commander, Disaster Assistance Response Team (DART) during earthquake relief operations in Turkey (1999), and J3 Engineer for the QG Force Interarmées de la Région de Montréal during the Ice Storm of 1998. Most recently, he deployed to Afghanistan from October 2008 to August 2009 as the deputy chief of staff for Governance, Reconstruction and Development (GR&D) at Headquarters Regional Command (South) in Kandahar. Colonel Dickson took over as director of the Canadian Army Land Warfare Centre in summer 2012.

JOE DOTY, PhD, is a retired US Army officer and the executive director of the Dr John Feagin Leadership Program at Duke University. Dr Doty is a graduate of the US Military Academy, West Point, NY, and served in both educational and leadership positions during his twenty-eight years in the Army, including battalion-level command. He concluded his service in the military as the deputy director in the Center for the Army Profession and Ethic (CAPE). Prior to arriving at Duke University in 2013, Dr Doty worked for three years as an ethics and leadership consultant in Singapore. His research focuses on leadership, ethics, character development, teaching, mindfulness, and human development. His latest publications are "Narcissism and Toxic Leaders," *Military Review* (Jan/Feb 2013), and "Ethical Leadership in Intercollegiate Athletics," *Journal of Values-Based Leadership* 7 (2): 48–58.

ALLAN ENGLISH, PhD, is an associate professor in the History Department at Queen's University in Kingston, Ontario, where he teaches a graduate course in Canadian military history. He is a member of the College of Peer Reviewers for the Canadian Institute for Military and Veteran Health Research and a fellow of the Centre for International and Defence Policy. He is currently conducting research in the areas of military and veteran health, command and control, leadership, and military culture. Allan English served in the Royal Canadian Air Force (RCAF) and Canadian Armed Forces (CAF) for twenty-five years in various operational and instructional positions as an air navigator.

PETER GIZEWSKI, MA, is a senior defence scientist/strategic analyst with the Defence Research and Development Canada, Centre for Operational Research and Analysis (DRDC CORA), Department of National Defence. He currently serves as strategic analyst to the Land Staff at the Canadian Army Land Warfare Centre (CALWC) and works in the Army's Land Futures Unit. He was educated at the University of Toronto (BA, High Distinction, Trinity College) and Columbia University (MA, MPhil), where he majored in international relations. Prior to joining the Department of National Defence he held various teaching and research positions in academia (including the University of Toronto and York University), at think tanks (including the Canadian Centre for Global Security), and in government (including the Department of Foreign Affairs and International Trade).

HEATHER HRYCHUK, MA, is a defence scientist/strategic analyst with Defence Research and Development Canada's (DRDC) Centre for Operational Research and Analysis. During her time with DRDC she has been posted to the Directorate of Air Strategic Plans and Canadian Forces' Aerospace Warfare Centre; the Chief of Force Development; the Canadian Forces Warfare Centre; and most recently, at the Strategic Joint Staff. In 2011, she completed a year-long deployment at ISAF HQ in Kabul. Prior to joining DRDC, Ms Hrychuk completed a thesis entitled "Lost in Translation: The Search for 3D in Afghanistan," and graduated with a master's in war studies from the

Royal Military College of Canada. She also holds a combined honours BA in law and political science from Carleton University.

E. KEVIN KELLOWAY, PhD, holds the Canada Research Chair in Occupational Health psychology and is professor of psychology at Saint Mary's University in Halifax, NS. A prolific researcher, he has authored over a hundred and fifty articles and chapters in addition to thirteen books. He is a fellow of the Society for Industrial/Organizational Psychology, the Association of Psychological Science, the Canadian Psychological Association, and the International Association of Applied Psychology. His research interests span a broad array of issues related to organizational behaviour with a special focus on leadership and occupational health psychology. He maintains an active consulting practice working with a variety of public and private sector organizations and is president-elect of the Canadian Psychological Association.

DANIEL LAGACÉ-ROY, PhD, is an associate professor and the head of the Military Psychology and Leadership Department at the Royal Military College of Canada, where he specializes in military professionalism and ethics and psychology and philosophy of religious conflicts. He previously taught ethics at the Dufferin-Peel Catholic School Board in Mississauga (ON), at the Université du Québec in Rimouski (QC), and at the University of Alberta in Edmonton (AB). He served in the Canadian Forces from 1987 to 1995 (Regular) and from 1998 to 2001 (Reserves). He published *Ethics in the Canadian Forces: Tough Choices* (workbook and instructor manual), the *Handbook on Mentoring*, and articles addressing various topics such as identity development and cultural intelligence. His future project is a book on war, religion, and violence. Dr Lagacé-Roy received his PhD (philosophy) from the Université de Montréal (QC).

ALLISTER MACINTYRE, PhD, completed thirty-one years in the Canadian Forces in 2006, having spent the final five years of his career as the deputy director of the Canadian Forces Leadership Institute. He holds a doctoral degree in social psychology and a master's degree in organizational psychology from Queen's University. Dr MacIntyre has worked as a researcher in Canada and Australia, taught psychology for three years at Royal Roads Military College, and has served on a number of international leadership and psychology panels. From 2002 until 2006 he served as the chair of psychology in the military section of the Canadian Psychological Association. For the past ten years, Dr MacIntyre has been employed as professor in the Department of Military Psychology and Leadership at the Royal Military College of Canada, Kingston, ON. He served as head of this department from 2010 to 2015. He has also held positions as an adjunct professor of psychology at both Carleton University and the University of Guelph. His academic and research interests include leadership, ethics, climate and culture, cohesion, and work stress.

DEANNA MESSERVEY, PhD, completed her doctoral studies in social psychology from Queen's University in Kingston, Ontario. Currently, she is a senior defence scientist on the organizational behaviour team at Director General Military Personnel Research and Analysis (DGMPRA). Dr Messervey is the primary scientific authority for the Defence Ethics Survey in the Department of National Defence. Her main areas of research are defence ethics, stress, decision making, and battlefield ethics.

DAMIAN O'KEEFE, PhD, completed his doctoral studies in industrial/organizational psychology at the University of Guelph. He has extensive applied research experience with both the Canadian Forces and the Australian Defence Force. As a research team leader, Dr O'Keefe was responsible for managing an applied research programme, which played a crucial role in the development of personnel selection policy for the Canadian Forces. He also taught at the Royal Military College of Canada and has presented his research at national and international conferences, such as the International Military Testing Association (IMTA) and the International Applied Military Psychology Symposium (IAMPS). As well, he has represented Canada on international working panels such as the Technical Cooperation Panel 10 (Survival Psychology), and Technical Cooperation Panel 3 (Human Resources), which are composed of senior research personnel from the United States, United Kingdom, Australia, New Zealand, and Canada. Dr O'Keefe is a faculty member at Saint Mary's University in Halifax, NS, where he teaches personnel psychology and industrial/organizational psychology.

Brigadier-General (Ret'd) G.E. (JOE) SHARPE, CD, OMM, joined the Royal Canadian Air Force in 1965 under the Regular Officer

Training Plan. He attended Royal Roads Military College in Victoria, BC, and graduated from the Royal Military College of Canada (RMC) in 1969 with a degree in applied science. He served in the Canadian Forces for the next thirty-two years in various operational, instructional air force, and joint staff positions, including deputy commanding officer of 425 All Weather Fighter Squadron, the inaugural commandant of the CF School of Aerospace Studies, and wing commander of 17 Wing Winnipeg. He served on the Joint Staff during the Gulf War as the command and control advisor and as the air component commander in the Joint Headquarters during the Winnipeg Flood in 1997. He completed his military career as a brigadier-general, serving on the air staff as the DG responsible for air force development. Brigadier-General Sharpe served for six years as the honorary colonel for the Canadian Forces School of Aerospace Studies in Winnipeg, Manitoba, and remains involved with the CF, assisting various organizations with their strategic planning activities. He was appointed as the colonel commandant of the Canadian Forces Military Police Branch in January 2011.

SHAUN TYMCHUK, MA, is a retired Canadian infantry officer with extensive experience in operations and training, and a graduate of the RMC War Studies Program.

Sub-Lieutenant ETHAN WHITEHEAD, BSc, RN, is a Maritime Surface and Sub-Surface Officer in the Navy Reserve of the Royal Canadian Navy. He graduated from the Laurentian University School of Nursing in 2014. He currently works as a Registered Nurse for Alberta Health Services in Westlock, AB.

DAPHNE XU, BA, graduated with a bachelor of social sciences (honours) in psychology from the National University of Singapore, and holds a specialist diploma in learning science from the National Institute of Education, Singapore. She has been with the SAF Centre for Leadership Development since 2008. Ms Xu's significant work contributions towards leader and leadership development during her tenure include research and curriculum development in the areas of leadership, ethics education, ethical reasoning for adaptive leaders, empathy, engagement, and core values inculcation.

Index